AFTERLIVES OF THE SAINTS

Afterlives of the Saints

HAGIOGRAPHY, TYPOLOGY, AND
RENAISSANCE LITERATURE

JULIA REINHARD LUPTON

STANFORD UNIVERSITY PRESS
Stanford, California

Stanford University Press
Stanford, California

© 1996 by the Board of Trustees of the
Leland Stanford Junior University

Printed in the United States of America

CIP data are at the end of the book

Stanford University Press publications are distributed
exclusively by Stanford University Press in the United
States, Canada, Mexico, and Central America; they are
distributed exclusively by Cambridge University Press
throughout the rest of the world.

For Kenneth

Contents

A Note on Texts

Unless otherwise noted, quotations from the first five books of the Hebrew Bible are taken from *The Soncino Chumash*, ed. A. Cohen; citations from the Book of Ruth are from the Soncino edition of *The Five Megilloth*; and citations from the Prophets, the Book of Job, and the New Testament are from the Oxford edition of the Revised Standard Version of the King James Bible.

I have used the Arden editions of *Measure for Measure* (ed. J. W. Lever) and *The Winter's Tale* (ed. J. P. Pafford). All other Shakespeare references are from the *Riverside Shakespeare* (ed. G. Blakemore Evans).

When citing Boccaccio, I have identified English translations as "E" and Italian page numbers as "I."

I have used M. C. E. Shaner's parallel edition of the "F" and "G" manuscripts of Chaucer's *Legend of Good Women* in the *Riverside Chaucer*, under the general editorship of Larry D. Benson.

Acknowledgments

Many people have influenced this book, whether through the direct impact of their intellectual example, comments and criticism, or research assistance, or through their more intangible contributions to the precious community-building that makes scholarly work possible. This is of necessity a partial list, and I regret any omissions.

I began writing about Burckhardt and the paradoxes of Renaissance periodization in my master's thesis at the Johns Hopkins University under the direction of Nancy Struever. At Yale University, Thomas Greene lent his erudition and editorial tact to what is now Chapter 5, on *Measure for Measure*, as well as to an early prospectus of the project. An earlier form of Chapter 5 appeared in *Exemplaria* 2.2 (1990): 375–401. Thomas Hyde's seminar on Renaissance mythography first introduced me to the confluences between mythography, iconography, and idolatry, and John Guillory, in his seminar on pastoral poetry, read *The Winter's Tale* in terms of Puritan debates about drama and religious imagery. My friend and fellow student Patricia Phillippy's work on palinodes influenced the early stages of the book's conception, and her later comments on almost every chapter have shaped its final form. Eric Nicholson has generously read the chapters on Boccaccio and Shakespeare, and his distinctive imprint is visible in them.

Since then, many colleagues and students at the University of California, Irvine, have contributed their insight and support to this project. Jane Newman, both my mentor and a dear friend, has read and commented on the entire manuscript; I am indebted to her for this and much more. I am also grateful for the advice and guidance of Juliet Flower MacCannell, always generous with both her theoretical expertise and her support of the professional endeavors of a younger colleague. In addition, I have benefited from the criticisms offered by Stephen Barney, Robert Folkenflik, Alexander Gelley, James Herbert, Wendy Hester, Dianah Jackson, Tracy McNulty, Matthew Potolsky, and Bridget Sandquist. Victoria Duncan, Tracy McNulty, Judith Pike, and Arielle Read provided research assistance. Interchanges with Linette Davis, Draza Fratto, and Lee Kress have led to some of this book's key formulations. Linda Bauer has taught me much about art history and iconography. I also owe a lot to discussions with Carolyn Austin, Vivian Folkenflik, Mieke Gelley, Betty Guthrie, the Reverend Sarah Koelling, Lori Miller, John Smith, Manya Steinkoler, and the other participants in reading groups held at UCI on women's spirituality, Rosenzweig and Lévinas, and Jewish texts and observance.

At UCLA, Michael J. B. Allen, Lowell Gallagher, Vincent Pecora, Eric Segal, Debora Shuger, and Alex Waintrub have offered excellent advice and suggestions. Jonathan Crewe at Dartmouth College and Timothy Murray at Cornell University have both contributed significantly to my final revisions of the book. To Rainer Nägele I owe not only generous comments on several chapters, but also models for thinking about Benjamin and theology that date from his seminars at Hopkins in the early 1980's. Bruce Fink's four-year seminar at UCI on Jacques Lacan shows its presence in many chapters here. Study sessions with Rabbi Elie Spitz and Rabbi Chaim Seidler-Feller on the Decalogue inspired many of the formulations in chapters 6 and 7.

A University of California President's Fellowship for 1992–93 allowed me to take a much-needed year off, during which time the bulk of this book was written. An Irvine Faculty Research Grant, the Organized Research Initiative in Women and the Image, and the UCI School of Humanities provided funds for research assistance, travel, and equipment.

I would also like to thank the editors at Stanford, especially Helen Tartar and Peter Kahn, for their work on this project. Ann Klefstad provided an especially fine reading of the manuscript.

To my parents and stepparents Mary Jane Lupton, Kenneth Baldwin, William Lupton, and Shirley Landon Lupton I owe a lifetime of debate about the troubled relations between religion and secularism. Conversations with Ellen Lupton about the definition of culture and with J. Abbott Miller about natural history have found their way into several chapters here. I am grateful to Frank and Rosalind Reinhard for providing emotional and financial support during hard times as well as good ones. Finally, it is an impossible task to measure the kinds of contributions that Kenneth Reinhard has made to this book and to the creation of the intellectual and domestic space out of which it has emerged. For this reason, the book is dedicated to him.

J.R.L.

Figure 1. Caravaggio, *Amor Vincit Omnia* (*Victorious Cupid*), ca. 1601–2. Reproduced by permission of the Gemäldegalerie, Staatliche Museen, Berlin, Germany.

Figure 2. Michelangelo Buonarroti, *Saint Bartholomew*, detail from *The Last Judgment* fresco on the ceiling of the Sistine Chapel. Reproduced by permission of the Sistine Chapel, Vatican Palace, Vatican State.

Introduction

Caravaggio's *Amor Vincit Omnia* (c. 1601–2) borrows its pose from Michelangelo's famous depiction of St. Bartholomew in the Sistine Last Judgment (Figs. 1 and 2).[1] Caravaggio's Baroque Cupid performs a series of operations on its Renaissance original: the Christian subject matter becomes classical, the monumental idealism is reduced to a blatantly erotic realism, and an allegorical tableau composed of a mythological personification and a collection of still-life objects displaces the eschatological narrative in which Michelangelo's tragic figure so sublimely appears. How do we approach this assimilation of a Catholic saint into the gallery of secular erotic art? Biblical typology, a major organizational principle in the program of the Sistine Chapel, also offers ways of understanding the transformation of Bartholomew into Cupid. Strictly speaking, typology describes the exegetical relationship between the Old Testament and the New, in which the prior text forms both the hallowed origin and the superseded beginnings of the latter work, a relationship that produces a network of figural correspondences and allusive ligatures between the two halves of the biblical canon. Typology has also been used at least as early as Saint Augustine to describe the possible rapprochement between pagan antiquity, demonized for its polytheism, and the new order represented by Chris-

tianity; in such a reading, certain aspects of classical culture, especially its philosophy and, eventually, its literature and art, lay the
foundation for the highest insights of Christian civilization, which
sublates the best of classical and Jewish thought as the ground of
modernity.[2]

Read from a typological perspective, Caravaggio's *Amor Vincit
Omnia* "conquers" Michelangelo's St. Bartholomew by subordinat-
ing its saintly pose to classical subject matter, annulling Christianity
by secularism in the same way that Christianity abrogates both Judaism and classicism. Moreover, Michelangelo's fresco is itself based
on ancient statuary; in secularizing Michelangelo's saint, Caravaggio
not only negates its religious content but also purifies and restores
the classicism of its aesthetic inspiration. Yet typology, praised by
critics such as Eric Auerbach and Northrop Frye for its unique historical consciousness as well as its salvaging of the Old Testament
for a Christianity increasingly distant from the Holy Land, performs
an act of violence as well as restoration. The Hebrew Bible, taken as
a distinct text with its own canonical organization and set of hermeneutic protocols, disappears into the Old Testament that takes
its place once the New Testament has been installed as its fulfillment. Or it appears to disappear: for in fact, rabbinic Judaism, more
or less coterminous with the birth of Christianity, far outlasts the
typological cancellation that purports to subsume the Torah.[3] The
figure of the modern Jew who has refused to enter into the New
Covenant belies the completeness of the world-historical transformation narrated by typology. So too, "classical culture," rather than
being an accurate picture of pagan religion or society, becomes the
dialectical construction of a Christian humanism that synthesizes
the Greek ideal of truth immanent in beauty with its own doctrine
of the Incarnation, leaving out anything that does not predict this
reconciliation.[4] Counter-classical studies of antiquity recover the
"cuisine of sacrifice" as the unphilosophical menu of an inveter-
ately pagan world (Detienne and Vernant) or compile the Hellenistic and Arabic encyclopedias of mythography, natural history, and
astrology that transmitted the classical paideia to Christendom (Warburg, Wittkower, Wind). These studies irremediably compromise

the idealist picture of the ancient world by revealing the allegorical machinery facilitating the symbolic syntheses of the Renaissance as well as the pagan scandals foreclosed by them.

Read from this perspective, Caravaggio's *Amor Vincit Omnia* represents not only the typological secularization of religious art but also a deflation of the Christian-classical reconciliations effected by Michelangelo's work and theorized by biblical typology. Rather than simply reversing the hierarchy between classical model and religious subject matter in order to perform an act of secularization, Caravaggio changes the nature of the relation between form and content. Whereas Michelangelo's piece effects an incarnational unity between classical statuary and Christian narrative so that the beauty of the Greco-Roman nude shines through the noble body of the martyred saint, in Caravaggio's painting the classical subject matter and the realistic depiction of flesh are "carnated" rather than incarnated, tacked on to each other in a material sign rather than unified in an aesthetic totality. The flesh of this most sensual Cupid weighs down both the learned mythological subject and the allusion to St. Bartholomew; no wings, either Christian or classical, could bear this boy's healthy, boldly exhibited body even an inch off the ground. Yet it is not simply realism that bears him earthwards. It is also allegory, evidenced by the panoply of crafted objects at the feet of Amor. These objects form a kind of caption or picture-writing that spells out the Virgilian *sententia* represented in the painting; the canvas divides like an emblem into the allegorical figure of love (a personification, not a person) and the image's legend or gloss, the *omnia* encapsulated in the attributes gathered about the boy.

Auerbach, in his reconstruction of typology as a poetic principle envisioned from the perspective of post-Romantic aesthetics, insistently distinguishes the artificial rhetoric of allegory from the historical consciousness of figural thinking (e.g., *Scenes* 54, 68). To this we should contrast Walter Benjamin's *Origin of the German Tragic Drama*, a book that constitutes a crucial intervention in typological theories of history and art. There, allegory appears as the mode that disrupts the syntheses of classicism: "in the field of allegorical intuition . . . the false appearance of totality is extinguished. For the *ei-*

dos disappears, the simile ceases to exist, and the cosmos it contained shrivels up" (176). If Michelangelo's *Last Judgment* represents the marriage of classical form and Christian meaning in the new totality called the Renaissance, Caravaggio's Baroque allegory punctures the dream of that totality, collecting the fragments of high Renaissance history painting in the still life that accumulates in the lower third of the painting.

The skin of Bartholomew, sloughed off by the saint as he rises in martyrdom to his new life in Christ, offers a provocative emblem for the remnants of typology. Art historians have long suggested that the flayed skin reflects the distorted features of Michelangelo himself, a consummate example of Renaissance self-fashioning and tortured introspection (Hibbard, *Michelangelo* 249). In Caravaggio's painting, all that remains of the flayed skin are the draperies that flow beneath Amor's provocatively raised leg. Yet we could also say that the painting as a whole identifies itself with that abandoned skin, taken as the husk or detritus of a deflated symbol—in Benjamin's expression, "the relic of a vanished totality" whose "cosmos [has] shrivel[led] up." Moreover, Caravaggio's painting performs its deflation by identifying with a motif already contained in the framework of the earlier piece. In Michelangelo's fresco, the saint's attribute is an anamorphic remnant, the site of the painter's distorted self-reflection and hence a warped mirror ripe for further artistic self-imaging. Rather than simply critiquing the first work, the latter painting parasitically exacerbates a motif already resident in the monumental worldview with which it interacts, an iconographic attribute that becomes the model as well as the object of Caravaggio's deflationary practice.

Read in this manner, Caravaggio's painting stages the typological rhythm determining the idea and aesthetic of the Renaissance as a dialectic between Christianity and secularization, and shows how typology always produces counter-logics that resist or dislocate its historical schematizations. It does so by ringing changes on the figure of a saint, from which it borrows both the dream of a resurrection in which body and soul are reunited and the figure of a material remainder produced by the symbolizing process of historical and spiritual transumptions. This book examines the ways in which hagiography and typology, sometimes alone and more often in tandem, enter into the construction of a Renaissance canon and period, during the centuries of Europe's most constitutive classical revival and in its retroactive consolidations in nineteenth- and twentieth-century historiography. This book is not about saints' lives in themselves, as either literary or historical phenomena, but instead addresses the structural effects of hagiography in the secular literature of the Renaissance. The central texts analyzed here—Boccaccio's *Decameron*, Vasari's *Lives of the Artists*, and Shakespeare's *Measure for Measure* and *The Winter's Tale*—all manifest key moments and aspects in the creation of a Renaissance canon for the post-Renaissance world. The epochal significance of these works, saturated in religious allusions as well as scenes of profane life and classical art, rests in neither the normative piety nor the subversive heresy of any of these writers, but rather in their crafting of myths of modernity precisely out of the religious material that formed such an important part of their daily vocabularies.

As a case study in literary history, this book establishes a family of hagiographic and typological conventions and motifs—annunciation, vocation, trial, martyrdom, iconoclasm, reliquary encryption, and so on—that together affiliate a number of apparently disparate works of Renaissance literature in a shared generic genealogy. These motifs make a repeated pilgrimage between medieval saints' lives and Renaissance literary works, tracing out a web of intersections, detours, and divergences that both link and distinguish religious and secular traditions. Such motifs come to describe the relation between medieval narrative and a secular literature that emerges as such through the typological cancellation of hagiography. Thus we can speak of hagiography undergoing the passion of secularization, or of later literature encrypting relics of the legends, or of comic tales and plays parodically "enunciating" biblical and hagiographic scenes of annunciation. I have tried to show how the scenarios transferred from religious discourse to secular literature project models of generic transformation that manifest the patterns and predicaments of literary secularization in the Renaissance and beyond.

Part I establishes the conceptual framework of the argument by reading each of the book's key terms—typology and hagiography—against another problem or method. Chapter 1, "Typologies of the Renaissance," argues that the mythos of the Renaissance borrows from figural interpretation in order to conceptualize Christian modernity's relationship to a civilization both chronologically and religiously alien. Much recent work on the period has emphasized the ideological and historical inadequacy of the very term "Renaissance"; often under fire is the anachronistic presentation of the epoch as secular, when in fact every detail of life was entrenched in religious paradigms and fraught by religious conflict. From such a perspective, it could be argued that the narrative of generic transformation I have developed, for all of its privileging of religious discourse, nonetheless depends too uncritically on a Burckhardtian picture of Renaissance secularism. Yet this book addresses not the religious life of the period but rather the series of canonizing retroactions, beginning in those centuries, that have constituted certain texts and artefacts as "Renaissance" works for the tradition of the humanities that has come after it. By comparing the ideas of Renaissance put forth by Jacob Burckhardt, Aby Warburg, and Walter Benjamin, Chapter 1 demonstrates the complicity of "typology" and "Renaissance," and the necessity to work through these terms to their limits rather than simply replace them with new, apparently more descriptive ones.

The next chapter plots the mutilation and suffering of the saintly body in the *Golden Legend* onto the hysterical symptom as formulated by Jacques Lacan. I do not use psychoanalysis as a key to the individual psychology of actual saints or of their literary representations, but rather as an account of the libidinal economies and material waste products of linguistic and social symbolization. Whereas Freud had implicitly equated "symptom" and "symbol" through his emphasis on the hermeneutic structure of neurotic formations, Lacan foregrounded what he called the *sinthome* as the remainder of such symbolization, the element of the "Real"—alternately glossed as trauma, *jouissance*, the void, or the impossible—that is negated, encrypted, and left over by the symbolic resolutions of primal scenes. The flayed body, the decapitated head, and the postmortem burial of the saint mark out the logical time of martyrdom, the traumatic cuts around which later literature will constitute itself as the "symptom" of hagiography, that is, as both a symbolic renovation and an incalculable surplus of Catholic narrative forms.

Part II, "The Novella and Its Renewals," shows how the genre of the prose novella instantiated by Boccaccio's *Decameron* forms a crucial episode in the constitution of a literature after hagiography. A brief chapter entitled "The Gleaner's Prologue" demonstrates that Chaucer's *Legende of Good Women* both imagines and falls short of the goal of constructing a literature after hagiography. The next chapter turns to Boccaccio's *Decameron* as the *Golden Legend* of the novella tradition. Boccaccio's collection of a hundred tales is a thesaurus of parodic approaches to hagiographic, liturgical, scriptural, and iconographic texts and conventions; as such, the *Decameron* plots the crucial juncture that channels medieval prose narrative into Renaissance fiction, drama, and biography. The *Decameron* begins with the mock-legend of a con man turned saint and ends with the serious tale of patient Griselda, a latter-day female Job. Framed by hagiographic parody on the one end and the palinodic reversal of parody at the other, the *Decameron* establishes a divine comedy / economy that resanctifies desanctification by ironizing the text's own secularizing tactics. Boccaccio's romantic recreations of martyrdom in the tragic tales of Day IV temporarily reroute this comedic circuit around the reemergent symptoms of the plague, a detour that in turn projects Griselda's relationship to Job beyond the dialectical terms of biblical typology that had appeared to contain it.

Shakespeare's *Measure for Measure*, the subject of the next chapter, appropriates and dramatizes the world of the novella, especially the genre's constitutive secularization of hagiography and its extension of typological exegesis to the relation between religious and secular literature. *Measure for Measure* counterpoints two opposing scenarios of male and female virtue, the tyrant-martyr conflict activated by Isabella in relation to Angelo, and the Antonine dilemma of the desert hermit imagined by Angelo in relation to Isabella. In the

play, virginity and marriage are not distinct alternatives that characters or critics can choose, but rather self-divided positions produced
by the overlay of contradictory roles in generically conditioned stories. These opposed generic legacies from the *Golden Legend* and its
renovations by the novella are brought into dialectical relation by
the play's typological debate between Justice and Mercy, an exchange that ultimately founders on an unlikely relic from martyrology, the nonsubstitutable head of the undecapitated Barnardine.

   Part III, "Iconographies of Secular Literature," examines the
visual traditions surrounding the saints as they pass into the representations of Renaissance secular culture. In triangulating hagiography, typology, and iconography, I am interested not so much in
the specific attributes and pictorial types of the saints, but rather in
the way in which typology and iconography represent two opposed
methods of reading the afterlife of hagiography, the first emphasizing the progressive logic of secularization, and the second pointing
to the contradictions faulting the historical narratives so produced.
Moreover, the "icon" of iconography brings into play a second historical pattern both embedded in and in excess of typology, namely,
the dialectic of idolatry and iconoclasm. On the one hand, iconoclasm represents the necessary middle moment of negation that allows "paganism" to be sublated into "classicism" under the rule of
Christian secularism. On the other hand, iconoclasm poses a repeated if always neutralized resistance to the incarnational ideal of
Western mimesis, inserting a negativity that persists beyond its synthesis into the typological unfolding of modern aesthetics.

   The chapter on Vasari's *Lives of the Artists* examines the use of
scriptural allusion, biblical typology, and the secularizing dynamics
of the novella in Vasari's masterful staging of the central drama of
Italian art. The governing narrative of Vasari's text crosses at key
points with the competing genre of natural history, which gathers
together the eccentric elements left over by Vasari's aesthetic design. The fable of creation *ex nihilo* that introduces the *Lives* contains
an iconoclastic moment that reemerges in Vasari's account of artistic innovation.

   Finally, the chapter on *The Winter's Tale* traces the historical cal-

culus that counterpoints four competing "iconographies of idolatry"—Jewish, Greco-Roman, Catholic, and Protestant—whose progressive correspondences with each other are traversed by the spa-
tiotemporal leaps of Shakespeare's romance.

This book is above all a study in the exegetical implications of
literary genres; I am interested, that is, in the narrative logics that
conceptualize literary change rather than in the historical contexts
and institutional frameworks of literary production and consump-
tion. The Protestant Reformation and its Catholic antecedents and
responses enter into this book not as concrete historical contexts
that would explain the form, meaning, and reception of particular
works, but rather as structural recalibrations of generic coordinates
that systematically reestablish what counts as old and new, as law
and grace, or as idolatry and iconoclasm at particular epochal junctures in literature's emergent history. As a dialectical pattern capable
of indefinite displacement and redeployment in new scenes of periodization, typology shapes any number of historical dualities, tran-
sitions, and crises, including the oppositions governing the relationships between the Old Testament and the New Testament, paganism and monotheism, Catholicism and Protestantism, the Middle
Ages and the Renaissance, and secular and religious worldviews.
Although these oppositions often simply function as parallels to each
other, as repeated moments of overturning in the spiraling path of
the West, the specific scenarios of historical and literary change at issue at any given moment usually organize these different typological translations in a hierarchy of abrogational rhythms: thus classicism can represent an antiquity parallel to that of Judaism, each of
which is canceled and renovated by Christianity (Vasari), and can
also function as the ground restored by Christianity across the mortified corpus of Jewish law (Hegel), or as the foundation rebuilt by
Renaissance secularism out of the ruins of medieval Catholicism
(Burckhardt). Especially when submitted to interpretive pressure,
these interfolded and apparently correlated oppositions can work at
cross purposes, as competing narratives of progress that retard each
other's fruition: in *The Winter's Tale*, iconoclasm and incarnational
aesthetics represent two opposed principles of renovation for the

West's ideology of representation. Although this typological and generic approach to literary secularization leaves out much that would be of interest to historically minded critics, I believe that sustained attention to the exegetical logics of literary form best accounts for the structural rather than local impact of hagiography on the canon of Renaissance literature.

The word "canon," so familiar to us in the current debates about the proper object of literary teaching and study, is of course a term borrowed from biblical studies, where it designates the authoritative list of texts that make up the *biblia*, or "books," for a particular denomination. In addition, the word "canonization" applies not only to the historical, legal, and hermeneutic process of entering a text into a particular configuration of scriptures but also to the juridical procedures that precede the official registration of a saint in the calendar of the Church. A book on hagiography in secular literature would seem to offer the ideal occasion to mediate the institutional, religious, and literary senses of canonization in a historicist analysis of Renaissance texts. In my view, however, the problem with current emphases on both institutionality and contextualization is that they tend to discount the role of such mechanisms as genre, citation, allusion, and imitation in retroactively producing the affiliations that link works in a tradition. If we remove such retroactive determinations in favor of an apparently more faithful act of historicization (whether of the original texts or the stages of their redeployment in later institutions), we have cut away a significant feature—indeed, the feature of signification itself—from the texts that we study.[5] Like the resources of allusion traditionally studied by literary scholars, biblical typology constitutes a pattern immanent in works of literature and the traditions in which they take shape, and thus allows us to restore the mechanisms of literary self-production to the center of contemporary analysis. At the same time, however, typology is not a benign set of poetic devices happily reproducing a Great Tradition, but rather underwrites a profoundly ideological apparatus whose world-historical motives demand constant assessment, surveillance, and reorientation on the part of the critic and teacher. By emphasizing the role of typology in the construction of a post-hagiographic literature, I hope to have offered a critique as well as an analysis of modern Western forms of traditionality, without recourse, however, to either a historicist position, which would emphasize the synchronic context of the works in question, or an institutional analysis, which would insist on the disciplinary production of the canon through the "power-knowledge" mechanisms of the university.

The phrase "afterlives of the saints" names not only a chronological moment in the history of forms but also a logical instance of the questions that continue to vex the idea of a secular literature. Two theses concerning the relation between sacred and secular literature are repeatedly exercised in this book. First, *secularization and Christianization are bound up in a dialectic that raises what it cancels*; hence what we generally call "secular literature" is actually Christian literature in a displaced but heightened form. Karl Löwith has argued that "Jewish Messianism and Christian eschatology, though in their secular transformations, . . . have developed those appalling energies of creative activity which changed the Christian Occident into a world-wide civilization" (*Meaning in History* 202–3). In a rather different project, John Guillory has similarly interpreted T. S. Eliot's ideal of literary culture as, in Eliot's phrase, "*unconsciously* Christian" (*Cultural Capital* 152). An unconscious Christianity is one whose formulas, emptied of their theological content, continue to operate all the more powerfully precisely because of their abstraction. Shorthand notations in this book for the structural collusion between secular culture and a certain brand of rationalized Christianity include "the Christian-secular dialectic" and "Christian secularization," phrases that refer to that process of modernization that has occurred within Christian culture, not as its undoing, but as the means of its endless expansion and ever deeper entrenchment in the eschatological dream of "a world-wide civilization," poised, like Caravaggio's Cupid, to conquer everything.

This identity of apparent opposites derives from the typological translation of the Hebrew Bible into the Old Testament and the repetitions of that revolution in later reforms of the Church. Just as the Old Law is both abrogated and internalized under the New Dispensation, so too, secular literature at once evacuates and intensifies the Christian narratives it inherits. Yet the role of biblical typology in the foundation of Christian secularization leads to a second thesis: namely, that *the Christian-secular dialectic always has remainders*, unsubsumed elements that can only be thought in relation to that dialectic, but that nonetheless exceed it. Here, we can rethink the notion of a "Christian unconscious" not as the continuing insistence of Christianity within a modernity postulated as its displacement, but rather as *what is unconscious to Christianity*, that is, what remains radically repressed by and hence disturbingly internal to it, the imploded husk of a previous representational tradition.

One such remainder is the difference between the Old Testament and the Hebrew Bible, two canons whose apparent identity is belied by the reordering of texts, the allocation of new emphases and selective amnesias, and the efflorescence of figural exegesis brought about by the subordination of the testament henceforth named "Old" to the New Testament. Another such remainder is the gap opened up by the Reformation in the history and self-representation of the Catholic Church. Although the Church has managed to retain its institutional identity through the (ongoing) crisis of the Reformation, it has nonetheless suffered a traumatic reinscription, reduced from the keeper of a universal faith to one embattled and increasingly defensive denomination of Christianity among others. Just as the biblical patriarchs are lauded in the annals of Christianity as the founders of a shared tradition, so too, the achievements of the Patristic period, scholasticism, and Gothic art are accepted as a common legacy by the inheritors of Western culture. And just as Jewish resistance to Christian conversion in the millennia following the Gospels disturbs the typological narrative of the New Covenant, the survival of the modern Church beyond its medieval golden age is perceived in the dominant Protestant and secular worldviews of English letters and Western capitalism as an embarrassing relic of another time.

One way to measure these epochal remainders is as a series of losses and gains: every text or discourse necessarily forfeits an original intent, import, and context when it receives a new meaning and orientation in the evolving narrative of history. Thus Auerbach, writing from his own historical position as an exile from the German tradition, describes the economics of typology: "What the Old Testament thereby *lost* as a book of national history, it *gained* in concrete dramatic actuality" (*Scenes* 51; emphasis mine). Yet the Hebrew Bible does not represent simply the lost origin of a single tradition (called "Judeo-Christian"), but also the surviving text of a different tradition formulated under the exigencies of Diaspora (rabbinic Judaism), for which it remains very much "a book of national history." Similarly, Catholicism is not simply the necessary precondition and antithesis to the modern Protestant culture that subsumes and replaces it, but exists beyond its resounding historical rejection in new forms of old memory (the Church of the Counter-Reformation and after). The *loss* of an original meaning implies both the idealism and the economics of nostalgia, in which an original significance, beautiful but naive, is exchanged in return for a place in the new canon. *Survival*, unlike loss, denotes those remnants of historical catastrophe that, at once persisting beyond their epochal revision and irrevocably reshaped by it, give the lie to the world-historical narratives founded on the assimilation or annihilation of their difference.

I would argue that the economies of both loss and survival in their interaction and contradiction need to be pursued in teaching as well as research on the "canon" of Western literature. Within the circuit of loss and gain, we always need to begin by reconstructing both an initial historical context and the later crises that will have retroactively rewritten the emphases and surface tensions of a text. From the perspective of survival, we need to correct the periodic retranscriptions carried out at the cataclysmic junctures of Western history by heeding those foreign elements *made foreign* precisely by the fact of persisting beyond the moment of their historic supersedure. As the distant historical origin of Western monotheism, the Jew is familiar to the Christian; it is only as a neighbor in the same city that he is a stranger. So too, there is nothing intrinsically alien about hagiography—until, that is, the world of discourse in which its relics are lodged is determined by humanist, rationalist, and Protestant values.

The corrective I propose to the exigencies of world history is not to pursue an ever more focused specification of individual contexts, but rather to attend to the fallout of epochal changes registered in generic transformations. The atavistic survivals and avatars of superseded discourses demonstrate both the ideology and the limits of the reigning historical narratives, without, however, positing a methodological domain external to them.[6] My name for this internal corrective to world history is "natural history." In this book, "natural history" refers most directly to that family of genres that treats the world as a Book of Nature; this includes the encyclopedia, the calendar, the herbal, the curio cabinet, and the still-life painting, like the collection of objects gathered about Caravaggio's Cupid. By extension, works of natural history tend to conceptualize time as a series of sedimented, unevenly distributed layers, strata of abandoned positions that record the drama of historical progress through its accidents and effluvia. Whereas from the perspective of world history, one position follows and subsumes another, from the perspective of natural history, one layer can contaminate, wrinkle, or undermine a contiguous one. One era can obdurately survive into the period that has supposedly surpassed it—like the irritating presence of the modern Jew in a Christian world, or the unbearable brightness of a Catholic president in a Protestant country. Or a later period can seep back into and reconfigure a chronologically prior level; thus under the critical gaze of the Reformation, Catholicism becomes tainted by the remnants of pagan idolatry suddenly visible in its gallery of saints.

I pose natural history not as a rival method to world history (an agon that would simply reinstate the authority of the competitor), but as the discourse that records the side effects of world-historical sea changes. We can read the phrase "afterlives of the saints" as an instance of both world history and natural history. In the redemptive telos of the Christian story, the death of hagiography as an autonomous genre is its means to new life, the *vita nuova* of the Renaissance; it is precisely the death of hagiography, its subsumption into new forms such as the novella, secular drama, and humanist biography, that guarantees its permanent installation in the canons of modern literature. Hagiography functions, then, as a consummate model and object of typological transformation for Renaissance literature, a generic paradigm that provides, for example, the terms for instituting Christian tragedy and tragi-comedy, as well as the canonization of the artist as the modern saint.

Yet we can also take "afterlife" not as the eternal reward won by Christ's sacrifice, but as the half-life of radioactive decay, or the bacterial decomposition of dead matter; from the perspective of natural history, "afterlife" means "side effect," the disturbing symptoms brought about by the work of cultural symbolization. A natural history of hagiography would glean those features and motifs of the saints' legends that neither are assimilated by the secular sublation of hagiography nor wither away into past history. These include the figure of the unconverted Jew as a survivor of typological translation, a motif that emerges in Griselda's repetition of Job at the end of the *Decameron*; the undisplaceable head of the Barabbas-like Barnardine in *Measure for Measure*; and Vasari's account of the Moses of Michelangelo admired by the Jews of modern Rome. Moreover, the epochal recharting of historical axes performed by the Reformation and the Counter-Reformation strangely equates the magical realism of the medieval saints with both the legalism of the Old Testament and the idolatry of paganism. Thus in *Measure for Measure*, the figure of the martyr falls on the side of the old Law; in *The Winter's Tale*, the Catholic and pagan calendars bleed into each other from the vantage point of their Protestant abrogation; and in Vasari's *Lives of the Artists*, hagiography represents both what is most progressive in Vasari's narrative method and the residual elements of natural history that interfere with his larger design. Finally, we must also be attentive to hagiography's hieroglyphic *Dingsprache* or language of things, the curiosity shop of religious objects that ornament the lives of the saints—flayed skins, talking heads, ointment jars, instruments of torture, relics, and broken idols. In passing into secular literature, these motifs *of* things themselves ossify *into* things,

rebuslike attributes of hagiography as a supplanted yet oddly persistent genre.

Read as an instance of both world history and natural history,
the "afterlives of the saints" names the symptom of hagiography's
own epochal displacement. The framework of world history pos-
tulates the dialectical unity between secularization and Christianization, a movement in which hagiography achieves its greatest
cultural power precisely through its apparent annulment by the classicizing, Reformational, humanist, rationalist, and empiricist initiatives of the Renaissance. Falling out from this movement, however,
is the afterlife of the genre's decay, the de-composing remnants of its
typological re-composition. In the archeological gaze of natural history, hagiography dimly glows as a fossilized discourse whose half-
forgotten shapes remain forever imprinted on the keystones of
modernity.

PART I

Typology and Hagiography

CHAPTER I

Typologies of the Renaissance

BURCKHARDT, WARBURG, AND BENJAMIN

In *On Christian Doctrine*, Augustine builds a scriptural precedent to defend Christian borrowing from classical learning:

> Just as the Egyptians had not only idols and grave burdens which the people of Israel detested and avoided, so also they had vases and ornaments of gold and silver and clothing which the Israelites took with them when they fled, as if to put them to a better use. . . . In the same way all the teachings of the pagans contain not only simulated and superstitious imaginings and grave burdens of unnecessary labor, which each of us leaving the society of the pagans ought to abominate and avoid, but also liberal disciplines more suited to the uses of truth, and some most useful precepts concerning morals. (XL.60)

Augustine uses the story of the Israelite women's gathering up of Egyptian jewelry and clothing on the eve of the Exodus to prefigure and justify the educated Christian's selective reliance on pagan learning (Ex. 3:22, 12:35). Augustine's exegetical maneuver builds a homology in which the Egyptians are to the Jews as Greco-Roman civilization is to Christianity: just as the Israelites took with them only the ornamental and utilitarian artefacts of the Egyptians, leaving behind all signs of idolatry, so the Christians should purify classical culture of its pagan elements by picking out its scientific and moral truths. This analogy depends in turn on Augustine's tacit equation of the Jews with the Christians according to the hermeneutic principle of biblical typology, in which each event of the Old Testament, granted full historical weight as an independent moment in time, gains its world-historical significance from unknowingly referring to the later, equally historical, moments realized by Christ and his Church. Like the pairing of prophets and sibyls on Michelangelo's Sistine Chapel ceiling, Augustine's reading of the episode from Exodus casts Christian culture as the historical fulfillment of both classicism and Judaism, insofar as Christianity clarifies, reorganizes, and sublates each of these alien civilizations into the authorizing yet superseded ground, at once historically autonomous and historically outdated, of the current program for cultural renewal. Biblical typology functions here both as a hermeneutic approach to a particular class of texts—those works acknowledged as neighboring on the Gospels without themselves being Christian—and as a theory of history, which grants significance to certain cultures, epochs, and events insofar as they are seen to refer to later moments in the narrative scheme of salvation.

By modeling the Christian *translatio* of the classical library on the relation between the New Testament and the Old, Augustine's appropriation of the scene from Exodus offers a "typology of the Renaissance" *avant la lettre*; hence Augustine's figure became a topos for humanist apologetics and self-representations in the period we now call the Renaissance, understood as the "rebirth" of classical culture out of Christianity. The solidification of the period term "Renaissance" by the great nineteenth-century historians, far from forgoing such structuring scriptural allusions, followed an abstracted, philosophized version of this typological rhythm. Indeed, the nineteenth-century "secularization" of historiography is itself an example of the typological dynamic, which raises Christian patterns of time to a new level of authority and explanatory power by purging them of any specifically religious content or transcendental reference.

This chapter examines the intellectual legacies, exchanges, and resistances that cross the careers of Jacob Burckhardt, Aby Warburg, and Walter Benjamin in order to demarcate the set of interpretive initiatives and historiographical motifs that make up both the historical profile and the nascent possibilities of Renaissance studies as a field of inquiry. Burckhardt's classic picture of Renaissance culture and the method of *Kulturgeschichte* that framed it depend on his disavowed dependence on Hegel's philosophical sublation of figural exegesis; in Burckhardt's historical vision, the culture of the Renaissance, presented as a synchronic cross section of daily life, manifests a world-historical narrative purportedly denied by his essayistic method and cultural pessimism. The assimilated Jewish scholars of the Warburg school, heirs to Burckhardt's cultural history, also inherited the Christian-secular dialectic at the heart of Burckhardt's periodization. Whereas Aby Warburg's emphasis on the iconography of the pagan gods and their afterlife in European texts and artefacts represented a potent yet unarticulated challenge to typological history, Erwin Panofsky's installation of the opposition between iconography and iconology, modeled on the Romantic distinction between allegory and symbol, reasserted the Burckhardtian genealogy of Warburg school practices. In 1927, Walter Benjamin, having recently completed *The Origin of the German Tragic Drama*, made an aborted effort to join the Warburg circle, his overture blocked by the cool reception of Panofsky. Benjamin's failed rapprochement with the Warburg school indicates both the affinity of his project with iconography and the unbridgeable gap between his methods and those of the Warburg scholars. I argue that Benjamin's reclamation of a Jewish remainder from the poetics of the period he called "Baroque" hit upon the passive resistance to typological historiography embodied by Warburg's emphasis on iconography as the vehicle of the *Nachleben der Antike*. To acknowledge the affinity with Benjamin's more radical project would have meant seriously confronting the Protestant biases of the German humanist tradition as well as the theological core of Western historical thinking, and this was something that Panofsky at least, and likely Warburg as well, were not prepared to do, given the depth of their identifications with German classical scholarship and its ideal of a secular culture based on historical consciousness.

This detour through German historiography constitutes my answer to the supplementation or outright rejection of the term "Renaissance" by many historians and historicist literary critics, who disparage the term's aesthetic biases or its emphasis on the Renaissance as neopagan or proto-secular.[1] Yet simply replacing the word "Renaissance" with an apparently less compromised alternative such as "early modern" usually means bypassing the way in which the establishment of a "Renaissance" epoch and canon took shape between the specific allusive and generic tactics of texts from the period on the one hand, and the scholarly and aesthetic discourses of the nineteenth and twentieth centuries on the other. This double temporal structure, always elusive, becomes increasingly difficult to foreground when we repress the histories of period terms by modernizing them, and when the task of contextualization takes precedent over the reconstruction of patterns and processes of generic transformation, within and also between historical moments. Rather than rejecting the word outright, we need to follow out the symbolic economies that support the conceptualization of "the Renaissance" in order to reach the limits and remainders of the term in alternative figurations and discourses. Here the work of Walter Benjamin on Baroque genre and iconography represents a crucial station in the vicissitudes of the postclassical canon, offering a model for Renaissance studies that would both address and redress the seductive syntheses of typological thinking.

Jacob Burckhardt: Renaissance 'Kulturgeschichte'

Burckhardt's 1860 *Die Kultur der Renaissance in Italien* succeeded in establishing if not inventing the mythos of the Renaissance as the birth of modern secular individualism.[2] "The Italian," Burckhardt writes, "was the first-born among the sons of modern Europe," because he was able to dissolve the corporate formations of medieval psychology, opening up the discovery of world and man:

In the Middle Ages both sides of human consciousness—that which was turned within as that which was turned without—lay dreaming or half awake beneath a common veil. The veil was woven of faith, illusion, and childish prepossession, through which the world and history were seen clad in strange hues. Man was conscious of himself only as member of a race, people, party, family, or corporation—only through some general category [*in irgendeiner Form des Allgemeinen*]. In Italy this veil first melted into air; an *objective* treatment and consideration of the state became possible. The *subjective* side at the same time asserted itself with corresponding emphasis; man became a spiritual *individual* [*geistiges* Individuum], and recognized himself as such. In the same way the Greek had once distinguished himself from the barbarian, and the Arabian had felt himself an individual at a time when other Asiatics knew themselves only as members of a race. (*Civilization* I: 143; *Kultur* 123)

In his theoretical writings Burckhardt disclaimed any Hegelian ties, rejecting providential narratives in favor of essayistic cross-sections of a culture's daily life. Yet Burckhardt's sampling from a moment in time continues to manifest the world-historical narrative that it claims to rescind. Such a narrative can be traced here in Burckhardt's sense for the expressive totality of the Renaissance (the notoriously influential pseudo-Hegelian *Zeitgeist*) and in the dialectic between the objective exploration of the outer world and the subjective development of self-consciousness that distinguishes "the Middle Ages" from "the Renaissance" in the process of separating the individual from his or her environment.[3] Whereas medieval people, like the allegorical works they crafted, veiled the particular with the general, the Renaissance individual was able to distinguish internal and external phenomena by developing them in relation to each other. Through this reciprocal articulation of subjective and objective particularity, the artists, humanists, and politicians of Renaissance Italy achieved world-historical significance, a meaning always produced by and immanent in the process of historical individuation rather than external to it as a transcendent principle.

Burckhardt's own historical method and project, termed *Kulturgeschichte*, entails a similar progressive particularization of the his-

torical field into its many cultural activities, from politics and religion to festive life and manners—a particularization, however,
which never falls into mere atomization, since all the elements add
up to a coherent picture of Renaissance life. As Hayden White has
argued, Burckhardt's denigration of allegory in favor of "'realistic'
representation" in his art-historical writing forms the aesthetic
equivalent and methodological ideal of the dialectical individuation
of human and world that Burckhardt discovers in the Renaissance
(261). Moreover, the relation of the Renaissance itself to ancient
culture is similarily integrated in its many-sidedness, a synthesis synonymous with the metaphor of rebirth that gives the period its
name. Whereas elsewhere in Europe, "men deliberately and with
reflection borrowed this or the other element of classical civilization" (*Civilization* I: 179), in Italy, "the Renaissance is not a mere
fragmentary imitation or compilation, but a new birth [*Wiederge-
burt*]" (*Civilization* I: 180; *Kultur* 165). Here Burckhardt distinguishes
between what Erwin Panofsky will later call the "renascences"—
the partial, allegorically driven revivals of Northern Europe—and
the Renaissance proper, which entails the symbolically integrated
reanimation of a cohesive classical past. The historical consciousness of the Renaissance, understood as the multiplicitous yet unified,
realistic yet selective restoration of the ancient past, mirrors the project of the cultural historian, who strives to recreate the infinitely
varied yet richly concatenated activities of a previous way of life
chosen by the historian for its high level of cultural achievement.[4]
For Burckhardt as later for Panofsky, the Renaissance presents the
model as well as the object of the historian's cultural inquiry, not
only because its artefacts coalesce into the unity of a distinct period
and way of life, but because they do so by themselves recreating an
earlier epoch's universe of form and meaning.

    In the historical narrative provided by German idealism, espe-
cially by Hegel, the classical period resurrected in and as the Renaissance was itself defined by the harmonization of subject with
object and form with theme. In his *Aesthetics*, Hegel defines the
classical work of art as a "perfection . . . grounded in the complete
interpenetration of inner free individuality and the external exis-

tent in which and as which this individuality appears" (I: 441). The classical work of art, like the aesthetic symbol, perfectly balances objectivity and subjectivity, or, in Burckhardt's definition of the Renaissance, the reciprocally "discovered" realms of world and humanity (*Culture* II: 279). Christianity, fundamentally at odds with the polytheism that animates classical art, nonetheless reachieves the classical immanence of divinity in humanity and meaning in form through the doctrine of the Incarnation.[5] What permits the resurrectional relay of pagan antiquity into modern Christianity is the intermediate, purely negative position occupied by Judaism in Hegel's work, and by the Middle Ages in Burckhardt's assumption of the dialectic. In Hegel's account of Judaism, the Mosaic prohibition against idolatry and the insistence on God's absolute Oneness radically sunders the pagan integration of the divine and the mundane—and thus calls out for their reconciliation in the new *symbolon* embodied by Christ.[6]

The two artistic responses to such a complete cleavage are *sublimity* and *allegory*: each mode places God beyond representation, the first by playing out the limits of cognition and mimesis in order to brush against the infinite, the second by insisting on the absolute conventionality of its own rhetorical conceits in order at once to demonstrate and to shelter the esoteric transcendence of allegory's subject matter. As negative representational modes, sublimity and allegory occupy parallel positions in the historical schemata posited by Hegel and adapted by Burckhardt. In Hegel's dialectic of religion, sublimity, associated already by Longinus with the Hebrew Bible, lies at the midpoint of a sequence that leads from classicism to Christianity via Judaism. In Burckhardt's narrative, allegory, the medieval signifying mode *par excellence*, defines the "Middle Ages" as the negative moment that counterpoints antiquity and the Renaissance, permitting the latter to resurrect the former through the negation of the middle.

Mapped onto each other, these parallel trajectories for the destiny of classicism produce some paradoxical but not surprising correspondences, given the hegemony of a secularized Protestantism in German historiography and philosophy:

Hegel	Burckhardt
Antiquity	Antiquity
[Beauty]	[Symbol]
Judaism	Catholic Middle Ages
[Sublimity]	[Allegory]
Christian	The Secular
Modernity	Renaissance

Catholicism and *Judaism*, opposites when understood in terms of the historical development of the one from the other, end up sharing the role of negated middle in these overlapping dialectics of history. So too, Christian modernity in Hegel's scheme and the secular Renaissance in Burckhardt's each put the emphasis on a different side of the Christian-secular dialectic while demonstrating its essential unity. Between these two thinkers, European history unfolds as a series of systematically recalibrated typological oppositions: Judaism negates paganism; Christianity, in confronting Judaism, revives paganism as "classicism"; and modernity, marking the rebirth of antiquity, cancels medieval Christianity in order to make way for both the Reformation and secularization. In each of these moments, the patterns of figural exegesis underwrite the movement of the ages, and are then themselves renounced in order to be renovated, moved into ever-higher heights of historico-rational freedom from their origin in the hermeneutics of Judeo-Christian revelation.

The Christian art of the high Renaissance, with its scriptural subject matter, classical forms, and incarnational motifs, exemplifies the synthesis of classicism and Christianity in modern culture. Indeed, the ease with which one can substitute a series of terms naming theological doctrines—incarnation, resurrection, transfiguration, transumption—in the place of either the philosophical term "synthesis" or the historiographical word "Renaissance" indicates the structural complicity between the German philosophy of history, the exegetical metaphors of Christianity, and the periodization of the Renaissance. The metaphor of rebirth that gives the Renaissance its name owes a great deal to biblical typology, which provides the model of its own sublation into secular modernity. For example, Christ's injunction that the Pharisee Nicodemus "be born anew" (John 3:7) is not simply a universal call to baptism and spiritual regeneration. It more specifically enjoins the active overturning of the Jewish legalism that Nicodemus represents. Pauline images of baptism as a rebirth out of spiritual death equate the prior mortification of the man newly born with the Law of the Old Covenant (e.g., Col. 2:11–14). In the baptismal metaphor of a *vita nuova* that anoints the secular Renaissance, antiquity lives again as modernity in the same way that Judaism undergoes rebirth in Christianity. Whereas Judaism must slough off its legalistic trappings and bridge the sublime gap between God and human in order to be regenerated in the New Covenant, the Renaissance sublation cancels the allegorical forms, corporate identities, piecemeal classicism, and fossilized spirituality of the Middle Ages, which constitutes the historical veil separating the Roman past from its Italian rebirth.

In Burckhardt's account of the Renaissance, hagiography, the medieval Catholic literary form *par excellence*, dramatizes the exegetical figures that allow for its own negation by secular culture. In a novellalike anecdote itself dependent on hagiography for its prose form, Burckhardt recounts the story of a town that debated how to honor a *condottiere* who had freed them from foreign aggression: "At last one of them rose and said, 'Let us kill him and then worship him as our patron saint.' And so they did, following the example set by the Roman Senate with Romulus" (*Civilization* I: 40). Not only are the conventions of hagiography used here to kill off and thus immortalize a hero, but the Roman example of Romulus rewrites and displaces the medieval paradigm, similarly immortalizing it through anullment. The great tyrannicides, patterned on classical models invoked as no "mere phrase" [*reine Phrase und Stilsache*], often occurred in churches, the only place where the despots and their families were sure to convene publicly. Burckhardt cites one conspiracy in which the signal for the bloodbath was "the words of the Creed, 'Et incarnatus est'" (*Civilization* I: 76–78; *Kul-*

tur 55); indeed, in Burckhardt's account, the tyrannicides effectively "incarnated" the Roman past by violating the sanctity of the Church at the moment when its chief doctrine was enunciated. In this brave new world, "Catos and Scipios hold the place of the saints and heroes of Christianity" (*Civilization* I: 179); that is, classicizing secularization and the installment of a new literary scripture took place through the razing and raising of medieval hagiography, a dialectic that borrows and renovates the paradigm of typological transumption provided by the New Testament.

Yet Italy, the baptismal font of the Renaissance, at once resurrects the ancient past and forms the superseded grounds of the modern present. Recall here Burckhardt's representation of the Italian as "the first-born among the sons of modern Europe"; seemingly straightforward, the phrase limits as well as celebrates Italy's place in the history of the modern West. For the Italian is the "first-born son" not only because he initiates modernity by renewing antiquity but also, following the story of Esau and Jacob, because Italy will ultimately *not* inherit the legacy of the classical past. In Augustine's gloss of the narrative, "Isaac is the Law and the Prophets; and Christ is blessed by the Law and the Prophets, even by the lips of Jews, as by someone who does not know what he is doing, because the Law and the Prophets are themselves not understood" (*City of God* XVI: 37). If Isaac represents the Law and the Prophets as they are inherited and reinterpreted by Christ, Esau, the first-born son who inherits nothing, represents the Jews not absorbed by the New Covenant, the elder brother who discounts himself from the renovated law. Here are the two faces of Judaism in Christian historiography: on the one hand, the Old Testament represents the heroic yet naive ground of modern faith that provides Christianity with its historic prototypes and patriarchs; on the other hand, the modern Jews who resist incorporation into the New Covenant instantiate the unrighteous remnant of the historical process who threaten to give the lie to its story of progress.

The implicit argument of Burckhardt's putatively athetic book runs like this: because Italy had no unifying political system such as feudalism or monarchy, it was free to invent modern forms of statecraft in its many petty despotisms and republics. In Burckhardt's phrase, the Italians could treat "the state as a work of art" in the laboratory-studios provided by their fragmented political geography, yet, precisely because of the absence of a unifying national structure, Italy itself could not coalesce into a modern nation-state. This destiny was reserved for the northern countries, which, like Jacob, inherited the cultural legacy intended for the first-born son. In Burckhardt's narrative of cultural rebirth, Italy, for all its innovations, is ultimately like Esau, who, logically set up to receive his father's blessing (here, classical civilization), instead both wittingly and unwittingly facilitates the ascendance of the younger son (the modern nations of northern Europe). The precocity of the Italian Renaissance made possible the maturity of European modernity, a destiny that the Italians themselves necessarily missed in the very act of founding.

In this Burckhardt's book registers the division of Italy in the modern European consciousness between the site of classical culture (both Roman and Italian) and the degraded, romantic vacation destination of its more economically and politically developed neighbors; in typological terms, Italy represents both the superseded yet glorious foundation of modernity (Isaac, the Old Testament) and the remnant of the sublation that its own experiments have made possible (Esau, Judaism after Christianity). Such a narrative is already implicit in early Protestant historiography; in 1523 Luther figured humanism as playing John the Baptist to the Reformation: "there has never been a great revelation of the word of God unless He has first prepared the way by the rise and prosperity of languages and letters, as though they were John the Baptists."[7] In Protestant historiography it is no accident that Italy, perennially *immature* because it was so brilliantly *premature*, is not only the cradle of secular humanism but also the seat of a Catholicism that it never outgrew.[8] In the logic of Burckhardt's narrative, just as Italy's lack of an overarching political structure enabled modern political experiment but prevented national development, so the tenacity and absurdity of a specifically *Roman* Catholicism both stimulated the fermentation of anticlerical sentiment and prevented the blossoming of a true Reformation. What, then, does Burckhardt mean by "the culture of the Renaissance *in Italy*"? The Italian Renaissance embodies the typological resurrection of antiquity through the negation of the Middle Ages; at the same time, it at once makes possible and falls short of the political maturity of the modern nations and the theological maturity of the Protestant Reformation.

Aby Warburg: Iconography and the 'Nachleben der Antike'

Aby Warburg, bibliophile and independent scholar (1866–1929), is most famous for gathering together in Hamburg a collection of books and researchers known as the Warburg school, an organization in many ways fashioned to be the repository of Burckhardt's *Kulturgeschichte*, because of its emphasis on the interplay between poetic, visual, and theatrical practices and because of its goal of tracing *"das Nachleben der Antike,"* the afterlife of antiquity, especially in the Renaissance (Gombrich, *Aby Warburg* 16). We have already noted the connections between Burckhardt and the Warburg school's most successful, committed, and prolific contributor, Erwin Panofsky (1892–1968); Panofsky's historiographical distinction between piecemeal renascences and the structurally unified Renaissance, mirroring his methodological opposition between the decoding work of iconography and the synthetic, contextualizing project of iconology, is founded on the aesthetic and historical discriminations of Burckhardt. Panofsky's "Iconography and Iconology," subtitled "An Introduction to the Study of Renaissance Art" —an essay that presents itself as both a methodological statement and a theory of historical periods—ends with a laudatory citation from Burckhardt.[9] In Panofsky as in Burckhardt, the Renaissance reconciliation of classical image with classical meaning mirrors the modern iconologist's hermeneutic integration of art and culture through the progressive articulation of past and present.

Aby Warburg also pays tribute to his Swiss predecessor in his early work on Botticelli (1893), an essay that links the painter's mythological inventions to both Ovidian poetry and the theatrical experiments of quattrocento Florence:

We here understand what Jacob Burckhardt, infallible as always in his general judgment, surmised in anticipation: "The tradition of pageantry in Italy, in its more elevated form, is a true transition from life to art." (Warburg, *Gesammelte Schriften* I: 37; trans. Gombrich, *Aby Warburg* 63)[10]

Here Warburg founds his own project of reconstructing the horizon of scholarly and visual motifs available to Botticelli on Burckhardt's *Kulturgeschichte*, which Warburg understands as the establishment of the confluence between art and life exemplified by the moving images of *das Festwesen*, the pageantry of feasts and festivals. In the preface to his 1902 essay "Bildniskunst und florentinisches Bürgertum" (Pictorial art and the Florentine bourgeoisie), Warburg sets for himself the task laid out but never achieved by Burckhardt himself, namely, to read art and cultural practices together in order to produce "a comprehensive [*zusammenfassende*] representation of the entire culture" (*Gesammelte Schriften* I: 93).[11]

Yet, despite the self-professed allegiances and clear continuities between Burckhardt's *Kulturgeschichte* and the researches of the Warburg school, there is an important historical difference between Burckhardt and most of the practitioners of the Hamburg circle, including Panofsky, Edgar Wind, and Fritz Saxl as well as Warburg himself.[12] All of these scholars were Jews, working in the high tradition of German humanism and classicism that attracted so many Jewish intellectuals of that time, even though that tradition was implicitly and explicitly founded on a Protestant logic and ethos that negated their discursive position on the canceled yet persistent ground of the Western tradition. Although this difference may seem merely sociological at first, I would argue that it had profound if subtle effects on the Warburg school's reception of the typological foundations of Burckhardt's Renaissance idea.

In his intellectual biography of Warburg, E. H. Gombrich recounts a quasi-mythical anecdote told by Warburg's older brother Max on the occasion of Aby's death:

When he was thirteen, Aby made me an offer of his birthright. He, as the eldest, was destined to enter the firm. I was then only twelve,

rather too immature to reflect, and so I agreed to purchase his birthright from him. It was not a pottage of lentils, however, which he
demanded, but a promise that I would always buy him all the books
he wanted. After a very brief pause for reflection, I consented. I told
myself that when I was in the business I could, after all, always find
the money to pay for the works of Schiller, Goethe, Lessing and perhaps also Klopstock, and so, unsuspecting, I gave him what I must
now admit was a very large blank cheque. (cited in Gombrich, *Aby
Warburg* 22)

The founding myth of the Warburg legend retells the story of Jacob
and Esau, an allusion that enacts a series of economic, intellectual,
and cultural transfers. The basic intent of the anecdote, of course, is
to dramatize Aby's not-so-foolish trading of commercial wealth and
responsibility (the Warburgs were a highly successful banking family) for scholarly freedom and independence.[13] The staging of this
scene in Aby's bar mitzvah year, however, also predicts (or rather
reflects back on) Warburg's rejection of his family's Jewish obser-
vances, as Max pictures Aby trading his birthright—a legacy that is
religious as well as economic—for a modern secular canon, the library of German classics that Max imagines purchasing for his older
brother. From this latter perspective Esau functions as a type of the
assimilator, who sells his Jewish birthright to the brother who will
become the patriarch and namesake of Israel. Finally, in the irony
provided by retrospect (and here lies the wit of the story), Warburg
will in fact have traded his birthright not for Goethe, Schiller, and
Lessing, but for the *Nachleben der Antike*, or what Burckhardt called
the Renaissance. These two canons, comically opposed to each
other in Max Warburg's tale—German versus international, in-print
versus rare, limited versus immense—are in fact deeply implicated in
each other, insofar as the idea of the Renaissance was fashioned in
large part by German intellectuals and historians who saw themselves as the classical tradition's rightful heirs, the ascendant Jacob
in relation to Italy's Esau.

   Whereas Christian typology takes Esau as a figure of Jewish im-
prudence and bad faith, the same character read from within Judaism represents Jewish self-negation, the bartering off of one's place

in the history of Israel in exchange for a transient profane pleasure.[14] Insufficiently Jewish from the one perspective (Esau as a figure of assimilation) and excessively Jewish from the other (Esau as a type of Jewish intransigence), the exegetical vagaries of the biblical character offer a poignant metaphor for the assimilated Jewish intellectual's double lack of birthright in pre-Nazi Germany, self-excluded from a "traditional" Judaism that seemed increasingly untenable, yet never fully included in a secular (Christian) society founded on the progressive spiritualization or reformation of everything residually Jewish in Christianity.

Apart from the obvious political exigencies that eventually led to the relocation of the Warburg school from Hamburg to London in 1933, how did the double exclusion represented by the figure of Esau mark Warburg's inheritance of Burckhardt's Renaissance? The key term here, the methodological category most closely associated with the Warburg school, is *iconography*, the study of the verbal meanings of visual signs. On the one hand, iconography, which since its inception in the Renaissance has been fundamentally associated with the study of pagan myth (and secondarily of Catholic imagery), demarcates that domain of classical culture for which, in the Jewish reading of Esau, Warburg was willing to sell his Hebrew birthright. On the other hand, iconography as the study of specifically allegorical and emblematic modes of representation stands at odds with the incarnational aesthetics that determine both the content and the structure of the Renaissance in the tradition of Burckhardt. By making an outmoded form of expression into the center of aesthetic inquiry, the pursuit of iconography infuses, within the very gesture of joining the German humanist tradition, a constitutional resistance to its Christological and typological narratives of periodization—without, however, articulating this resistance in terms of either the positivity of an alternative tradition or the negativity of a concerted critique.

"Iconography," etymologically "to write with images," names a field of inquiry and aesthetic expression fundamentally at odds with the Jewish prohibition against idolatry and graven images, a commandment that helped determine Warburg's view of antiquity as a storehouse of potentially dangerous magical influences. Warburg, that is, was acutely aware of the structural complicities between "iconography" and "idolatry" explored at greater length in my chapter on *The Winter's Tale*; departing from the idealism of the German classical tradition which he saw himself continuing, Warburg was drawn to antiquity precisely as the site of demonological, astrological, and superstitious beliefs and behaviors. Warburg's antiquity is characterized not by the *stille Grösse* of Winckelmann, but rather by the Dionysiac dance of what Warburg calls the *Nympha*, the "idealized female figure in motion" of classical statuary which Warburg reencounters in Renaissance images of Venus and Flora, Judith and Salome, serving girls, angels, and young boys (Gombrich, *Aby Warburg* 65, 108).[15] Yet, unlike Nietzsche, whom he cites with some frequency, Warburg maintained a critical relationship to the irrational forces of a paganism he saw resurging in contemporary politics, a criticism conditioned not only by humanist rationalism but also by Mosaic law, a code that emphasized the demonic thread of pagan antiquity at the expense of its ideal beauty. It is no accident that Warburg linked his childhood discovery of anthropology in the form of *Indianer-Romane* to the time when he first broke the dietary laws, as if his lifelong dedication to the study of pagan religion flowed directly out of his departure from Jewish observance.[16]

If Warburg's anthropological rather than aesthetic emphasis already manifests a certain distance from idealism carved out from within the discourse of German classicism, the Faustian outlines of his biography—the descent into a madness equated with classical antiquity, the dangerous bartering of religion for knowledge, the romance with an irrational past figured as Woman—indicate the ability of German humanism to assimilate Warburg's career to its own patterns of the intellectual life. The very darkness of Warburg's vision of antiquity finds ample precedent in the German tradition. From this perspective, Warburg's emphasis on the iconography of idolatry locates him as one of the last great cultivators of the German humanist tradition before the rise of Nazism, making him the heir of both Burckhardt's Renaissance and his cultural pessimism.

Through the study of classical iconography, Warburg has effectively "joined the club" of German humanists and cultural historians, exacerbating its Faustian and Dionysian strands while remaining committed to its belief in the aesthetic and moral ballast provided by the classical tradition.[17]

Yet iconography is *not* the chosen method of either Burckhardt the art historian or Burckhardt the cultural historian, since iconography, as Erwin Panofsky points out, limits itself to "the identification of . . . images, stories and allegories," rescinding the right to conceive of artworks as "manifestations of underlying principles . . . [or] 'symbolical' values," a task reserved for what Panofsky calls iconology (*Meaning* 29, 31). Whereas Panofsky aligns iconography with allegory as a purely analytic and convention-bound mode of expression and interpretation, iconology approaches the symbol, insofar as it intuits the deeper meanings and unifying themes that weave a work of art into the multifaceted world of its period. Panofsky fashions this distinction, explicitly founded on the opposition between dead writing and living speech (*-graphy* and *-logy*) as an associate of the Warburg Institute (*Meaning* 32); it is as if he is reacting against the potential dissonance between Warburg's iconographic project and the tradition of German humanism, a tradition that, since Goethe, Hegel, and the Romantics, tended to be profoundly antiallegorical in its aesthetic and historical vision. The Romantics' Pauline valorization of the incarnational logic of the symbol at the expense of the dead letter of allegory facilitated the structural identification between the apparently opposed theologies and aesthetics of classicism and Christianity, a homology organized, as we have seen, around the negated middle ground reserved for Judaism (and, in Burckhardt's schema, for the Middle Ages).

As Panofsky's defensive distinction indicates, iconography as both a mode of expression and a method of analysis overlaps with the techniques of allegory; if anything, it suffers from an even greater tendency to hieroglyphic obscurity and cryptic wit, since the task of interpreting philosophical abstractions, religious doctrines, or poetic texts in visual images requires a punning dexterity that leads, often intentionally, to the hermetically sealed more than

the hermeneutically open. Warburg, as Gombrich is at pains to insist throughout his biography—perhaps for the same defensive reasons that Panofsky invents iconology—was not interested in iconography per se; that is, he did not limit himself to deciphering the
intended meanings of a particular image. Like Panofsky, he read images symptomatically, as unconscious expressions of deeper movements or psychological currents; in this sense, he ascribed to the
hermeneutics if not the aesthetics of the symbol, since he understood individual works to express or incarnate other, "deeper," tendencies. Yet in Warburg's work iconography comes in the place of
typology, an allegorical substitute that disturbs the dialectical flow of
Christian-secular world history.

At first glance, iconography and typology might seem closely
affiliated, since both can be seen as species of allegory whose contents and methods often overlap. Thus typology, as in the design of
the Sistine Chapel cycles, often provides both the details and the
overall organization of an iconographic program.[18] But Eric Auerbach—the scholar most responsible for reclaiming typology as a category for literary criticism, and, like Panofksy, a man exiled from
the German humanist tradition that he supported and elaborated
to the end—adamantly distinguished typology from allegory, in
terms that repeat the idealist opposition between symbol and allegory.[19] According to Auerbach,

> a figural schema permits both its poles—the figure and its fulfill-
> ment—to retain the characteristics of concrete historical reality, in
> contradistinction to what obtains with symbolic or allegorical per-
> sonifications, so that figure and fulfillment—although the one "sig-
> nifies" the other—have a significance which is not incompatible with
> their being real. (*Mimesis* 195)

Unlike an allegorical sign, a typological *figura* does not lose its own
claim to historical reality when it is made to signify a later event or
divine meaning, which sub-sumes without con-suming the prior
occurrence: "It remains an event, does not become a mere sign"
(*Mimesis* 196). By distinguishing typology from allegory, Auerbach
highlights (and celebrates) the way in which figural exegesis implies
a philosophy of history as well as a hermeneutic system. Typology

raised to an aesthetic and historical principle becomes a way of sav-
ing medieval literature from its own deadeningly allegorical procedures. It should come as no surprise that Auerbach grounds his figural reading of Dante on Hegel's comments on the *Divine Comedy* in
the *Aesthetics*, where Dante is made to embody or enact through
his very means of expression the incarnational vision of Christianity,
thus taking his place in the history of world literature.[20]

Whereas Burckhardt's period term "Renaissance" crystallizes
and renovates a foundational metaphor of Christian-secular historiography, Warburg's phrase "*das Nachleben der Antike*" demonstrates
the disturbance that iconography produces in the exegetical correspondences of typology. The word *Nachleben* or afterlife does not
name a distinct epoch or period, but rather sets the historian the
task of tracing the vicissitudes of particular image-complexes in their
passage through many discourses: the figure of the pagan *Nympha*,
for example, as her dance metamorphoses through history, or the
changing constellations of the Zodiac in Greek, Egyptian, Arabic,
and European sciences of the stars. Burckhardt's *Kulturgeschichte* favors the synchronic cross section, the picture of a period—this synchrony, however, always displays a key moment in a world-historical narrative, and thus ratifies the providential scheming it purports
to eschew. Warburg's iconography pursues the diachronic strand,
the afterlife of an allusion—not as a dramatically structured story,
but as the dissemination, breakdown, and recomposition of images
across time and space. Burckhardt's synchrony reinforces the unities
required for narration, whereas Warburg's diachrony reads artefacts
as sedimentations rather than incarnations of history.

The key word in Warburg's phrase is *Nachleben*, not *Leben*: the
prefix *nach-* points to the remnants and deformations as well as the
successful rebirth of ancient images; *Nachleben* carries the sense of
"survival," of living beyond or after, evoking the atavistic remainder
of a superseded position more than the inner-historical transcendence of a cultural monument. Although Warburg retains Burckhardt's (and later Panofsky's) distinction between authentic and inauthentic revivals of antiquity, his work always reconstructs the
degradation of classical images in their trajectory through Hellenistic, Arabic, or medieval traditions of scholarship as crucial chapters

in the transmission and restoration of the antique "originals." These originals in turn always bear traces of pagan ritual and superstition that prevent their full assimilation to the classical ideal; for Warburg, the classicism of an image is always retroactive, the *Antike* only appearing in its *Nachleben*. Like the phrase "migration of symbols" coined by Rudolph Wittkower, another scholar affiliated with the Warburg library, the expression "*Nachleben der Antike*" implies a tradition always in diaspora; even its originary moments are internally distanced from the symbolic harmony of meaning resident in form. In Warburg's analysis, moreover, an artist's ability to purify a particular image of its historical accretions never becomes the defining achievement of a period or culture, since contaminated and restored images can coexist not only in the same epoch, but even in the same work. So too, the *getreuen Wiederbelebung*, the true resuscitation, of a classical motif often comes about as the result of a resistance to rather than an affirmation of the reigning style or intellectual tendency of the artist's milieu.[21]

Finally, Warburg's emphasis on the unconscious charges or "engrams" that imported images can carry into a work in excess of the receiving artist's intentions brings his method closer to a psychoanalytic theory of intertextuality than to *Kulturgeschichte* in the manner of Burckhardt. The word "engram," which Warburg borrowed from the psychologist Ewald Hering, indicates the deposit or "writing" of energy in a memory trace (Gombrich, *Aby Warburg* 241–42); as a species of the engram, iconography comes to encompass a writing-with-images that now implies a whole energetics of unconscious inscription and involuntary recall, as well as the conscious selection and transmission of a tradition through the use of allegorically coded visual signs. Although the "psychic polarities" that dominate Warburg's psychology of artistic expression now feel dated and simplistic, his belief that images can function as an "organ of social memory" that records and transmits archaic perceptions, gestures, affects, and traumas points toward the possibility of a psychoanalysis of allusion.

But now I am going through a familiar gesture in the minor genre of *homages-à-Warburg*: namely, showing how his work predicts some important critical innovation of which the current writer just happens to be an exponent, while also pointing out the yoke of idealism that prevented him from bringing to fruition the nascent originality of his thought (a task reserved for us).[22] Such a gesture insufficiently mediates the present critical moment (whether it embodies psychoanalytic criticism, feminism, historical anthropology, or cultural studies) with the historical logics out of whose interference the peculiar outline of Warburg's contribution emerges for us. My method in this book is not "psychoanalytic intertextuality," taken as a modern critical technique applied to Renaissance works, but rather the dialectical analysis of generic transformations and iconographic migrations. (By "dialectical" I mean here that I always try to implicate the method of analysis in the history of the object to which it is applied.) This includes following the discourses of genre and iconography themselves as they have crucially passed through the allusive machinery of post-classical texts, and noting how they have been shaped by the modern reflection on, retroactive consolidation of, and dissonant intervention in the Renaissance as a canon and a period. In this project, biblical typology is not simply a theological motif and narrative principle to be rediscovered, in the style of Auerbach, in the creations of late medieval and Renaissance authors. Biblical typology represents here one of the foundational principles of modern periodization per se, and thus must be dialectically engaged rather than simply rejected or replaced. So too, the point in these past few pages has been to show how Warburg's work disturbed the German tradition that it joined by putting *das Nachleben der Antike*—an afterlife that takes shape in the literalizations, misreadings, and redistributions performed by iconography—in the place of its supposed synonym or subset, "the Renaissance." Such a substitution occurred neither as the result of a conscious program to subvert German humanism nor as the prophetic intuition of future critical movements, but rather, at least in part, as the result of the paradoxes attendant on Warburg's conflicted historical position as a Jew dedicated to explicating the exegetically intricated canons of pagan antiquity, Christian hermeneutics, and post-Renaissance secularism.

Walter Benjamin: Allegory and the Baroque

If such a reading feels tendentious when applied to Warburg, so self-consciously alienated from anything resembling a living (or "surviving," *nachlebende*) Jewish tradition, its outlines come into focus when we read Warburg's iconographic research against Walter Benjamin's negative critique of *Kulturgeschichte* and his positive analysis of Baroque and modern allegory, projects that developed in tandem with his ongoing if often oblique pursuit of the Judaism encrypted in modernity. Benjamin's *Ursprung des deutschen Trauerspiels*, written between 1924 and 1925, was published in 1928, after its submission as a *Habilitationsschrift* or qualifying work to the University of Frankfurt, where it was ultimately rejected (Steiner, "Introduction" 7–11). In December 1927, Hugo von Hoffmansthal sent Erwin Panofsky the volume of his journal *Neue deutschen Beiträge* in which Benjamin's chapter on Baroque melancholy had appeared, along with a note indicating that Benjamin was interested in earning the attention of the Warburg circle (*"die Aufmerksamkeit dieses Kreises erwerben"*) (cited Brodersen 91). It is clear from Benjamin's correspondence with Hoffmansthal that Panofsky's reply was discouraging:

> Thank you for sending me Panofsky's odd letter. I was aware that he is an art historian "by profession." But based on the nature of his iconographic interests, I thought I could assume that he was the same kind of man as Émile Mâle, e.g., someone who would be interested in important things, if not to the same extent, even if they have nothing to do with his profession in all its manifestations. (Benjamin to Hoffmansthal, February 8, 1928; *Correspondence* 326)

Note that Benjamin singles out iconography as the point of contact between his own work and that of the Warburg school; in the letter to Hoffmansthal, he associates iconography with cross-disciplinary exploration, representing it as that feature of artefacts that exceeds the purview of a "profession in all its manifestations," a discipline, that is, conceived as a reflective totality made up of reinforcing regions of interest. Although Panofsky's discouraging reply terminated Benjamin's attempt to gain a position at the Warburg

school, a copy of the *Trauerspiel* book did make its way into the collection of the Warburg library, inscribed in Aby Warburg's hand
with a greeting to Fritz Saxl, dated July 4, 1928 (Brodersen 90). In
his introduction to the *Origin of the German Tragic Drama*, George
Steiner, calling Panofsky's skeptical response "the most ominous
moment in Walter Benjamin's career," speculates that Warburg's circle "would have afforded Benjamin a genuine intellectual, psychological home," and even that a later invitation from Panofsky in
London "might have averted his early death" (Steiner, "Introduction" 19); Steiner, who speaks here as one of the most prominent
preservers of German humanism in exile, imagines Benjamin's career following a path more like his own. I would argue instead that
Benjamin's presumption of common ground with Aby Warburg and
his associates bears witness to the unarticulated critique of a typologically organized historiography in Warburg's work, and that
Panofsky's rejection of the overture reveals the insupportability of
that critique when approached from within the Burckhardtian
framework of Renaissance *Kulturgeschichte* and German humanism.

The second half of the *Ursprung des deutschen Trauerspiels* is devoted to a study of allegory, which Benjamin salvages from its fatal
demotion by Goethe's valorization of the symbol. Whereas the symbol epitomizes the aesthetic reconciliation of form and meaning,
allegory for Benjamin belongs to the domain of theology, which
forms the disavowed grounds of aesthetics. Thus begins the section
on "Allegory and *Trauerspiel*," which stages the ascendancy of symbol over allegory as a Baroque tyrant-martyr drama:

> For over a hundred years the philosophy of art has been subject to
> the tyranny of a usurper who came to power in the chaos which fol-
> lowed in the wake of romanticism. The striving on the part of the
> romantic aestheticians after a resplendent but ultimately non-com-
> mittal knowledge of an absolute has secured a place in the most ele-
> mentary theoretical debates about art for a notion of the symbol
> which has nothing more than the name in common with the gen-
> uine notion. This latter, which is the one used in the field of theology,
> could never have shed that sentimental twilight over the philosophy of
> beauty which has become more and more impenetrable since the end
> of early romanticism. . . . The unity of the material and the tran-

scendental object, which constitutes the paradox of the theological symbol, is distorted into a relationship between appearance and essence. . . . But the foundations of this idea were laid long before. In classicism the tendency to the apotheosis of existence in the individual who is perfect, in more than an ethical sense, is clear enough. What is typically romantic is the placing of this perfect individual within a progression of events which is, it is true, infinite, but is nevertheless redemptive, even sacred. . . . In contrast the baroque apotheosis is a dialectical one. It is accomplished in the movement between extremes. In this eccentric and dialectic process the harmonious inwardness of classicism plays no role, for the reason that the immediate problems of the baroque, being politico-religious problems, did not so much affect the individual and his ethics as his religious community. (*Origin* 159–61)

Benjamin opposes the theological conception of the symbol, in which the work of art manages to join the heterogeneous realms of spirit and matter without harmonizing them, to the aesthetic conception, which reduces matter to a manifestation or appearance of spirit by enforcing a semiotic model of the artwork. The aesthetic understanding of the symbol is *incarnational*, especially when the plastic image of classicism ("the apotheosis of existence in the individual who is perfect") is temporalized into a story of historical salvation in Romanticism, which places this perfect individual within a "redemptive, even sacred" "progression of events." The model here is the Christian resurrection of the classical symbol effected by biblical typology, which restores the paganism it negates by passing the classical ideal through the stations of the Cross.[23]

But doesn't incarnation belong to theology, the discourse to which Benjamin credits the "genuine"—that is, allegorical—understanding of the symbol? Recall here Hegel's discussion of the fracturing of the classical symbol by Jewish monotheism, a schism reasserted rather than reconciled in the two possible responses to it (sublimity and allegory) and overcome only in the symbolic ideal of Christian incarnation. Rather than associating the theological symbol with Christianity, Benjamin seems to locate it in the sublime-allegorical period, since he opposes the nonsynthetic unity of matter and spirit "accomplished in the movement between extremes" to the "harmonious inwardness" of classicism. Such a monotheism would remain at odds with both classical paganism and its complement in that Christianity-compatible-with-classicism that we have associated with German humanism and the idea of Renaissance. Benjamin finds traces of such a monotheism in Baroque theology and religious iconography:

> even the story of the life of Christ supported the movement from history to nature which is the basis of allegory. However great the retarding, secular tendency of its exegesis had always been—seldom did it reach such a degree of intensity as in the work of Sigmund von Birken. His poetics give, "as examples of birth, marriage, and funeral poems, of eulogies and victory congratulations, songs on the birth and death of Christ, on his spiritual marriage with the soul, on his glory and his victory." The mystical instant [*Nu*] becomes the "now" [*Jetzt*] of contemporary actuality; the symbolic becomes distorted into the allegorical. The eternal is separated from the events of the story of salvation, and what is left is a living image open to all kinds of revision by the interpretive artist. (*Origin* 182–83)

Whereas the "story of the life of Christ" forms the narrative core of typological historiography, in Baroque allegoresis even the Christian mythos can be transformed from the transcendent meaning to which all significant historical events refer into a network of received images ready-made to allegorize current events and mundane occasions ("birth, marriage, and funeral poems"). In semiotic terms, the life of Christ shifts places from transcendental signified to arbitrary signifier, dissolving the mystic instant in which historical events glow with their eternal referent into the mere now of contemporary events that no longer point beyond themselves to a story of redemption, since the story of redemption has instead been made to point to these profane instances.

Benjamin subsumes this reading of the Christ story under "the movement from history to nature which is the basis of allegory." "History" here seems to indicate that sphere of significant events opened up by the Christian temporalization of the classical symbol, whereas "nature" for Benjamin delimits an archaeological scene of history in ruins. In typological representations, the ruin frequently

serves as a figure for the Synagogue destroyed by the New Covenant, thus visualizing the proper succession of historical periods.
For Benjamin the ruin, rather than signaling the advent of another
epoch's renewal, itself constitutes a kind of rebirth, a rebirth *as
ruin*—namely, the survival of a work beyond the period of its cultural currency: "the decrease in effectiveness, whereby the attrac-
tion of earlier charms diminishes decade by decade, [becomes] the
basis of a rebirth [*Neugeburt*], in which all ephemeral beauty is completely stripped off, and the work stands as ruin" (*Origin* 182; *Ursprung* 160).[24] In Benjamin's version of the Renaissance metaphor,
ruins do not simply represent the devastated foundations of new
and more glorious buildings, as in the typological displacement of
the Synagogue by the Church, but rather persist beyond their supersedure, giving rise to a beauty and a historicity that differs from
and is produced by the synecdochic logic of *Kulturgeschichte*. Rather
than restoring texts to their original contexts and meanings—the
historicist dream that animates the humanist concept of "culture"—
Benjamin emphasizes the death of the context and the consequent
dessication of the work as it loses legibility and assumes a new profile as ruin, an aspect borrowed from typological discourse and
turned against it.

This landscape of ruins is populated by the flora and fauna that
spring from the pages of herbals and bestiaries, the genres of natural history that Benjamin opposes to the conception of nature embodied by the "early Renaissance":

> nature was not seen by [the Baroque] in bud and bloom, but in the
> over-ripeness and decay of her creations. In nature they saw eternal
> transience, and here alone did the saturnine vision of this generation
> recognize history. Its monuments, ruins, are, according to Agrippa
> von Nettesheim, the home of the saturnine beasts. In the process of
> decay, and in it alone, the events of history [*das historische Geschehen*]
> shrivel up and become absorbed in the setting. The quintessence of
> these decaying objects is the polar opposite to the idea of transfig-
> ured nature as conceived by the early renaissance. (*Origin* 179–80; *Ur-
> sprung* 157)

Whereas the "bud and bloom" of "transfigured nature" evoke the
pregnant relation of type to fulfillment in the fullness of Renais-

sance time, "over-ripeness and decay" denote the leavings of the historical process, its unintended by-products rather than its pre-destined *telos*. (Thus the term "natural history" comes to name among other things all those genres and motifs concerning the book of nature that did *not* lead to the modern sciences.) In passages such as this, Benjamin does not simply oppose history to nature as tran-sience to eternity; he recovers a temporality beyond typology in the guise of natural history, a grafting of one term to another rather than a synthesis of the two. For Benjamin, the "nature" of natural history is more historical than the "history" of *das historische Geschehen*, since it refuses to backlight the events of the *saeculum* with their Christological significance, instead charting the vicissi-tudes of Christian signification—its sources, aims, objects, and prod-ucts—in the very structures of historical thought.

To this end, Benjamin writes toward the close of the book:

> All the material, with its far-reaching implications, which it has been possible to uncover by a method which occasionally seemed vague, occasionally reminiscent of cultural history [*kulturhistorisch anmuten-den Methode*], forms a whole when seen in relation to allegory, comes together in the idea of the *Trauerspiel . . .* a critical understanding of the *Trauerspiel*, in its extreme, allegorical form, is possible only from the higher domain of theology; so long as the approach is an aesthetic one, paradox must have the last word. Such a resolution, like any res-olution of the profane into the sacred, can only be accomplished his-torically, in terms of a theology of history [*Geschichtstheologie*]. (*Origin* 215–16; *Ursprung* 192)

This is one of those passages from the *Trauerspiel* book so thick with the intimacy of an uncommunicated thought that one hesitates to gloss it. Nonetheless, certain motifs should by now be familiar, es-pecially the opposition between aesthetic ideology, ruled by the symbol, and what Benjamin calls "a theology of history," operating under the regime of allegory. Although one might expect this *Geschichtstheologie* to name the idealist core of secular historicism, Benjamin instead reserves genuinely historical thought precisely for such a theology ("Such a resolution . . . can only be accomplished *historically, in terms of a theology of history*"). Whatever such a theol-ogy of history might be, it surely diverges from the *kulturhistorisch an-*

mutenden Methode that Benjamin fears his book resembles, for cultural history, as we have seen in Burckhardt, was made in the image of the aesthetic symbol. Once again, then, "theology" appears in the region of the negated middle, between classicism and its renovation in the incarnational symbol, whether that renovation is identified with Christianity, the rise of modern aesthetics, or both. So, too, "history" once more has two valences, the dominant historiography ruled by secular typology and an alternative historicity that falls out from typology as its ruins, taken as the object of a more searching, because less synthesizing, dialectical thought.

This "theology of history" beyond typology resembles the project of Benjamin's contemporary Karl Löwith (1897–1973), the German historian of Western philosophies of history. As Löwith recounts in his 1940 memoirs, *Mein Leben in Deutschland vor und nach 1933*, he was the son of an assimilated Jewish father and a Lutheran mother, and a veteran of the First World War who had married a Protestant woman. The rise of Nazism brought about Löwith's first, and forced, identification with Judaism. In exile during the war, his work henceforth would attempt to confront Western historical thinking with its theological origins, not in the service of a more complete secularization of historiography (which he saw as an impossibility), nor in order to embrace a Jewish vision of historical process as against the Christian one, but rather to wrest from the New Dispensation a historico-religious discourse more authentic than that produced by the collusion between a neutralized Christianity and a messianic modernity in the mainstream of German thought. Löwith's 1949 *Meaning in History*, staged as a series of essays on historians, philosophers, and theologians from Augustine to Burckhardt, puts forth the thesis that the basic tropes of modern historiography are fundamentally Christian in theme and structure, and yet that a Christianity true to its own premises must think the absolute nonrelation between historicity and eternity, and thus rescind the very project it makes possible. In Löwith's account, the disavowal of that nonrelation in both explicitly Christian and putatively secular historiographies has led to the pseudo-secularism of Hegel's philosophy of history, and more catastrophically to the inner-historical messianism of the Third Reich as well as the evangelical-imperialist dissemination of Western civilization across the globe.[25]

Although *Meaning in History* proceeds almost entirely within the terms and canon set by Christianity, Löwith ends the book by presenting the Jews as the only people in whom religious and historical thought are or could be truly integrated:

> The possibility of a belief in the providential ordering of world-historical destinies depends on [the Jewish] belief in a holy people of universal significance, because only peoples, not individuals, are a proper subject of history and only a holy people is directly related to the Lord as a Lord of history. Christians are not a historical people. Their solidarity all over the world is merely one of faith. In the Christian view the history of salvation is no longer bound up with a particular nation but is internationalized because it is individualized. In Christianity the history of salvation is related to the salvation of each single soul, regardless of racial, social, and political status. . . . From this it follows that the historical destiny of Christian peoples is no possible subject of a specifically Christian interpretation of political history, while the destiny of the Jews *is* a possible subject of a specifically Jewish interpretation . . . one has to conclude that a Jewish theology of secular history is indeed a possibility and even a necessity, while a Christian philosophy of history is an artificial compound. . . . The perplexing situation is that the attempt at a philosophy of history depends on the Hebrew-Christian tradition, while this very tradition obstructs the attempt to "work out" the working of God. (195–96)

Löwith argues that the universal message of Christianity is at odds with a coherent theology of history, since the Christian shift from national to individual election meant that the arena of salvation would henceforth be played out on the battleground of each single soul, as a question of the relation to eternal life. Yet profane history continued to affect the possibilities of individual redemption, and the singular stories of each person's damnation or salvation in turn reflected the historical actuality of Christ's coming and the reorganization of world epochs brought about by that event. In order to present a theology of history, the new universalism depended on

a secreted reservoir of the very nationalism annulled in the announcement of the Christian message to all people and peoples.
Löwith calls the Christian philosophy of history an "artifical com-
pound," since it splices a reserved remainder of the negated Jewish
conception of national redemption onto the Christian dogma of
individual salvation in order to create a theology of secular time.[26]

Like Benjamin's deployment of Baroque theology in the service of a critique of incarnational aesthetics, Löwith latches onto
key moments of crisis in the history of the post-classical West in
order to "introduce Christianity into Christendom" (158), a citation
from Kierkegaard that distinguishes the antiinstitutional radicality
of Christian thought from its neutralization in both the church and
the state as bodies working in history, which use the paradigms of
Christian eschatology to create *teloi* for and within secular time
(197). So too, in his "Theologico-Political Fragment" written in
the early 1920's, Benjamin distinguishes the messiah from the ends of
history in order to reassert the sublime gap between the sacred and
the profane articulated by allegory: "nothing historical can relate
itself on its own account to anything Messianic. Therefore the Kingdom of God is not the *telos* of the historical dynamic; it cannot be
set as a goal" (*One Way Street* 312). Both Löwith and Benjamin are
interested in a "theology of history" that takes shape at the site of
the breakdown of Christian-secular historiography, and both men
link the possibility of such a theology to the constitution of a religious group as a community: Löwith contrasts the Hebrew nation
to the Christian individual, and Benjamin opposes the "harmonious
inwardness" of classicism to the "politico-religious problems" of
the Baroque, which "did not so much affect the individual and his
ethics as his religious community" (*Origin* 160–61). A "theology of
history" takes shape in Benjamin's work as in Löwith's not as a specific content or program, but as a recurrent obstacle entangled in
the Judeo-Christian dialectic of reform that allows or even necessitates the rethinking of that dialectic.[27]

Benjamin's source for a *Geschichtstheologie* drawn from the ab-
scesses that collect in the narrative of Christian modernization is
not, however, the exiled Jewish Lutheran Karl Löwith, but the con-

servative Catholic, Nazi apologist, and juridical historian, Carl Schmitt, author of the 1922 tract *Political Theology*.[28] In the *Origin of the German Tragic Drama*, Benjamin cites Schmitt's definition of the sovereign as he who can declare a state of emergency (*Ausnahmezustand*); understood as a suspension in the normative working of the law, the state of emergency holds the same place in the world of politics that the miracle holds in the realm of nature.[29] Following his hero Hobbes, Schmitt is a "decisionist," insisting that the juridical decision, rather than manifesting an underlying norm or natural law, introduces the radical and nonpredictable cut of the new into the legal order; whereas the decision transposes a creationist model of the world into the political sphere, the ideal of the norm takes its inspiration from the natural sciences (46–47). Schmitt opposes his reactionary political theory, grounded in Counter-Reformation theology and the apologetics of the restored monarchies of the nineteenth century, to all rationalizing, secularizing, and Protestant theories of the state. Benjamin was far from ascribing to Schmitt's politics, but nonetheless found in Schmitt's marked Catholic difference from the Protestant dialectic a *locus communus* from which he could demarcate a historical theology distinct from the dominant German idealist one.

Quoting Schmitt without naming him, Benjamin writes of Baroque politics:

> For as an antithesis to the historical ideal of restoration [the baroque] is haunted by the idea of catastrophe. And it is in response to this antithesis that the theory of the state of emergency is devised. If one wishes to explain how "the lively awareness of the significance of the state of emergency, which is dominant in the natural law of the seventeenth century" disappears in the following century, it is not therefore enough simply to refer to the greater political stability of the eighteenth century. If it is true, that "for Kant . . . emergency law was no longer any law at all," that is a consequence of his theological rationalism. The religious man of the baroque era clings so tightly to the world because of the feeling that he is being driven along into a cataract with it. The baroque knows no eschatology; and for that very reason it possesses no mechanism by which all earthly things are gathered in together and exalted before being consigned to their end. (66)

Here, Benjamin uses passages from Schmitt's *Politische Theologie* in order to recover a Baroque *Geschichtstheologie* no longer readable in the light of Kant's "theological rationalism." In Benjamin's setting of the Baroque scene, "catastrophe" stands in the place of "eschatology"; whereas the latter allows for the totalizing historical horizon of the Second Coming, in which every event receives a meaning in the revealed narrative of salvation (the essence of the typological vision), the threat of catastrophe introduces the possibility of the complete destruction of the world without a correlative sublation and retranscription, the apocalyptic counterpart to creation *ex nihilo*.

In such a vision, the tyrant-martyr, hero of the Baroque *Trauerspiel* in Benjamin's account, both differs from and doubles the political saints of Burckhardt's Renaissance. In the anecdotes recounted by Burckhardt, the assassination of tyrants in churches, the canonization of *condottieri* through murder, and the installation of the new culture-heroes in the place of the old religious ones were all acts of modern canonization that served both to kill off and to renew the martyr stories of the Middle Ages; in the passion suffered by hagiography in the drama Burckhardt calls "the Renaissance," secularization exemplifies rather than takes exception to the progress of typological history. In Benjamin's excursus on the despots of the *Trauerspiel*, however, both tyranny and tyrannicide mark moments of exception or emergency in the normal workings of the law, including the law of typology, exceptions embodied by the very idea of the "Counter-Reformation" as a reaction-formation symptomatically installed against and after Europe's dominant movements of renewal and reform. Unlike the Machiavellian New Prince of Burckhardt's humanist Renaissance—an exuberant if violent figure of the new individualism—the tyrant-martyr of Benjamin's Baroque *Trauerspiel* is left over from the wars of religion, a remnant rather than a renewal of medieval hagiography and thus an index of both the limits of secularization and the origins of secular historiography in biblical typology.

In Benjamin's book, the word "Baroque" stands as the antithesis to the aesthetic ideology embodied by the term "Renaissance," insofar as the Baroque names the allegorical difference resistant to typological reading that iconography had isolated in Warburg's research. From Burckhardt to Warburg to Benjamin, we can trace the displacement of the period term *Renaissance* by its substitutes *Nachleben der Antike* and *Baroque*, as well as the concomitant supplanting of the typological *symbol* by *iconography* and *allegory*.

Author	Period	Signifying Mode
Burckhardt	Renaissance	symbol
Warburg	*Nachleben der Antike*	iconography
Benjamin	Baroque	allegory

Yet "Baroque," one could counter, merely names the historical period of seventeenth-century Germany, a term it shares with the Italy of the same century: the period term "Baroque" doesn't compete with or replace "Renaissance," it simply comes after it—a fact demonstrated by Benjamin's own occasional use of the word "Renaissance." In this regard, recall the precocity of the Italian Renaissance in Burckhardt's implied narrative of modernity, in which Italy facilitated the birth of the modern state by the premature brilliance of its local exercises in statecraft. If Burckhardt's Italian Renaissance suffers from *precipitousness*, Benjamin's Germany suffers from chronic *belatedness*: its Baroque occurs instead of, rather than after, the Renaissance. As Kenneth Reinhard and I have argued elsewhere, the supposedly national literary history announced by the book's subject, "*German* Tragic Drama," is continually overshadowed by Benjamin's attention to the flowering of literature on other stages of European history, especially the English drama of Shakespeare and the Spanish drama of Calderón (*After Oedipus* 49–50). Not only does the German Baroque occur in lieu of a Renaissance, but the Baroque itself finds fuller expression elsewhere. Whereas for Burckhardt the prematurity of the Renaissance made possible the maturation of Europe, for Benjamin the belatedness of Germany both requires and gives the lie to the redemptive logic of modernity. Germany, that is, required such narratives in order to rationalize the late blooming of its own national destiny, whose catastrophic consequences in turn exposed what Löwith called the Christian-secular dream of "fulfil[ling] history by and within itself" (*Meaning in History* 159). Although Löwith's 1949 analysis of the paradoxes of this task are both more far-reaching and more reductive than Benjamin's in the 1920's, Benjamin's antitypological reflections on the origin of the German tragic drama provide a complementary critique of the ends of the German philosophy of history.

Cultural History and Its Discontents

In his 1937 essay "Eduard Fuchs, Collector and Historian," Benjamin mounts a brief but explicit critique of *Kulturgeschichte*:

> But the absurdity of a dialectical history of culture [*Kulturgeschichte*] as such lies deeper, since the continuum of history, blown apart by dialectics, is nowhere scattered over a wider area than in that part people call culture. In short, cultural history only seems to represent a deepening of insight; it does not present even the appearance of progress in dialectics. For it lacks that destructive element that guarantees the authenticity of dialectical thought and of the dialectician's experience. It may well increase the burden of treasures that are piled up on humanity's back. But it does not give mankind the strength to shake them off, so as to get its hands on them. (*One Way Street* 360–61)

Benjamin's target here is not Burckhardt's *Kulturgeschichte* per se, but rather the attempt by Marxist critics to mount a materialist version of cultural history. According to Benjamin, "that part people call culture," granted the unity of a reflective totality under Burckhardt's pictorializing gaze, needs to be broken up and its sundered parts reenvisioned in terms of their relationships to different modes of production; instead, in Benjamin's analysis, Marxist critics, purporting to carry out such a program, too often tend simply to multiply the objects of cultural inquiry, reinforcing rather than challenging the contextual unity of the field called "culture." In Benjamin's analysis, what appears to be a democratization and pluralization of the objects of research instead simply "increases the burden of treasures that are piled up on humanity's back"; that is, the more objects for "cultural" analysis we have (and the more tele-scoped their historical range, so that what we increasingly get is a history of yesterday), the less we seem able to encounter them, to make them into tools and weapons for new forms of expression and critique.[30]

Benjamin's analysis is still relevant today, when cultural studies is gaining increasing prestige and ethical authority in academic cir-cles, often supported by critics who cite Benjamin's essays on me-chanical reproduction and the author as producer as historical prece-dents for current discourses of cultural materialism. Yet, as Ben-jamin himself points out, "cultural materialism" is a contradiction in terms, since "culture" should be precisely the category most fun-damentally shattered and redistributed by a genuinely materialist practice. When the word "studies" appears after the word "culture," we are led to believe that this shattering has taken place, insofar as an anthropological definition of culture has replaced (or subsumed?) the elitist, Burckhardtian, determination of the term. Two pur-portedly distinct meanings of the same word are at stake: the "cul-ture" of cultural studies, often used in alliance with such terms as "ideology," "context," "interdisciplinarity," "globalism," and the "politics of x," is sharply distinguished from the "culture" of "high culture," synonymous with "intellectual aristocracy," the "traditional disciplines," "Western civilization," and "national boundaries." This division of the kingdoms is problematic for many reasons—for ex-ample, the fact that many non-Western civilizations have long-standing traditions of "high culture," which is by no means the purview of Europe alone. I would argue that the devolution from a high-church to a low-church "culture" preserves the idealist his-tory of the term without dialectically challenging that history; in-deed, if anything, the "culture" of cultural studies is a more totaliz-ing because more comprehensive and inclusive concept than the narrower, more selective and discriminating definitions of Burck-hardt or Warburg.

Benjamin, on the other hand, eschews the word "culture" al-together for the word "art," which for him continues to carry immense creative and critical potential. In the same essay Benjamin singles out "the interpretation of iconography" as one of the "essential elements of any future materialist critique of works of art," since "explication of iconography not only proves indispensable for the study of reception and mass art; above all it guards against the excesses to which any formalism soon beckons" (*One Way Street* 362–63). Although his footnote is to Emile Mâle rather than Aby Warburg, at this late date in his writing Benjamin remains engaged with the challenges that iconography poses both to formalist idealism and to pseudo-materialist contextualism. For Benjamin, iconographic analysis avoids the formalist reification of works, but not by "contextualizing" them—for "context" still implies the difference between the work and its outside, and thus enforces the reification it purports to reject. Iconography, on the other hand, as the network of image-meaning complexes activated by either the work or its reception, constitutes the very text-ure of the text as a temporally changing nexus of citations and retroactions, of readings and rereadings. Iconography delimits both a representational code and its instantiations, the dimensions of both *langue* and *parole*, and thus resists becoming an external frame or context of the work while always remaining denaturalized, in need of interpretation, since its systems are forthrightly semiotic rather than mimetic. So too, genre, as Fredric Jameson has demonstrated, is a term absolutely crucial to the breaking down of both formalist and contextual hypostatizations, since genre, effecting a contract between the author and the audience in relation to a once and future tradition, situates the work in the matrix of conventions that make up not the context, outside, or prehistory of the work, but the very being of the work in time. To borrow a formulation from Benjamin, genre and iconography force us to think about the way "works incorporate both their pre-history and their after-history—an after-history in virtue of which their pre-history, too, can be seen to undergo constant change" ("Eduard Fuchs," *One Way Street* 351).

For similar reasons, this is a book on hagiography in *Renaissance*, not "early modern," literature—a word retained not out of a reactionary nostalgia for Burckhardt's picture of Italy's cultural flowering, but rather because that deeply ideological period term, with its roots in self-representations that stem from the centuries so designated, has itself had an effective history that does not go away by simply replacing it with a new word. A genuine critique of the term does not entail finding a more accurate substitute, but rather following out the word's historical determinations between the works described by it and the century of historiography that canonized the period. This task is all the more necessary when the word "Renaissance" not only names the period of the works examined in this book, but is also a prime example of the dynamic analyzed here, namely, the role of biblical typology in the constitution of the secular scripture we call literature.

CHAPTER 2

The Denouement of Martyrdom

THE SYMPTOM IN PSYCHOANALYSIS

AND HAGIOGRAPHY

In Freud's early work on hysteria, the symptom emerged as a linguistic formation, a psychosomatic symbol produced through condensations, literalizations, and displacements of elements encountered in a traumatic scene. One problem that troubled Freud, however, was the intransigent persistence of the symptom in the face of all analysis of it into its components and prehistory. A certain archaic pleasure, as well as an entrenched network of secondary gains, seemed to maintain the symptom in excess of its rhetorical structure and hermeneutic analysis. Jacques Lacan derived this persistence of the symptom from the element of *jouissance*, the bit of traumatic pleasure both canceled and produced by the signifying operations of the neurotic components of the symptom, a kernel of enjoyment that clarifies both the tenacity of the symptom and its mercurial, chaotic ability to leap beyond pure repetition to something resembling new creation. In *Seminar XXIII*, conducted in 1974–75, Lacan renamed the classical "symptom" of psychoanalysis the *"sinthome"* in order to distill among other homophonies both the figure of the *saint homme* and the name of St. Thomas Aquinas, *"sinthomadaquin,"* from the signifying matrix of the symptom (Nov. 18, 1975). Lacan's conception of the symptom unfolds around key phrases and doctrines drawn from Catholic theology, including St.

Thomas Aquinas's theory of beauty as *claritas*, the Judeo-Christian etiology of creation *ex nihilo*, and the Catholic doctrine postulating the real presence of Christ in the Eucharist. These allusive ligatures binding sanctity and the symptom signal a point of departure for a reading of psychoanalysis and hagiography that neither demystifies sanctity by subsuming it under the aegis of neurosis nor historicizes psychoanalysis by reducing the specificity of its terms to those that it borrows from other discourses.[1]

The symptomatic reading of a literary and ideological complex such as hagiography needs to account for both the semiotic structure of the genre's conventions and for the kinds of *jouissance* that such structures at once obstruct and preserve. The latter includes the fascination, horror, ecstasy, or disgust evoked and contained by literary representation, quantities implicated in both the affective hold of literature on its audience and the delight that stems from the very act of symptomatic formalization and signification—*jouissance* is "a sense *joui* by the subject" (Miller, "Formal Envelope" 21). The symptom in its Freudian formulation provides a model for the rhetorical and intertextual citations, imitations, and exclusions that constitute a tradition; from this perspective, the secular novella, for example, emerges as a symptom—a transformative repression—of the saint's life. The symptom taken from its later Lacanian revision does not oppose this hermeneutics of literary change so much as it isolates within its historiographical dynamics those aspects of the saint's life that, precisely through their resistance to intertextual mutation, provoke the swarming of allusions, the installation of historical narratives, and the construction of forms and figures of literariness. These traumatic points, in their refusal to be displaced, are also the sites at which the endlessly recirculating machinery of tradition can produce something new, a creation *ex nihilo* in the sense of fashioning something around a nothing.

The figuration of art as a symptom is a common motif in historical analyses that take works as "manifestations" of a particular period or context. In his essay "Iconography and Iconology," Erwin Panofsky defines iconology as a symptomatic study of culture, in which "we deal with the work of art as a symptom of something

else which expresses itself in a countless variety of other symptoms"
(31). In the *Origin of the German Tragic Drama*, Benjamin's antitypological intervention in the iconological methods of the Warburg
school, Benjamin writes that "martyrdom prepares the body for
emblematic purposes" (217). If Panofsky's medical terminology takes
the symptom as a symbol in a pre-Freudian mode, Benjamin's account of martyrological dismemberment parallels both Freud and
Lacan. It evokes Freud's dynamic sense of the symptom as an act of
distortion or *Entstellung* in response to repression as well as Lacan's
rearticulation of the symptom as a knot in signification rather than
a key to latent meaning. Whereas Panofsky's iconology emphasizes
the way in which Renaissance forms of signification express deeper
spiritual and historical currents, both gaining meaning from and
giving unity to the period in which they were created, Benjamin's
reconstruction of Baroque allegoresis insists that emblematic and
iconographic forms of expression were not only the expressive vehicle but themselves the expressed content of Baroque martyrology.
That discipline did not use emblems to represent torture so much as
it used the disarticulating apparatus of torture to carve up the body
into material for emblems. Benjamin suggests that the painful breakdown of the corpus in scenes of martyrdom is designed to produce
a constellation or complex of relations between dismembered, reified elements whose discrete meanings do not serve to reconsti-
tute the fragmented body into a new and higher unity. In Lacanian terms, the martyrological emblem is less a "symptom," in the
sense of a symbol or manifestation of a larger cultural current, than
a "sinthome," in the sense of a Baroque flowering of pure signification. It is a *"joui* in sense" that elicits the translation of meanings
from one level to another, while obstructing that very translation.

Taking Jacobus de Voragine's massively influential compendium
of saints' lives, *Legenda Aurea* (The golden legend), as a thesaurus of
hagiographic exempla, this chapter shows how "martyrdom prepares the body for emblematic purposes" by analyzing three recurrent moments in scenes of holy torture: the display and initial mutilation of the saintly body, the curtailment or "cutting short" of
torture effected by decapitation, and finally, the reliquary rites sur-

rounding the burial of the saint. These three moments do not occur in every martyr's legend, nor do they exhaust the range of torturous signification exercised by scenes of martyrdom. Nonetheless, this sequence maps out a general formula for the denouement of the martyr's passion that accounts for the final movement of many legends. These scenes gain their fixed, quasi-algebraic character insofar as they tend to separate out of their signifying framework into citable images of the narrative process. The display of the saint's body manifests the *iconicity* of the saint; the stroke of decapitation that enlists the saint in the commemorative calendars of the Church codifies the *canonicity* of the saint; and the interment of the saintly corpse rejected by the pagan political order founds the *reliquary function* of the hagiographic and literary text. Display, decapitation, and encryption become rebuslike "attributes" not of individual saints but of hagiography as a genre, dislodged emblems of the narrative's structure and movement.

Scourging, Flaying, Racking

Jacobus de Voragine's thirteenth-century *Legenda Aurea* was not so much a "legend *in* its own time" as a "legend *of* its own time," a summary compilation of preceding traditions of hagiography presented in an accessible, coherent, and widely disseminated form. Over the period of its reception in the late medieval and Renaissance periods, the work's generic self-identification as "legend"— derived from the Latin gerundive meaning "something to be read" —itself underwent successive rereadings. The *Golden Legend* is a calendar and a lectionary, a list of feast days and a collection of readings—*legenda*—appropriate to each one. In most medieval contexts, "legend" referred to a saint's life, and, in the period after Jacobus de Voragine's work, it came to designate a life from the *Golden Legend* itself. By the end of the fourteenth century, however, "legend" increasingly meant story, in both the fictional and historiographic valences operative in the Renaissance (*OED*). By the seventeenth century, "legend" had come increasingly to connote an inauthentic or nonhistorical story. Whereas in the Renaissance the term could encompass both history and literature, with the entrenchment of the Reformation and Counter-Reformation, the word began to indicate neither history nor literature, but rather a bastardization of both—legends, and above all the *Golden Legend*, are unhistorical history and unpoetic poetry. The successive rereadings of the *Golden Legend* and its generic designation is itself something that must be read (*legendum*) as a formative episode in the constitution of a literature after hagiography.[2]

The saints' lives of the *Golden Legend* fall into two basic groups, the martyr-stories—mostly tales from the persecution of the early Christians—and the *vitae* of the hermits, fathers, and latter-day saints.[3] The martyrdoms, which form the focus of this chapter, derive from the early *Acta* or court proceedings of the early witnesses of the faith (martyr = witness), and from the commemorative lists and local calendars of the saints, periodically formalized and generalized in the "universal" martyrologies or calendars of the Eastern and Western churches beginning in the fifth century.[4] In the history of their increasing elaboration, the minimalism of these early sources and forms blossomed into exquisite bouquets of tortures miraculously endured or suspended through the grace of God. In his structural analysis of the *Golden Legend*, Alain Boreau divides the sequence of tortures that make up the central drama of martyrdom into three basic groups: preparatory tortures (e.g., arrest, incarceration, public humiliation); principal tortures (beating, mutilation, and fire); and mortal tortures (most commonly decapitation) (118–20).[5] Among the principal tortures number those torments that serve to stretch or lacerate the flesh of the saint, including scourging, flaying, racking, and their variants. Thus whipping serves to abrade, dent, and gouge the flesh of the saint, exposing the organs; in the passion of St. Vincent, "the torturers drove iron rakes into the saint's sides, so that the blood streamed from every part of his body, and his entrails hung out between the broken ribs" (*Golden Legend* 115). Flaying turns the saint inside out, exposing his organs and flesh and leaving his skin an empty sack—the most famous attribute of St. Bartholomew. Racking the saint stretches the cutaneous envelope and mangles the body's skeletal support, distorting the shape and scope of the body without removing any of its parts. Christina's pagan father commands "her flesh to be torn with hooks, and her tender limbs to be broken" (367), a sentence that combines the lacerating effects of scourging with the anatomical torsion performed by the rack. This is the double punishment of St. Margaret as well, who was "bound upon the rack, and beaten cruelly, first with rods, then with sharp iron instruments, so that all her bones were laid bare" (352); stretched on the rack and then beaten, Margaret's body is treated like the skin of a drum, drawn taut so that the rhythm of the saints can be beaten out on it.

These torments distend, perforate, or rend the saint's body, treating it as a flexible, infinitely infolded surface able to be stretched, torn, and opened up to view. Rarely do these torments lead to death; rather, they prepare the body for the final immolation by tenderizing, precooking, scoring, or seasoning the flesh of the saint—as when salt or boiling water is applied to the open wounds of the martyr, aggravating the lesions that emboss the epidermal surface (*Golden Legend* 365, 640). Christologically, such scenes combine the "Ecce homo" of Christ before the people with his flagellation: in these preparatory punishments, the body of the saint is displayed precisely through its flagellation, the whips and rods of which groove, puncture, and weal the skin of the saint.

This display that is also a splaying and flaying constitutes the saint as an icon within the narrative, a public spectacle and fascinating image of patience in suffering that often leads to the conversion of the pagan viewers. It is not simply that an iconography of the saints develops around the cults and legends of the martyrs as a supplemental commentary external to their lives, but that a certain iconicity, a being-as-image, coalesces within the framework of the legend. The relation of this iconicity of the saintly body to its mutilation is registered in the prominent role of the instruments of torture in the visual attributes of the saints: the knife or skin of Bartholomew, the wheel of Catherine, and the grill of Lawrence all provide a picture-writing that identifies portraits of the saints through the means of their bodily affliction. The images of the saints reconstituted in the portrait gallery of divine history are marked—

both identified and marred—by the singular traits of mutilation that ensured their place therein. In such portrayals, the visual integrity of the saints as forms or *Gestalten* coalesces around the piecemeal hieroglyphics of their attributes, their rebuslike picture-language recalling formally as well as thematically the martyrological laceration of the saints' bodies.

Indeed, the status of the image is thematized in many saints' lives, insofar as the Christian's refusal to sacrifice to the idols of the heathen state leads to martyrdom. The saint's ridicule, demystification, or smashing of pagan idols points to the poverty of religious representation, yet the display of the mutilated saint that follows as a consequence of such iconoclasm lays out in advance the reconstitution of iconography in the dissemination of Catholicism. The displayed martyr is a proto-icon who both destroys and stands in for the rejected idols; indeed, in the Protestant discourse on the religious image, hagiography will come to mark the structural and historical complicity between pagan idolatry and Catholic iconography.

In *Seminar II* (1954–55), Lacan sets forth the imaginary order as the mode of representation that psychically configures the body at once as a beautiful form or unifying *Gestalt* and as an entity prone to morcellation and dissolution. The subject, Lacan says,

> sees himself. He sees himself from the other side, in an imperfect manner, as you know, as a consequence of the fundamentally incomplete nature of the specular *Urbild*, which is not only imaginary, but illusory. The perverted inflection which analytic technique has been acquiring for some time is founded on this fact. Within this perspective, one would like the subject to aggregate all the more or less fragmented, fragmentary pieces of this thing in which he fails to recognise himself. One wants him in effect to gather everything which he experienced in the pregenital stage, his scattered limbs, his partial drives, the succession of partial objects—think of Carpaccio's *St. George* skewering the dragon, with small severed heads, arms, and so on. (244–45)

The *Urbild* or primal image of the other serves to consolidate the ego in an act of specular identification that confers on the subject its first sense of possessing and inhabiting a unified body. At the same

time, that organizing image that gathers together the partial drives of
the subject remains frighteningly susceptible to psychosomatic dis-
integration. Lacan's reference to Carpaccio's painting of St. George
manifests the double function of the iconography of the saints,
whose portrayals at once present images of conversionary identification and, through the piecework of their attributes, decompose
the ideal forms they mirror forth.

In his early work, Lacan takes up the fragmented body of
Kleinian fantasy—"images of castration, mutilation, dismemberment, dislocation, evisceration, devouring, bursting open of the
body"—and links it to the phenomenon of aggressivity in the regime of the imaginary (*Écrits* 11). In this account, bodily disinte-
gration is the *cause* as much as the *effect* of violence, insofar as aggression occurs as a defensive response to the fantasy of morcellation
that rises up from the specular coherence of the body as its evil
twin. In the mirror games of rivalry, bodily fragmentation is at once
the prefiguration and the afterimage of competitive aggression. The
apparition of the *corps morcellé* indicates the element of the real in a
theater of images whose theoretical provenance in the writings of
Melanie Klein draws iconographic sustenance, in Lacan's analysis,
from the theological paintings of Bosch (*Écrits* 11–12).

In his much later seminar on the *sinthome*, Lacan continues to
associate bodily self-representations with the imaginary in order to
emphasize the continuity between the imaginary and the real already anticipated in his work on aggressivity:

> An empty sack isn't any less a sack, that is, it is not imaginable as skin
> but for the existence and consistency of the body. We must take as
> real this ex-istence and this consistency, since the real is the holding of
> them [*le réel, c'est de les tenir*]—hence the word *Begriff*. The imaginary
> shows here its homogeneity with the real. (*Seminar XXIII*, Nov. 18,
> 1975)

Lacan aligns "consistency" with the rule of the imaginary that dominates our thought and experience, and "ex-istence" with the real,
as what subsists outside of ("ex-") the representationally configured
world of everyday reality. The body conceived as an empty sack

"consists" insofar as it presents a coherent shape in its most minimal form, as an outline capable of holding something.[6] The cutaneous sack "ex-ists" by virtue of its emptiness, collapsed on itself and only articulable through inflation with more emptiness: "the sack . . . is that which swells [*se gonfle*]" (Nov. 18, 1975).

If the display of the saintly body presents the saint as image, as the proto-icon that prefigures all future iconography of the saints, this image partakes of the real insofar as it materializes the body as empty husk and pure surface without an underlying content or signified. The skin of St. Bartholomew is precisely such an empty sack or draped fabric, a sloughed hide and deflated container that could never be (re)embodied. Whereas Bartholomew's skin is the metonymic attribute that identifies the saint, the iconicity extracted and displayed in his epidermal cloak serves as an attribute of hagiography as a genre, an anamorphic image that detaches from a phase of hagiography's formal structure and crystallizes it.

This flayed skin, moreover, bears a "precipitous" relationship to aggressivity in the scenario of martyrdom; presented as the object and product of violence—violence's precipitate—the mutilated body of the saint also animates the disturbing specter of physical disarticulation that triggers aggressivity. In Lacan's formulation, the subject is always in the fantasy, indeterminately implicated in the positions of both the saint and the persecutor yet reducible to neither. The tyrant, embodying the persecuting agency of the superego, instantiates the symbolic Other whose enjoyment we suffer. The saint who is being beaten figures the imaginary other, its reduction to the pure corporeality of the image both ensuring and threatening our sense of consistency and integrity. Moreover, both the symbolic Other and the imaginary other are bound to the real. Thus the symbolic function of the ego-ideal is anchored by an element of obscene enjoyment which hagiography lodges at the heart of the law. This law encompasses both the rule of the pagan tyrant, who, in the cases of the saints Barbara and Christina, is also the father of the saint, and, more disturbingly, the law of the God who authorizes this scene of sacrifice. On the other side of the relation, martyrdom stretches and desiccates the specular reflectivity of the saint's displayed body into an anamorphic distortion produced by the rivalrous play of mirrors. This disturbance in the visual field indexes the real lack in the symbolic Other, the element of inconsistency in the law signaled by both the diabolic perversity and the ultimate impotence of the tyrant's machinery of pain.

According to Lacan, the beauty of an object stems not from its formal coherence (as in classical aesthetics) but rather, following medieval canons, from a brilliance irreducible either to any specific content (the order of the imaginary) or to its formal structure (the symbolic): "The *synthomadaquin* has that indefinable something called *claritas*" (*Seminar XXIII*, Nov. 18, 1975). Here Lacan deliberately supplements the Greek conception of beauty as form with its medieval Latin inflection as *claritas*, a word that implies a brilliance that blinds as much as it illumines. The very name of the *Golden Legend* implies an aesthetics of shimmering reflectivity, a wealth of sheer light as material substance that betrays a poverty of form rejected in the Renaissance rediscovery of classical *disegno*. Lacan attributes the conceptualization of this beauty bordering on the sublime to medieval scholasticism; what knots Saint Thomas to the symptom in Lacan's later neologism, the *sinthomadaquin*, is this doctrine of beauty as *claritas*, the pure appearance without underlying essence that charges the object with both its imaginary allure and its real presence. As early as *Seminar VII* (1959–60), on the ethics of psychoanalysis, Lacan had derived from Thomas Aquinas the idea that "the beautiful has the effect . . . of suspending, lowering, disarming desire . . . the fantasm is 'a beauty that mustn't be touched,' in the structure of this enigmatic field" (*Seminar VII* 238–39).[7] The iconicity of beauty "disarms" the subject, erecting an impediment to both desire and aggressivity within the sequential unfolding of signification, its circulation at once held in orbit and kept in check by the sublimely beautiful point at its center.

After her racking and scourging, St. Margaret returns to her prison cell, "which instantly was filled with a great brightness [*mira ibi claritas fulsit*]" (*Golden Legend* E 353; L 401). This light radiating from Margaret's cell finds its counterpart in the prefect's inability to look upon the wounds of her scourged and racked body: "the pre-

fect, unable to bear the sight of such an outpouring of blood, hid his
face in his mantle" (353). In the linked images of the effusion of
blood and the effulgence of light, it is as if the very obscenity of
Margaret's ruptured body leads to the pouring of a divine light from
the apertures of her flesh (353). In Lacan's expression, Margaret has
a beauty that cannot be touched, a terrible aspect that, sending the
prefect's face behind his cloak, impedes rather than inspires desire.

The distension of the saint's body emblematizes the distension
of the narrative itself during this phase of the torture, which is open
to seemingly endless dilation through the sequential addition of further torments. The martyrdom of Christina proceeds from the
scourging and breaking of her body to the binding of the saint on a
wheel, her torture with fire and oil, an attempted drowning, en-
capsulation in a heated iron cradle, immolation in a furnace, exposure to wild animals, amputation of breasts and tongue, and finally
arrows in her heart (367–68). This episodic amplification of martyrdom inaugurated by the scourging of the flesh treats the narrative
itself as an elastic tegument capable of indefinite expansion. This
moment in martyrdom marks the site of episodic proliferation and
fantastic extrapolation in the history of the genre, the chaste interval of the early *Acta* burgeoning into the legendary excrescences of
medieval hagiography. If the display of the saint's body crystallizes
her as icon, a stopping of the narrative emblematized in the hagiographics of the saints' attributes, the stretching of the saint thematizes the stretching of the narrative (and the imagination) in the emblematic parade of further torments.

In *Seminar XXIII*, Lacan posits the symptom as a fourth order,
the element binding the real, imaginary, and symbolic together,
their fields interlocked in the Borromean structure of a trefoil knot.
The three orders, that is, are the areas demarcated by three loops; if
any one is disconnected or mistied, all three would come undone.
The *sinthome*, declares Lacan, comes into service precisely when the
knotting of the three orders is faulty—when a line that should cross
under, for example, crosses over instead. The *sinthome* rebinds the
orders either at the point where they are improperly joined or at
one of the other ligatures threatened by the deficient tying of the

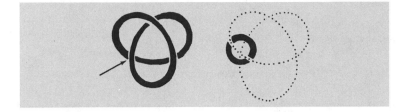

Figure 3. *Left*, a mistied trefoil knot. *Right*, a mistied trefoil knot corrected by the symptom. Adapted from Jacques Lacan, *Séminaire XXIII: le sinthome*, as reproduced in *Ornicar?* 9, "Séminaire du 17 Fevrier 1976," figures 2 and 5. Reproduced by permission.

knot. It is not simply, then, that Lacan reorients the symptom from the symbolic to the real; he emphasizes the presence of the real in a set of configurations that changes in relation to which juncture of orders is supplemented by the secondary shackling of the symptom.

In martyrology, the ostensive distension performed by such torments as flaying, scourging, and racking rebinds the three orders at the adjacency of the imaginary and the real. Yet the symptom lashes the imaginary and the real together in compensation for a crisis that threatens to unjoin the dialectic of the symbolic and the imaginary in the seamless production of social meaning. In the fantasy that a saint is being beaten, the fascinating screen composed of the saint's suffering body at once indicates and covers over the lack in the Other that jeopardizes the perceived coherence of the natural and social orders. In Slavoj Zizek's analysis, "sacrifice is a 'gift of reconciliation' to the Other, destined to appease its desire. Sacrifice conceals the abyss of the Other's desire, more precisely it conceals the Other's lack, inconsistency, 'inexistence,' that transpires in this desire" (*Enjoy Your Symptom* 56). The *Golden Legend* localizes that disturbing lack in the perversity of the pagan tyrant and the impotence of Roman law in late antiquity, but from the vantage of the Christian world order, whose sacrificial logic of symbolization will have been instituted in its place. The saints are rebels against one order, but only in the name of another: a theocratic City of God that will finally reinforce rather than dissolve the disciplines of the earthly *polis* (Pagels 119). The ostensive distension of the saint in martyrdom points to the lack in the Other and then pays off that lack with the pound of flesh offered in sacrifice.

As Edith Wyschogrod has argued, the life of the saint presents to its readers both an exemplum submitted for Christian *imitatio* and a radically unrepeatable exception designed "to '*show*' unrepresentability itself" (*Saints and Postmodernism* 13). Wyschogrod thus locates an antinomian moment at the heart of hagiography's institutional apologetics, homiletics, and etiologies. The reference to "showing" suggests both the foregrounding and the twisting of pictorial representation suspended in the peculiar iconicity of the saint's peeled and stretched body. The *ecce sancta* constituted by the "showing" of the saintly body, I would argue, fastens the reflective surface of the *Golden Legend* over the emergence of inconsistency in the domain of the symbolic. The trusswork of the symptom frames the peculiar iconicity of the saintly body, giving it the lie while supporting it within the symbolic scene of representation. That body offers up at once a mesmerizing image of specular identification and a pure surface without depth, the empty husk of sanctity exposed.

Decapitation

In the *Golden Legend*, Jacobus de Voragine lists competing accounts of the death of Saint Bartholomew:

> Saint Dorotheus says that he was crucified; . . . Saint Theodore says that he was flayed. In many other books we read only that he was beheaded. But these contradictions can be made to agree, by saying that he was first crucified, then flayed while still alive in order to increase his suffering, and finally beheaded. (*Golden Legend* 483)

Jacobus de Voragine's method of textual criticism resolves contradiction not by adjudicating between sources on philological grounds but rather by collating and reconciling competing accounts to create a coherent narrative (Boreau 104–5). Here, the proposed menu of bodily display (crucifixion and flaying) followed by decapitation carries the authority of a formula, a fixed temporal and logical relationship between set elements. Decapitation, although it is not the only kind of mortal wound, is by far the most common cause of death in the *Golden Legend*, and it is an affliction rarely suspended by a miracle. In the *Golden Legend*, decapitation marks an ending function, a time to conclude; it epitomizes or capitulates the narrative function of closure, with which it is identified with a quasi-algebraic regularity. In hagiography's law of genre, flaying must come before beheading, since decapitation arrests the spectacular sequence of tortures with the caesura of death.[8]

Whereas ostensive distension accentuates the skin, surface tension, and anamorphic contortion of the bodily envelope, decapitation by definition focuses on the head, foregrounding the saint not as suffering flesh but as rational subject. This emphasis on the saint as person, however, occurs in the very act of severing the seat of reason and identity. Thus St. Longinus, who keeps speaking the word of God after his teeth and tongue are torn out, is finally silenced by decapitation (*Golden Legend* 189); the head, which houses the mouth, is the true site of rational discourse, and its removal ends all speech. In this and similar sequences, the loss of body parts other than the head involves incomplete, discontinuous dismemberments reorganized, subsumed, and brought to a close by decapitation, just as castration in Freud's scenario of psychic development orders the polymorphous perversity of the partial drives under the aegis of a phallus established by the threat of castration. The loss of the head is not simply one dismemberment among others in a potentially infinite metonymic chain, but rather a symbolic recomposition of bodily fragments into a subjectivity gathered up by its very cancellation.[9]

As we saw in the last section, the ostensive distension of the saint through stretching, twisting, fracturing, and rupturing opens up more than the corporeal surface of the saint. The narrative structure itself opens to the paratactic prolongations of romance. The decapitation of the saint interrupts this potentially endless flow of tortures; cutting off the head also cuts off and cuts into the narrative sequence, producing a definitive break in the texture of the martyrdom. Moreover, the set of dismemberments that often comes between scourging and decapitation begins the final articulation— etymologically, the division into joints or members—of the mar- tyrdom, a progressive discrimination of the narrative structure recapitulated and finished off by the stroke of decapitation. This succession of punctual cuts introduces difference into the self- generating tissue of image and spectacle and draws its mushrooming montage of icons to a close by distinguishing between the indefinite multiplicity of the preparatory tortures and the absolute singularity of the mortal blow.

This slicing is also a splicing, a grafting of the individual into the transhistorical order of the saints. Through decollation, the be- headed saints join the corporate body of the Church, where they are effectively reheaded by Christ. The hagiographic subgenres ac- tivated and thematized by decapitation are the commemorative lists, liturgical calendars, and modern canons of the saints, genres that provide the governing framework for the encyclopedia of the *Golden Legend* that informs the hundred days of Boccaccio's *Decameron* and the commemorative and cataloguing functions of Vasari's *Lives of the Artists*. The universal martyrologies of the Church are summa- tional calendars that subordinate the fantastic embroidery of the leg- ends to the bare enrollment of the saints in the *Namenregister* of the elect. The *Roman Martyrology* used today, based on earlier calendars dating from as early as the ninth century, commemorates the saints by the simple listing of the name, station, place, date, and means of death:

> *The Third Day of September*
> At Capua, the holy martyrs Aristaeus, Bishop, and Antonine, a boy.
> On the same day, the birthday of the holy martyrs Aigulph, Ab- bott of Lérins, and the monks his companions, who after their tongues and eyes had been cut out, were beheaded by the sword. . . .
> At Cordova in Spain, St. Sandal, Martyr. (*Roman Martyrology* 191)

Such canonical lists and calendars interpellate the saints into the corporate body of the Church; the very headlessness of the saints, the effacement of their particular features in the common fate of decapitation, is formally registered in the minimalist act of listing the names of the martyrs.

Notations tabulating the progress of torture and death in the *Roman Martyrology* share with the *Golden Legend* the hagiographic formula that places decapitation after mutilation and display. Thus St. Anectus was "scourged by ten soldiers, his hands and feet were cut off, and, being beheaded, he received the crown of martyrdom" (*Roman Martyrology* 132). Saint Febronia was "first of all scourged with rods and stretched on the rack, then torn with combs, and burnt with fire. Lastly, her teeth were pulled out and her breasts and feet cut off, and being sentenced to capital punishment, she passed to her Spouse, adorned with many sufferings" (130). The torments progress quasi-logically from scourging, racking, or combing—the abrading and anamorphic deformation of the body without subtraction of parts—to a cluster of dismemberments whose initial cuts (hands, feet, teeth, breasts) are both repeated and subsumed in the mortal sentence of capital punishment, which closes the sequence with the tonic conclusiveness and punctual spareness of a grammatical period.

Febronia, once decapitated, "passed to her Spouse"; for the female saints in particular, to lose one's head in martyrdom is to regain the head of Christ as Bridegroom, for "the husband is the head of the wife, as Christ is the head of the Church" (Eph. 5:23). Both men and women martyrs are eunuchs for Christ who, in a frequent turn of phrase, earn the "crown of martyrdom" by substituting one head for another (*Golden Legend* 354). The single stroke of the headsman's ax brings the potentially endless sequence of mutilations and partial dismemberments to a halt through a mark that forever fixes the saint in the ranks of the elect. The sharp edge of the calendar entry prunes the fantastic growth of miracles initiated by the display of the body. The canonical lists of saints and feast days discipline the generic excesses of hagiography through the restrained inscription of names and dates, which provide "legends" in the sense of an explanatory tag or caption rather than an elaborated tale—mere "headings" without chapters to follow. These summaries are also "sums" in the mathematical sense, the tally or account sheet of decapitational subtractions.

Yet if the decapitation of the saints figures the simultaneous constitution and cancellation of subjectivity in a moment of symbolic subsumption and summation in a larger, faceless order, several legends of the martyrs separate out another kind of subjectification that inheres in the severed head left over from decapitation. Ever loquacious, St. Paul's severed head "pronounced in Hebrew the name of Jesus" (*Golden Legend* 44); here the voice appears at once disembodied and strangely material, localized in a rejected body part that, like the head of Orpheus, continues to speak after death. St. Dionysius, once felled, "stood erect, and took his head in [his] hands" (621); here, the decapitated head reemerges beneath rather than above the shoulders in an off-center restoration of the body. St. Cecilia survives the three blows allowed in Roman law for three days before she finally dies (695); her neck is miraculously resistant to the interpellative cut inflicted both by the pagan persecutor who follows the letter of the Roman law and by the formula of torture and death prescribed by the logic of hagiography. To this list we could add the head of St. John the Baptist on a charger and the later discovery or "Invention" of the same head found buried in an urn (*Golden Legend* 502–10), framings that extract an object remainder from the symbolizing function of decapitation. The majority of the martyr legends deploy decapitation as a simple action, more often briefly noted than lengthily described, whose purpose is to articulate and close the narrative sequence by crowning and canonizing the saint with martyrdom.[10] This group of legends, however, isolates the product or by-product of decapitation left over by the narrative cut, worrying the narrative function of punctual closure into a thinglike accretion.

In *Seminar XI*, Lacan attributes to the drives the production of a "headless subject":

> The object of the drive is to be situated at the level of what I have metaphorically called a headless subjectification, a subjectification without subject, a bone, a structure, an outline, which represents one

half of the topology. The other side is that which is responsible for the fact that a subject, through his relations with the signifier, is a subject-with-holes [*sujet troué*]. (*Seminar XI* 184)

Here Lacan associates the figure of headlessness with a two-part movement. The first phase alienates the subject in "the gaps that the distribution of the signifying investments set up in the subject" (101), namely, the relentless march of the signifying chain. The decapitation of the saint at once conceptualizes the saint as rational person, cuts off her reasoning capacity, and integrates her into the corporate assembly of the Church. So too, the alienation of the subject in the demanding circuit of the drive produces a "subjectification without subject" in which, Lacan says further, "the subject is an apparatus," an automaton spoken by the order of signifiers that assimilates it. We could say that the acephalic saints, like the headless subject of the drive, achieve a subjectivity *in name only*, a subjectivity not simply reduced to but indeed produced by the symbolically inscriptive function of the saint's day intercalated in the calendar of the liturgy.

And yet Lacan traces a second movement, not the positive embodiment of the subject as an autonomous agent who could master the symbolic order, but rather the emergence of a "subject with holes" who falls out of signification. This second phase isolates the measured lack endlessly displaced in the signifying chain and momentarily frames it as a hole or void, an unquantifiable negativity that borders on the overwhelming positivity of *jouissance*. Whereas the movement of alienation describes the canonizing function of decapitation, the moment of separation accounts for the talking heads of hagiography. These de-capitational phenomena—decapitations, that is, of decapitation itself—return to the symbolic cut that interrupts the unfolding sequence of tortures, rolling its incisive conclusion into an addendum precipitously ahead of the narrative closure decapitation normally brings off. St. Dionysius carrying his head beneath his shoulders as well as the head of John the Baptist buried in an urn map the topology of an *interior acephalism*, in which the subtraction of the head from the body is sunk beneath the shoulders as a heterogeneous bubble of loss and enjoyment; interior acephalism separates out decapitation's *closure* as a moment of uncanny *enclosure*. So too, the thrice-hacked neck of St. Cecilia incarnates the cut performed by decapitation while delaying and hence fundamentally changing its conclusive stroke by knotting the punctual function of decapitation into a point of narrative impasse, of arrested development.

We had analyzed the splaying of the saint's body, which abstracts the pre-iconographic iconicity of the saint, as the symptomatic binding of the imaginary to the real in compensation for the lack in the symbolic Other. Decapitation and its uncanny vicissitudes retie the symbolic to the real in reaction to the threat of imaginary proliferation. The *point de capiton* introduced in Lacan's early seminar on psychosis (*Seminar III*) anticipates the binding function of the *sinthome* in *Seminar XXIII*. In Lacan's theory of *capitonnage* (buttoning, quilting), a single signifier, such as the proper name granted in circumcision or baptism, serves to enlist the subject in the symbolic order.[11] For each subject, language is configured differently, depending on which points anchor, scan, and orient the set of signifiers. These key signifiers are installed by moments of ritualized trauma such as circumcision, which literally cuts the name into the body, or by the haphazard coincidences of language and *jouissance* that introduce the *infans* into discourse. In either case, the buttoning of the subject to the symbolic order involves an element of the real, insofar as the act of primal repression talismanically wrests certain signifiers (labeled by Lacan as S_1) from the ranks of ordinary signification (S_2), charging these unary or master signifiers with a horrific, thinglike density. Like the *sinthome*, then, the *point de capiton* effects a primitive binding of orders that plants the subject in the dialectic of symbolic and imaginary signification through the operation of a traumatic point, a nonsignifying blind spot.

Hagiographic decapitation enacts such a *capitonnage*. If decollation announces the denouement—literally the unknotting or disentangling—of martyrdom, it does so by definitively binding the martyr to the *sacra conversazione* of the saints through a thematic and structural incisiveness foregrounded and real-ized in the legends of severed heads. Moreover, decapitation, thematizing this process within the framework of hagiography, becomes a traumatic point of repetitive narrative production in the afterlives of the saints. As we will see in the chapters to come on the *Decameron* and *Measure for Measure*, Renaissance literary texts symptomatically rework scenes of martyrological decapitation in order to both stall and install the rule of secularization by isolating the traumatic lining of its symbolizing movement.

Reliquary Interment

Yet the martyrdom of the saint does not end with her death. After the mortal blow a series of postmortem anecdotes and miracles begin to collect, often beginning with the problem of burying the saint. The tyrant's rage against the resistance of the martyr extends to the corpse, whose proper burial is often outlawed by the persecuting agency. St. Sebastian's body is "thrown into a sewer, lest the Christians preserve and venerate it as the relic of a martyr" (*Golden Legend* 109), a fate shared with the starved and racked body of St. Petronilla, which is eventually "thrown into a *cloaca*" (301); in these legends, the tyrant treats the corpse quite literally as sewage, a waste product to be flushed away rather than honored through burial. In the aftermath of St. Vincent's passion, the Roman governor Dacian orders the corpse to be exposed to wild animals, but angels and miraculously tamed scavenger birds protect it; when Dacian then orders the body to be weighted with a stone and thrown into the sea, the corpse fails to sink (115–16). Here, the attempt is not simply to deny the body burial, but to make it disappear—something that, as in a modern horror film, it simply will not do. In the legends of Chrysanthus and Daria (633) and of Vitalis (246), the sentence to live burial condenses the refusal of proper funeral rites with the martyrdom itself.

Through refusing burial, the tyrant attempts to inflict a second death on the executed criminal by denying the martyr any place in the cemetery of memory. Such scenes attempt to double biological death—the physiological passing of the organism—with symbolic

death, in these cases the exclusion of the subject from all memori-
alization. The actions of the pagan tyrant emerge into the frame of
Christian narrative from the mythic backdrop of Greek tragedy and
epic, where the greatest fear and shame is not death itself so much as
the lack of burial and its ceremonies. In Sophocles' *Antigone*, Tire-
sias announces the effects of Polyneices' exposure to wild beasts on
the proper exercise of divinatory and sacrificial rites:

> All the altars of the town are choked
> with leavings of the dogs and birds; their feast
> was on that fated, fallen Polyneices.
> So the gods will have no offering from us,
> not prayer, nor flame of sacrifice. The birds
> will not cry out a sound I can distinguish,
> gorged with the greasy blood of that dead man.
>
>   . . .
>
> What use to kill the dead a second time? (1016–22, 1030)

Romantic readers found in *Antigone* a prototype of modern Christian tragedy interred within the Greek canon. Yet for all their apparent similarity the hagiographic and Sophoclean scenarios are
fundamentally different. In the Greek drama, the refusal of burial
disastrously interferes with divine communication; the key word in
Rebecca Bushnell's analysis of the scene is the *asēmon*—meaning-
less, indistinguishable, a-semantic—cries of the birds (*Prophesying
Tragedy* 62). In the Christian scene, on the other hand, God's Word,
in the form of ministering angels and miraculous preservations,
comes into play precisely in response to the ejection of the corpse;
far from silencing the divine, the exposed, battered, and truncated
cadaver of the saint triggers God's further revelations. In *Antigone*,
lack of burial threatens to disturb or suspend relations between mortals and immortals; in the *Golden Legend*, the same act instigates brilliant synapses of intervention, which momentarily connect the symbolic and the real, the order of men and the order of God, around
the rejected corpse of the saint.

In *Antigone*, the state's treatment of the dead body as detritus is
literalized in the droppings of the carrion-glutted birds, an image
that emblematizes the complete degradation or fall of the cadaver

from the symbolic order of the *polis* and its halls of human memory into the defiles of a natural cycle suddenly disengaged from divine as well as human circuits of meaning. In the legend of St. Vincent, on the other hand, the impossible buoyancy of the stone-weighted corpse miraculously halts the sinking of the body into the sea. This liquid suspension of the cadaver's fall, however, does not trace the upward movement of an idealization, since it is precisely the physical properties of the saint's body that are at stake. Both the tragic and the hagiographic narratives maintain the status of the corpse as refuse, as fundamentally undisposable debris, which, like the interminable half-life of radioactive waste, returns with uncanny persistence and disturbing effects to haunt the order that has foreclosed it. In the Greek drama, however, the insistence on the corpse as detritus flags the continuing scandal of its sacrilegious degradation, whereas in the *Golden Legend*, the unsinkable character of the floating corpse is precisely the means and sign of its sublimation.

In *Seminar VII*, Lacan defines sublimation as the process that "raises an object . . . to the dignity of the Thing" (112). Sublimation, that is, takes an object of exchange, representation, and value and charges it with the overwhelming materiality and singular, indestructible weight of the real, momentarily wresting it from the circuit of signification. Far from describing a movement from the material to the ideal or from the sensual to the intellectual, sublimation in Lacan's account travels the reverse path: it drives an object constituted in desire and representation toward the material limits of symbolic ideation. In hagiography, the tyrant's treatment of the saint's corpse as offal is not reversed; it is revalued by the miraculous preservation of the cadaver. The saint's body takes on its thaumaturgic function in the postmortem cults precisely as a waste product, a nonexchangeable gift. In hagiography, the degradation of the saint demonstrates the limits of both exchange and waste disposal in a sublime object that cannot be thrown away, recycled, or swapped for something else.

If the tyrant's attempted foreclosure of the saintly body from rites of mourning strives to impose a second death on the Christian martyr, the miraculous retrieval and pious preservation of the corpse grants the saint the inner-historical afterlife provided by cults and legends. The *postmortem* anecdotes of the saint's immediate converts and companions, united as a group by the task of burial, narrativize the preservation of the dead saint by the institutions of worship. Burying a martyr is enough to create a martyr: St. Nicodemus, retrieving Petronilla's body from the *cloaca*, "in his turn was imprisoned, beaten with thongs weighted with lead, and thrown into the Tiber, whence the clerk Justus recovered his body and buried it with honor" (301). In the legend of Quiricus and his mother Julitta, the gathering of the saints' dismembered bodies figures the ingathering of a Christian community constituted rather than riven by the experience of persecution: "In order to prevent them from being buried by the Christians, the prefect ordered the martyrs' bodies to be cut piecemeal, and to be scattered to the wind. But an angel collected the members, and they were buried by the Christians under the cover of the night" (317). By providing the symbolic rites forbidden by the pagan state, these scenes spell out and knit up the symbolizing cut of the executioner's stroke by dramatizing the establishment of the saint's cult in the canonical practices of the Church on earth.

The posthumous anecdotes that collect around the remains of the saint demarcate in advance the regime of a literature after hagiography—in its image and in its wake. The life of St. Lucy begins as an episode in the afterlife of St. Agatha:

> Lucy, the daughter of a noble family of Syracuse, saw how the fame of Saint Agatha was spreading throughout the whole land of Sicily. She went to the tomb of this saint with her mother Euthicia, who for four years had suffered from an incurable issue of blood. . . . And when all the people had left the church, the mother and her daughter remained and approached the tomb, and kneeling down devoutly, began to pray. And it happened that the maiden suddenly fell asleep, and dreamt that she saw Saint Agatha standing amidst the angels, decked with precious stones; and Agatha said to her: "My sister Lucy, virgin consecrated to God, why dost thou ask of me something which thou thyself canst straightway grant to thy mother? Go, thy faith has cured her." (*Golden Legend* 34)

The legend of St. Lucy elaborates a narrative element within the genre of the saint's legend—the miracles associated with the tomb and cult of the saint—into an independent chapter, in which Agatha sanctions the faith of Lucy through a miracle of healing, passing on the mantle of holiness to a new martyr in the history of salvation. Moreover, this scene of hagiographic influence itself "issues" from the scriptural account of the woman suffering from an issue of blood, an ailment mirrored by the virtue that Jesus feels going forth from him as he cures it (Luke 8:46). In the legend of St. Lucy, a menstrual disorder forms the communicating medium between biological and hagiographic generations. The title of John Donne's "Nocturnal upon St. Lucy's Day" casts Donne's secular love poetry as a nocturnal on hagiography, a well-wrought urn preserving the reliquary fragments of the legends of the saints; as such, it stems from the currents of cultic burial, devotion, and allusion that channel one life into another in the ducts and passages of the *Golden Legend*.

Housed in individual churches, the saint's relics formed the object above all of local devotions, often confined to a single town or region: the entrenched parochialism that a "universal" or "Roman" calendar such as the *Golden Legend* is designed to correct.[12] Jacobus de Voragine's calendar lists canonical saints rather than local ones; he also devotes many entries and parts of entries to the historic "inventions" and "translations" of the saint's body or body parts. These transferrals of relics, often from the East to the West, served to dislocate the heterogeneous practices of individual parishes and reorganize them into more synchronized and centralized rites through a specifically Roman calendar. The *Romanitas* of these calendars bespeaks the Western focus of the world-historical vision inherited by the Roman Catholic Church from the Roman Empire. Thus the Feast of the Decollation of John the Baptist "was instituted for four reasons . . . namely, to celebrate his beheading, the cremation and gathering up of his bones, the finding of his head, and the translation of his finger and dedication of his church" (502). The Feast of the Decollation is essentially a collation of postmortem practices.

The body's dispersal and recovery enacts the dissemination of Christianity among the Gentiles, the *translatio* of power among the different branches of the Church, and the homogenization of parochial worship in the canonical consolidations and coherent historical scheme of the Roman calendar.[13]

Although the burial of the saint evokes elegiac topoi shared with pagan poetry, the hagiographic work of mourning emphasizes not the artistic production of elegies, epitaphs, and funerary monuments that would substitute a symbolic representation for the dead person in the inner-historical transcendence of memory, but rather the miraculous properties of the saint's dead body—the perfume of its odors, its freedom from decay, and the curative virtues of its members and fluids. The rites surrounding the burial and worship of the saint snatch the corpse from the foreclosed region of the second death, a realm that continues to infuse the reclaimed cadaver in the Christian community assembled by its burial. The properties of the relic incarnate the saint's continued efficacy on earth through the material sampling of the saint's remains, rather than through elegiac examples that would replace the lost object with memorial representations. The radical nonsubstitutability of the saint's relics and their presence in a particular place become the fount or footing of sacred figurations and universalizing and "translating" impulses.

St. Andrew's tomb produced "manna in the form of flour and a scented oil" (13); from the bones of St. Catherine of Alexandria "an oil issues continually, which strengthens the limbs of the weak" (715). In his commentary on All Hallows Day, Jacobus de Voragine glosses such fountains of sanctity: "The saints' bodies are the storeroom of God, the temple of Christ, the alabaster vase of spiritual ointment, the fountain of divine grace, and the organ of the Holy Ghost" (643). The passage figures the corpse of the saint as the ointment jar attributed to Mary Magdalene, a metaphor that presents the interred relic as itself an urn, vase, or baptismal basin. By conflating the reliquary and the relic, the container and the contained, this topology of an encased encasement maps the opposition between outside and inside as the indeterminate product of a single surface folded on itself. Such an urn cannot be capped or closed: thus a constitutive emptiness continually pours out of the open rim of its libational structure. Interment incorporates a void into the iconic projection of the saint's flayed and splayed body, effectively hollowing and hardening its fluctuating pictorial plane into a sculptural artefact.

In *Seminar VII*, Lacan takes the jug of Heidegger's essay "Das Ding" as the prototype of creation *ex nihilo*:

> Now if you consider the vase from the point of view I first proposed, as an object made to represent the existence of the emptiness at the center of the real that is called the Thing, this emptiness as represented in the representation presents itself as a *nihil*, as nothing. And that is why the potter, just like you to whom I am speaking, creates the vase with his hand around this emptiness, creates it just like the mythical creator, *ex nihilo*, starting with a hole. (*S VII* 121)

Lacan reconceives the theological doctrine of creation *ex nihilo* by presenting it as creation not out of nothing so much as *around* a nothing. For Lacan, creation is always *ex nihilo* insofar as it introduces an articulated emptiness into the fullness of the real, a void that allows for the binary play of presence and absence in signification and representation.

In *Seminar XXIII*, Lacan returns to the problematic of creationism under the rubric of the symptom, where he explicitly connects artistic creation to the formations of the symptom; something in art, he suggests, aims at and isolates what is presented in the symptom: namely, a creation *ex nihilo* that instantiates "something of one" (*il y a de l'Un*), a shape, mark, or outline that emerges against, and brings into focus as such, a ground only retroactively prior to it.[14] That ground is both the inarticulate real, which precedes and is forever canceled by the stroke of creation, and the order of signifiers brought into a new concatenation by that unary mark as it perforates the real. Creation *ex nihilo* introduces a void into the texture of the real, effectively carving it up through the work of signifiers; this void is then internalized as a real hole in the chain of signifiers, which are rewoven into relationship with each other around this occluded point. In Lacan's version of creationism, the Uni-verse is a

jug or vase that turns around a void, which, ex-isting beyond the order of law and social meanings, gives reality its con-sistency. So too,
the symptom gives the subject its consistency, its minimal formal
coherence as a sack or container, by embodying the void that hol-
lows out that baggy skin. In Slavoj Zizek's analysis, "symptom is the
way we—the subjects—'avoid madness,' the way we 'choose something' (the symptom-formation) instead of nothing (radical psychotic autism, the destruction of the symbolic universe) through
the binding of our enjoyment to a certain signifying, symbolic formation which assures a minimum of consistency to our being-in-
the-world" (*Sublime Object* 75).

The relic, both a thing encased in an urn or casket and itself a
vessel or fountain that generously pours out the gift of its emptiness, is one figure for creation *ex nihilo*. If the saint as rejected turd
materializes the disgusting positivity of the waste left over by symbolic exchange, the saint as ointment jar or reliquary models the
negativity of a void that sets into motion a play of differences irreducible to it. The first evokes the overwhelming proximity of epiph-
any at the onset of the Christ narrative, and the second formalizes
the radical emptiness of Christ's tomb, which marks the openness of
that life's conclusion. In the logic of the relic, the funeral urn is also
a chamber pot, and the fountain is also a sewer. Between these two
images of refuse and reliquary, the interment of the saints folds
ephiphanic presence into the constitutive emptiness of the vessel as
the two limit-points of the real that demarcate and define hagiographic representation.

Thus the presence of the saint in the relic resembles the presence of Christ in the Eucharist. In another crossing of psychoanalytic discourse and Catholic theology, Lacan's seminar on transference borrows the phrase "real presence" from the Catholic doctrine of the Mass in order to conceptualize the appearance of pure
desirousness in the dialectic of the transference (*Seminar VIII* 302–5).
Like the Real in Lacan's teaching, the "real presence" of Christ in
the bread should be understood neither empirically, as an actual
chemical transformation, nor symbolically, as a mere reenactment
or commemoration, but rather as something more on the order of

hallucination, the carnation on the altar of reality of a thinglike voice, gaze, or weight out of the very operations of language.[15] The relic indexes the ghostly region of the second death within the confines of everyday reality; it is precisely as a leftover from the refusal of mournful symbolization that the relic takes on its sublime quality. The relic is a piece of the real, a fragment of the saint's rejected remains; as such, it is neither noumenal—since by definition the relic preserves the body and not the soul of the saint—nor strictly phenomenal, since its curative properties hallucinatorily suspend the laws of nature, shooting *physis* through with rays of the divine.

The postmortem anecdotes contained within the expanding frame of the legend spin strings and loops of miniature saints' lives and miracle tales out of the single point of consummated martyrdom. This thicket of subsidiary material mournfully brings the legend to a close by tying up the loose ends of the martyrdom's denouement and universalizing the terms of its commemoration, while it manically inflames the open structure of the cut by preserving the local relics of its symbolizing function. The potted head of John the Baptist that falls out of decapitation already ties the logic of the relic to that of the severed head. Insofar as the postmortem anecdotes collect around the by-products of canonization, their function of narrative elaboration resembles the gesture of that other *saint Thome*, doubting Thomas, who would only believe in the reality of Christ's resurrection when he could stick his finger directly into the wound of Christ. The apostle verified the Resurrection by rankling rather than suturing the rim of the wound, causing the real presence of Christ to manifest itself around the probing finger. Like the *ex nihilo*, the doubt of St. Thomas represents the *sinthome* as a real thorn in the side of the symbolic, a foreign body that vexes a differential cut into an abyssal void.

Decapitation creates a break or cut in the narrative's ostensive dilation; with the postmortem anecdotes, we could say that *the text swells where it is cut*. The elaboration of the narrative in the aftermath of martyrdom at once darns up the breach of beheading by mournfully transcribing its symbolizing function in the Roman calendar, and aggravates the wound by refusing to allow the narrative to close up around the intercalation of that severing. To return to Lacan's Borromean topology of the symptom, we could say that reliquary interment effects a double binding of the three orders. As a work of mourning, the postmortem addenda reinforce the signifying bond of the symbolic and the imaginary in compensation for the traumatic cut of decapitation. Yet this work of mourning occurs in reaction to the symbolic death imposed by the tyrant as well as to the mortal blow of decapitation. Foreclosed from the symbolic, the saint's corpse returns in the real of hallucination. Thus the logic of the relic, refusing all compensatory substitutions in favor of the real presence of the saint in her remains, reattaches the symbolic and the real at the point of their psychotic disentanglement.

On either side of the symbolizing cut, the narrative swells, first through the distension of martyrdom by the multiplication of tortures, and then through the assemblage of accessory anecdotes that extend to include the memorial program of hagiography itself. The first phase projects the symptom as warning sign, as in the swelling of a pimple, boil, or blood vessel before it bursts. This "projection" of the symptom is temporal (so the preliminary swelling of the narrative "projects" or "predicts" an emergent crisis) and spatial (this swelling "projects" or "protrudes" from the narrative economy as a bump or abscess). The second phase takes the symptom as side effect, as in the swelling of flesh around a splinter or after a fall. Whereas the initial burgeoning of episodes treats the narrative as an inflated tegument forever punctured by decapitation, the postmortem puffing up of the narrative treats the breach as an open lesion both sutured and irritated by its mournful reworking.

The postmortem segment of the legends allows a secular rereading of the *Golden Legend* within the framework of hagiography. In carrying on the task of burying, worshipping, and translating the saints, secular literature figures itself as *the mourning for hagiography* in a memorial economy of symbolization. Through the inverse techniques of exemplary *imitatio* and lambasting parody, secular literature idealizes the lost object in the act of announcing its death and supersedure. Alternately, secular literature can also identify itself with the *relic of hagiography*, the leftover of hagiography's own subsumption by the secularizing mechanisms of exemplary idealization and parodic ironization. Such a figuration is necessarily momentary, localized and marginal, as fragmentary as the relic itself, since it is the waste product of broader, more "canonical," dialectical procedures. Thus we can look for relics of the relic embedded in the sublationary structures of such forms as the humanist exemplum and the anticlerical novella, as well as modern tragedy and tragicomedy in both their literary instantiations (Shakespeare, Racine, Goethe) and their Romantic theorizations (Hegel, Hazlitt, Coleridge).

Whereas the casting of literature as the work of mourning for a prior genre must emphasize the imitative, citational, and recyling mechanisms that make up the traditionality of tradition, the logic of the relic lays out the possibility of creation *ex nihilo*: a genuinely new creation that takes place through the introduction of a void— an empty tomb or an unhealable wound—into the texture of literary history. Yet what makes the Renaissance secular poet like God is not an originary act, a starting from scratch, as in post-Romantic doctrines of originality or "creativity." Instead, the Renaissance poet introduces or exacerbates swellings, punctures, and voids in the preexisting fabric of literature, fundamentally reorienting its directions of signification. The splayings, cuts, and interments of hagiography present three such moments for the Renaissance creation of secular literature *ex nihilo*. These phases in the denouement of martyrdom present charged points in which the genre of the martyr's legend thematizes its own structure, petrifying and separating its narrative functions into objectlike knots that emblematize—in the hieroglyphic manner of a saintly attribute—particular types of artefactuality for hagiography and its literary afterlife. It is not simply that secular literature empties out inherited forms, following the negative procedures of parody or ironization, but that this tradition of Renaissance texts articulates these hagiographic motifs *as empty*, as evacuated tombs whose very immobility mobilizes the hagiographic and post-hagiographic genres they will have come to define. The *Golden Legend* cannot, of course, itself be said to create *ex nihilo*; to the contrary, this wearying monument of and to compilation manifests a tradition reduced to pure repetition. Rather, the stretched skins, severed heads, and preserved fragments that formulate the logical time of martyrdom offer the overdetermined points of hagiography around and against which secular art can create itself as such. It is in this sense that secular literature is the symptom of hagiography: not only the return of the repressed in displacements and condensations, but the articulation of and identification with a *nihilo* that enables and defines true creation. In the process, Renaissance literature is, in the words of Donne's poem on St. Lucy's Day, "re-begot, / Of absence, darkness, death: things which are not."

Finally, a coda: although I have used the psychoanalytic conception of the symptom to interpret hagiography, I have not addressed the way that religious discourse might return as itself a symptom that disturbs the secularizing, demystifying, and even typological tendencies of psychoanalysis (the latter visible, for example, in Lacan's "Catholic" reading of Freud's "Jewish" science). Such an analysis would need to follow out both vectors of the logic of the symptom. One would need to show how Freud's and Lacan's genealogies of morals and religion replay the very narratives of patricide and memorial internalization—the typological narrative of modernity *par excellence*—that they purport to expose. One should also show how psychoanalysis, in both consciously articulating and symptomatically repeating the typological rhythm of repression and its return, is able to encounter the remainders of that rhythm and make them the voided centers of new creation *ex nihilo*. This means attending to the way in which psychoanalysis has worked to recover as much as to demystify the psychic truth of religious doctrines and practices (circumcision, transubstantiation, the unspeakable name of God) discounted by the rationalizing imperative of philosophy and the spiritualizing drive of modern theology. Indeed, psychoanalysis recovers those truths precisely insofar as their original effectiveness has been canceled by the dialectic of modernity, retrieving them as the remnants of typology around which a new, postsecular, ethics might be formed.

PART II

The Novella and
Its Renewals

CHAPTER 3

The Gleaner's Prologue

CHAUCER'S LEGEND OF RUTH

Chaucer's *The Legend of Good Women*, subtitled "The Seintes Legende of Cupide," is a collection of biographies about classical women who died for love.[1] The lives are introduced by a substantial Prologue that explores the scope of authorial responsibility under medieval forms of literary production—in particular the constraints of translation and patronage—in the dream-vision form favored in so many of Chaucer's minor poems. Chaucer's identification of his work as a "legend" Anglicizes the Latin gerundive *legendum* ("that which is having to be read"), a word that originally designated the day's reading in a lectionary or calendar (as we saw in the previous chapter), and soon came to indicate any saint's life or collection of lives. The subtitle to Chaucer's poem, "The Seintes Legende of Cupide," explicitly registers the hagiographic provenance of the word "legend" as a precise generic term with its own history of formal conventions and prescribed uses. Yet Chaucer's extension of the word "legend" to the lives of "good women"—that is, to female figures who exemplify classical "verray vertu and clennesse" rather than Christian "holynesse" (G 296–97)—already presses the word "legend" toward its modern sense of story, history, or account; indeed, the *OED* gives Chaucer's work as the first example of this usage in English.

Peeling off the sense of "legend" as story from "legend" as "saint's life," Chaucer's text takes up the directive of the *legendum* as something-having-to-be-read in order to force a particular blossoming of secular literature in the interstices of hagiographic conventions. It is, however, a distinctly *early* blossoming, its prematurity measured not by chronology (by most counts, the poem was written between 1380 and 1387), but by the inherent limitations of Chaucer's proposed project and the successes and failures besetting the execution of that project relative to other works of the period and of the poet's own canon. The unripeness of secularization in the *Legend* makes this biographical experiment an appropriate proem to the more foundational grafting of hagiography onto romance and *fablieux* exemplified by Boccaccio's *Decameron* as well as Chaucer's *Canterbury Tales*. This brief chapter serves as a "prologue" (literally, "the word that comes before") to my analysis of the novella in the sense that it briefly examines a logically preliminary effort at secularization in a closely related yet distinct narrative form, namely, biographies of famous women. Moreover, this preamble proceeds by reading the Prologue to *The Legend of Good Women*—a subgenre for which Chaucer is justly famous—in terms of its own pre-texts and fore-words, in particular Chaucer's allusion there to the Book of Ruth, a text that emerges in Chaucer's poem as both a forerunner and a countermodel to Christian hagiography and its secularization.

Chaucer's rereading of the medieval *legendum* is itself founded on a theory of writing as reading, *legere*, figured in the Prologue as a process of gleaning. The narrator addresses the community of male lover-poets:

> For wel I wot that ye han her-biforn
> Of makyng ropen, and lad awey the corn,
> And I come after, glenyng here and there,
> And am ful glad yf I may fynde an ere
> Of any goodly word that ye han left. (F 73–77)

The metaphor of gleaning compares language to a field of corn whose best crops have already been reaped by previous writers, leaving only the ears passed over by the first harvesters for the verbally destitute contemporary author. The new poet is belated, left to express the few things that previous authors have left unwritten; in the scenario of writing as gleaning, all the new author gets is the leftovers of the past.

The topos of belatedness, however, does not exhaust the metaphor of writing as gleaning. As the poem's editor, M. C. E. Shaner, points out, the figure stems from the biblical injunction to leave gleanings "for the poor and for the stranger" (Lev. 19:9), a law dramatized in another biography of a famous woman, the Book of Ruth, in which the widowed heroine from Moab, both poor and a stranger, follows behind the harvesters in the field of her Jewish in-law Boaz.[2] As the editors of the *Riverside Chaucer* point out, the narrator's self-description as one who "come[s] after, glenyng here and there" may echo Ruth's plan to "glean among the ears of corn after him in whose sight [she] shall find favour" (Ruth 2:2). The gathering of the remnants of the harvest by the indigent foreigner recycles waste into a gift, both a *good*—a righteous deed on the part of the landowner—and *goods*—a comestible product. Ruth does not simply receive a donation, but rather works to collect what has been missed by the harvesters, and it is her act of gleaning that gives these leavings the value of an obligation fulfilled by the other. Moreover, as a widowed in-law, herself the remainder of a marital exchange, she is not only entitled to glean the fields of Boaz, but also to be gleaned—taken up and remarried—by him.[3] Finally, as a righteous convert, a foreigner who chooses to be Chosen, Ruth comes to exemplify Jewishness not as a natural, inherited identity, but as a reclaimed remnant that always carries an element of residual foreignness into the prophetic genealogy of future appropriations and translations.

In the Chaucerian analogy of writing as gleaning, the new author does not simply cull words and motifs from earlier writings, but rather articulates what was left unwritten by previous works. The act of writing retroactively discovers an idea, phrase, or figure intimated but not expressed, picked up but then dropped, by previous works, in order to receive as a gift what had before been without value. Thus Ruth not only follows "after him"—the posture of the late poet—but goes "after him *in whose sight* [*she*] *shall find favour*"; so too, Chaucer's narrator is "*ful glad* yf [he] may fynde an ere / Of any *goodly word* that ye han left." The element of favor and gladness that links the two passages beyond the topos of the precursor points to the gleaner-poet's transformative relationship to the remnant of the Other. Ruth makes it possible for Boaz to execute his obligations to her as a widow, a foreigner, and a relative, restoring her to the structure of kinship that constitutes the bond between generations. So too, the new poet searches for what was left unsaid by previous writers in order to take it up as a legacy, a "goodly word" in the sense that it has been reclaimed as *goods*, capable of use and exchange in future literary transactions.

Chaucer's evocation of gleaning intervenes in two apparently similar analogies of writing-as-collecting: the classical topos of the writer as selective reader, and the New Testament figure of the good preacher as he who separates the wheat from the chaff. The sense of the Latin verb *legere* as reading derives from the primary meaning of *legere*, "to collect, gather together, choose"; in classical poetics, the poet is one who picks and chooses from the best of past works in order to make his own text, just as a bee digests the pollen of diverse flowers into honey. The biblical image of gleaning, rendered as *colligere* in the Vulgate, echoes the *legere* of classical poetics but shifts the emphasis from collecting the best (the classical apian metaphor) to garnering what the other has left behind (the Hebrew Book of Ruth).[4] In his German translation of Ruth, Luther chose the word *auflesen* to signify gleaning; *auflesen*—to pick *up*—implies raising the reject into the order of goods, whereas *auslesen*, or picking *out*, would imply selecting the best from what is already good, along the lines of the classical model. Gleaning is always a secondary collecting, a gathering up of what has fallen out of an earlier selection. If we resituate the apian metaphor within the logic of gleaning, then the bees could only gather nectar from flowers that had been disregarded or dropped—like the bouquet scattered by Proserpina (Ovid, *Metamorphoses* V.399–401), or blossoms cut inadvertently by the plowman in the field (Virgil, *Aeneid* IX.576–81). Moreover, this recollection of discarded flowers instates them as a retroactive gift, a valentine made in the present in order to be sent from the past, since picking up what has fallen away turns the reject into an offering.

The Mosaic law of gleaning also works against the more common Christian allegory of reading, the separation of the wheat—the best, the substance, the spirit—from the chaff—the unusable husk, the letter, the leftover. Chaucer's God of Love himself invokes this image when he chastises the poet for only representing bad women in his former works: "But yit, I seye, what eyleth the to wryte / The draf of storyes, and forgete the corn?" (G 311–12). The repetition of the word "corn" at once links and distinguishes the two passages, since in the New Testament allusion, "corn" represents the precious kernel carefully removed from a pile of worthless detritus, whereas in the Old Testament reference, the corn figures something scarce but edible that someone else has left behind.[5] Although the gleaner integrates fallen matter into the social order of use and exchange, she integrates it *as detritus*; so too, the "goodly word" recovered by the later poet retains the signs of having been *made good* by the act of its gathering. The "goodly word" taken up by the new poet both enters into the economy of literary discourse and continues to bear witness to the remnants of symbolic circulation, as akin to the chaff as it is to the wheat.

To paraphrase Emmanuel Lévinas, the French phenomenologist and post-Holocaust theologian, the gleaner is "responsible for the other's responsibility," which includes his responsibility for her. Lévinas poses the ethic of responsibility for the other's responsibility as a Jewish rejoinder to the Christian reading of "love thy neighbor," itself drawn from the same chapter of Leviticus as the law of gleaning (Lev. 19:18).[6] The dominant reading of the line, Lévinas argues, "assumes the prototype of love to be love of oneself," so he proposes a retranslation: "Be responsible for the other as you are responsible for yourself" ("The Pact" 225). Responsibility brings with it the idea of *response*, of an originary answering to and for someone else who precedes the subject, an alterity that breaks the self-reflexive narcissism of a charity that would found all relations to other people on the model of an irreducible self-love.[7] In the Book of Ruth, the Levitically sanctioned act of gleaning joins the giver and the receiver in a covenant of responsibility that is neither disequilibrated by the inequity of debt nor specularized in a symmetrical relationship of reciprocal exchange. Although Boaz directs the harvesters to leave extra grain for her, Ruth must still actively gather it; insofar as her gleaning rights are regulated by law, she is not indebted to Boaz, who is fulfilling his obligations to her as the other who logically precedes him rather than performing a voluntary act of charity that would confirm and expand his sense of self.[8] Ruth receives without either giving or being given to—there is no trade-off of goods or services—yet she owes nothing. No debt accrues. In the place of a calculable debt, however, emerges an infinite responsibility. Ruth is responsible for Boaz's responsibility since she makes possible his ability to give; his responsibility is in her provenance, under her care, and can be activated only in relationship to her as something foreign to him. Boaz is responsible "for" the other's responsibility in a different, negative sense, since Boaz marries Ruth not as her next of kin but as her next to next of kin; the closer relative, unwilling to marry Ruth as dictated by levirate law, formally hands over his obligation to Boaz: "Take thou my right of redemption on thee; for I cannot redeem it" (Ruth 4:6). In marrying Ruth, Boaz quite literally takes responsibility for the responsibility of the other by assuming the levirate rights and obligations regarding Ruth from a third party who has proven himself inadequate to the law. In this case, the "for" attached to responsibility means not "in support of" but "in place of," as a substitute; it is the difference between "caring *for*" someone by taking up a relationship to him, and "standing in *for*" someone by taking over his duties.

The new poet's reception of the "goodly word" is also a means of taking responsibility for the responsibility of the earlier text, not only on the model of Ruth, who ratifies the gift of the other by gathering it, but also in the manner of Boaz, who assumes the obligations not executed by the closer kinsman. It is no accident that a good part of the Prologue to the *Legend* is spent debating the proper site of authorial responsibility. In the dream-vision, the God of Love accuses Chaucer of misogyny in his *Romaunt of the Rose* and *Troilus and Criseyde*; Alceste, Chaucer's Beatrice-like intercessor figure, in turn defends the poet by asking why he should be held accountable for the intentions of works he is simply translating (F 362–72; G 340–52). The answer lies neither in holding the original author responsible (thus leaving the translator off the hook, as Alceste would have it) nor placing all responsibility with the new poet (thus proclaiming the innocence of the original, as the God of Love argues), but rather in deeming that the writer-as-gleaner is "responsible for the responsibility of the other." That is, the translator is liable for the ethical import of the original, not because that import should be transparent to him, but, on the contrary, because the intentions of the source text can never be fully evident to the translator. The meaning and intent of the original author functions as an unknown quantity that the translator can never measure, and yet for which he remains answerable. The new poet assumes the responsibility of the other *as other*, as that which he is *accountable for*, but cannot *calculate*.

Such a logic is played out in the intertextual transactions of the legends that follow the Prologue. Lisa Kiser has argued that Chaucer dramatizes the inadequacies of the wheat/chaff model by taking the stories of such classically "bad women" as Dido, Cleopatra, and Medea and presenting them as "good women" by blatantly editing their ancient sources (98). In the case of Cleopatra and Medea, the procedure is so crude that it verges on parody: Chaucer simply leaves out what doesn't fit the theme (Cleopatra's politics, Medea's child-killing) in order to present these women as heroic martyrs for love. In the case of Dido, however, I would suggest that Chaucer experiments with the alternative model of gleaning, for here, he privileges the minor Ovidian reading of Dido in the *Heroides* over the dominant Virgilian one, but within an extremely sensitive, even faithful, paraphrase of the *Aeneid*. The life begins with an homage to Virgil:

Glorye and honour, Virgil Mantoan,
Be to thy name! and I shal, as I can,
Folwe thy lanterne, as thow gost byforn,
How Eneas to Dido was forsworn.
In thyn Eneyde and Naso wol I take
The tenor, and the grete effectes make. (924–29)

Chaucer will "follow" the lantern of Virgil as a guide and beacon, just as Dante did in the *Inferno*; yet he also follows Virgil as the gleaner does, picking up what the earlier poet has left behind. (The word "byforn" is shared by the two passages.) And he does this by reading "thyn Eneyde" with "Naso," with Ovid's *Heroides*; in his life of Dido, Chaucer isn't simply leaving out what he doesn't like ("the chaff"), but rather picking up variant readings of the past from the textual field in which he works. Chaucer uses Ovid to retrieve another Dido at once implied by and opposed to Virgil's characterization; Chaucer gleans Ovid as a gleaner of Virgil. Chaucer's "Legenda Cleopatrie, martiris" is a patently irresponsible reading of history; the life of Dido, however, is not only a more historically "responsible" text in its attempt to collate and reconcile opposing accounts, but a legend that is in Lévinas's phrase "responsible for the Other's responsibility," since it plots the contours of one reading within the parameters of another, as a remnant that needs to be acknowledged and redeemed as such by a later text. Through Chaucer's intervention, the *Aeneid* makes restitution to Dido: like Boaz and the kinsman, Chaucer takes responsibility for Virgil's responsibility for Dido, not by selecting out what doesn't fit, but by making one text stand in for and supplement another. This restitution, moreover, becomes a gift *to* the new poet made into such *by* the poet's own act of gathering; in this, Chaucer resembles Ruth.

Dido, then, enters the *Legend of Good Women* in the same way that the poet gleans "*goodly* words" from the works left by earlier writers; she has been *made good* (an ethical revaluation) and *made into goods* (an object of future textual exchange). This making good occurs through the retrieval of secondary accounts that fall out of the central stories of the past—a reclamation that does not negate the residual status of these supplementary narratives. Furthermore, the means of that making good is the blunt identification of classical histories with hagiography, by labeling each ancient story a *legenda martiris* without transforming the terms of either side of the equation. Chaucer's strategy of conflation differs from that of two works with similar projects. Boccaccio's *De claris mulieribus* simply leaves out Christian women, since their standards of virtue exist on the other side of the epochal divide separating the ancients from the moderns. Christine de Pisan's *Book of the City of Ladies*, largely devoted to classical figures, ends with a compilation of saints' lives, presented as the "high roofs of the towers" that crown the history of good women (217). In Christine's project, the saints appear as a later and higher form of historical development, existing within the same architecture as the ancient women, but with a distinctly greater calling.

 Like Boccaccio, Chaucer leaves out Christian women, yet like Christine, he uses hagiography—not, however, as a separate body of *historical material*, but as a genre of *historical writing* that imposes an alternate set of values on the classical stories it processes. In Chaucer's hands, hagiography becomes a kind of sieve, a filtering device that can either separate the wheat from the chaff, the good from the bad, in order to produce a crudely moralized classical canon, or glean past texts for overlooked histories, alternate characterizations, and divergent moral and hermeneutic codes, thus opening hagiography up to precisely those elements that exceed the Christian worldview distilled by the genre. Whereas the first operation attempts to Christianize classical literature by tailoring ancient materials to hagiographic paradigms, the second strives to secularize Christian literature by making its conventions responsive to the call of competing pre-Christian pasts. Such a gleaning is not reducible to a leisurely grazing or browsing, since it is regulated by an ethico-legal imperative, an *obligare* that deflects the Latin *legere* into a responsibility for the past in the two senses detailed above: both a *relationship to* earlier texts as the repositories of forgotten remainders, and a *substitution for* such works when their representations appear wanting.

 By tentatively dialecticizing hagiography into secular literature through the classical sources the legendary form is made to adapt, Chaucer's *Legend of Good Women* momentarily delimits a secular literature after hagiography. By imagining a secularized Christianity from within a Christianized classicism, Chaucer's poem demonstrates how the potential interchangeability of these two moves underwrites the possibility of a secular literature in the modern (Christian) West. As Linda Georgianna has decisively demonstrated, a "Protestant Chaucer," forged above all through the work of the Reform martyrologist John Foxe in the sixteenth century, has profoundly influenced Chaucer studies, at the expense of a Chaucer who would of course have been historically Catholic. The Chaucer so produced epitomizes the Christian-secular dialectic, insofar as Chaucer comes to represent everything that is progressive—at once proto-Protestant, anticlerical, and humanist—in late medieval culture, leaving behind the embarrassing ceremonialism and legalism of the Catholic Church. In the allusion to gleaning, however, Chaucer's attempts at secularization are facilitated by neither a Catholic nor a Protestant paradigm of reading, but by a Jewish one. To the two Chaucers discriminated by Georgianna, the Catholic Chaucer of the poet's historical moment and the Protestant Chaucer received in the history of English letters, I would add an unlikely third: namely, a "Jewish" Chaucer, a Chaucer who only emerges as the remainder of the world-historical appropriation of Judaism by Christianity as it is repeated in the Protestant overturning of Catholicism. In Chaucer's time, of course, the Jewishness of Leviticus and the Book of Ruth would have been canceled by the typological order of the Christian scriptures, just as the legal ethics of gleaning would have disappeared seamlessly into the Christian ideal of charity; we need only recall the unmitigated anti-Judaism of the Prioress's Tale to sense the absurdity of attributing a specifically Jewish reading to Chaucer's allusion to Ruth. It takes a third critical and historical position to glean gleaning as a metaphor of writing (this much is commonplace) and as itself a remnant left over by both the classical and Christian figurations of *lectio*. The generic conceit of the *Legend of Good Women*—to eulogize classical martyrs of love, and thus to conflate the models of ancient literature, hagiography, and courtly love—establishes one program for secular literature in the Renaissance. Yet if we read that transaction for its remainders, we encounter a remnant, not Christian and not classical and also not the synthesis of the two, in something that could be called "secular" or "modern" literature. In this case, that chaff is an ethics and poetics derived from a passage in the Hebrew Bible—here, responsibility for the other's responsibility—insofar as it is not accounted for by the later logics that founded themselves on it.

It is the divide that opens up between "legend" as saint's life and "legend" as story, between the "seints legende" and the "legend of good women," that this book aims to demarcate, analyze, and trouble. For articulating that gap also entails exacerbating it, in order to repunctuate the synapse of secularization that discloses and crosses over the generic breach within the word "legend." Such a reorganization of the afterlives of the saints is already inscribed in the term "hagiography" itself, and its place in the canons of the Jewish and Christian scriptures. Whereas in the Christian Old Testament the Book of Ruth falls between Judges and 1 Samuel, the Hebrew Bible groups Ruth with the Ketuvim, or "Other Writings," along with such generically disparate works as Job, Esther, the Song of Songs, and Ecclesiastes, since these texts fit neither into the tightly knit narrative and legal framework of the Pentateuch (Torah), nor into the post-Mosaic historical project of the Prophets (Nevi'im). This heterogeneous collection of proto-literary texts is designated in Greek as the Hagiographa, literally, "sacred writings." Between the Hebrew Ketuvim and its Greek translation, "hagiography" takes shape as that sacred writing left over from the central categories of the canon. This definition points the way to a reading of literature as the afterlives of the saints, taken as a progressive station along the road of increasing spiritualization, and also as the retroactive gleaning of an abandoned remnant: both the remnant of the Hebrew scriptures and of the Christian reordering of those writings. The provenance of that remainder indicates that, if there is indeed a possible literature beyond the Christian-secular dialectic, it will not be more secular than the secular (that is, more "authentically," because less Christianly, secular), but rather, *more sacred than the sacred,* because founded on residual models of the holy, whether Jewish, Catholic, or radical Protestant, as each is drained off by the rhythm of a secularizing reform aimed at the spiritualizing synthesis of classical and Christian representation. (Recall Löwith's Kierkegaardian project to "introduce Christianity into Christendom" in *Meaning in History* [70].)

Yet *The Legend of Good Women* does not yet incarnate literature after hagiography, in either its dominant (Christian-secular) form or its symptomatic (antitypological) manifestations, and the reason for this lies within the limitations of gleaning itself as a model of literary change. As the picking up of discarded materials, gleaning is still locked within an economy of recycling that would maintain the literary tradition through a process of endless repetition, whether conceived as citation, imitation, allusion, or revision. Boccaccio's *Decameron*, borrowing its title from "hexameral" accounts of creation, activates the theological topos of creation *ex nihilo* in order to name a new kind of literary productivity whose critical *negations* (a move fully readable within the operation of repetition) coalesce around traumatic *negativities* that exceed and thus reorganize the transmission of tradition. Since its model of gleaning, however complex, follows a logic of following behind, Chaucer's *Legend of Good Women* can only serve as a Gleaner's Prologue to Boccaccio's *Decameron*.

CHAPTER 4

New Wine in Old Skins

THE 'DECAMERON' AND SECULAR LITERATURE

The Griselda tale, the one hundredth novella in the *Decameron*, has been key to interpretations of the *Decameron*'s project as a whole, especially insofar as this modern saint's life stands in an inverse relation to the opening novella, the systematically parodic mock-hagiography of the blasphemer and sodomite Ser Ciapelletto. Thus Enrico de' Negri's "The Legendary Style of the *Decameron*" gradually builds its hagiographic analysis of Boccaccio's book from the "stylistic joke" of I.1 up to the crescendo of Griselda's story, its "liturgic mode . . . reminiscent of the *sacre rappresentazioni*, the sacred texts, and above all, the Book of Job" (178, 189). Vittore Branca has similarly linked the tales by describing the *Decameron* as "a gallery of figures ranging from Ciappelleto / Judas to Griselda / Virgin Mary" (quoted in Almansi 37). Stories I.1 and X.10 set up two opposed models of secular literature, the first operating through the negative strategies of reversal and inversion, the second through the positive *imitatio* of scriptural and hagiographic motifs. Moreover, these two models are dialectically linked, since the apparently positive tendencies of the Griselda story constitute a reversal of Ceperello's reversals, a palinodic retraction and reinscription of the previous 99 tales.[1]

Given this dynamic, what secularizing scenarios are left out or

left over by the dialectical interplay between Cepperello and Griselda, between negation and the negation of negation? Here, the
relics of martyrology that mark the tragic narratives of Day IV provide three competing yet related models of intertextual transformation—dismemberment, encryption, and symptomatic inflamma-
tion. The tales of dismemberment (IV.1, 5, and 9) periodically
punctuate the progress of Day IV; reliquary interment occurs within
the three novellas of severed hearts and heads; and the motif of
swelling burgeons out of the central cut of IV.5 into a second cluster of stories (IV.5, 6, and 7). The distribution of these hagiographic
motifs among the tales of Day IV extends such motifs' narrative
functions (articulation, elaboration, and ostension) beyond the
progress of Day IV to Day IV's position in the *Decameron* as a whole.
These martyrological motifs clarify the economy that installs Griselda as the sublated counterpart of Ciaperello while impeding it
by pointing to an alternate model of a literature after hagiography
that settles out of the dialectic of Christianization and secularization.

From the False Saint to the Pattern of All Patience

The story of Ser Ceperello that inaugurates the hundred tales of
the *Decameron* falls into four basic sections, each keyed to a particular religious convention or paradigm that it ironizes (see Mazzotta
58–62). The speaker Panfilo frames his story with a sermon praising
God as "maker of all things [*il quale di tutte fu facitore*]" (E 68; I 49),
a homily that implicitly compares the secular poet of the *Decameron*
(or "ten days") to the divine Author of the Hexameron, the "six
days" of Creation. The story that follows tells the *vita* of Ser Ceperello, a blasphemous sodomite who finds himself on the brink of
death in the home of usurers. On his deathbed, this sinner gives a
false confession to a credulous priest in order to protect his money-
lending hosts. In the postmortem aftermath, "Ser Ceperello" becomes "Saint Ciapelletto," a holy figure worshipped by the local
community. Boccaccio's novella proceeds by citing and ironizing
key genres of religious writing: the hexameral sermon, the hagio-

graphic *vita*, the religious confession, and the circulation of posthumous anecdotes that ensure the canonization of a saint.

Through these parodic allusions, the story of Ser Ceperello dramatizes "the making of a saint" as a process of literary rather than divine creation. The title "Ser," indicating the hero's profession as a notary, insistently signals the devious affiliation between the secular writer and the false saint, the clerk and the cleric, the Ser and the Santo. The end result of this narrative equation is to press the term "legend" from its medieval sense of a saint's life toward its modern sense of fable or story; in registering the difference between the saint's life and the novella, Boccaccio's tale simultaneously draws the legendary and the fictional closer together.[2] The story's parody of hagiographic canonization predicts the literary canonization of the *Decameron* as a triumphantly secular text, a work that, in a common critical cliché, bravely moves from the City of God to the city of men, from the *Divine Comedy* to the *comédie humaine*. Such a shift, however, occurs not as a change of focus or content, a personal redirection of interest and perspective, but rather as a set of procedures performed on the genres inherited from religious discourses. The decameral poet, like the God of the Hexameron, creates *ex nihilo*—not, however, in the sense of making something out of nothing, outside the realm of conventional forms, but rather in the sense of producing literature through the negation of existing language. This process describes the tale's internal dynamic, in which the hero's false confession reverses the terms of his initial *vita*, and, more important, the story's treatment of inherited texts and genres.

Take Boccaccio's interaction with Dante in Story I.i: the references to sodomy, blasphemy, and usury locate the milieu of the tale in the circle of the violent against God in the *Inferno*, Cantos XIV–XVII. As Giuseppe Mazzotta points out, Boccaccio takes from Dante the Thomistic critique of these overlapping verbal, monetary, and sexual economies as forms of unnatural or sterile production and makes such production a model of his own fictional practice (*World at Play* 59n). The usurer, like God, creates something (interest) out of nothing (money, a pure signifier). As with the subtitle naming the *Decameron* a "galeotto," Boccaccio constitutes the secularity of his text by identifying his art with a moment condemned in Dante's poem. In the canonical maneuvers of I.i, Boccaccio creates secular literature *ex nihilo* by colonizing those demonized, censured, or emptied spaces that already riddle the received terrain of religious discourse, taking each as a *de-camera* or empty room for post-hexameral creation.

The tale of Griselda that closes the *Decameron* differs radically in tone and tendency from the negative poetics of the book's opening novella. Griselda is a virtuous peasant girl who is suddenly chosen by Gualtieri, the local marquis, to be his wife, only to be subjected to a series of tests—the loss of her children, her humiliating return almost naked to her father, and her service at Gualtieri's apparent remarriage to a young noblewoman who turns out to be their own daughter. Patient through all of these trials, Griselda is finally restored as wife and mother at the end of the tale. Enrico de' Negri's 1952 reading of the tale as the culmination of Boccaccio's "legendary style" insists on the high seriousness of X.10: "This is the scheme, as old as the *Vitae Sanctorum*, of the *exempla* of humility and of sufferance. . . . In fact, the tale is the result of so many parables as no writer, before or after Boccaccio, has ever dared to cope with. The counterpart must be sought in the legends depicted by painters" (189). Linking the tale of Griselda to the Book of Job as well as to the lives of the saints, de' Negri derives the peculiar effectiveness of the story from the inherited iconography of suffering that infuses the story's contemporary setting with the clarity and insistence of myth. In this, de' Negri's reading restates the tradition established by Petrarch, who had found in Boccaccio's story an allegory of the patient soul in its relation to a testy but ultimately just God.[3]

In the decades since de' Negri's essay, the moralizing voice of Petrarch has been displaced by the equivocations of the story's narrator Dioneo, whose sexual and poetic license and spirit of ironic negativity have been emphasized by such readers as Millicent Marcus, Giuseppe Mazzotta, Patricia Phillippy, and Joy Potter. Despite the salutary subtlety of this shift from the moralistic statement of the story to the ethical ambiguity of its enunciation, however, I would argue that no amount of "reading against the grain" can erase the striking difference in project and attitude that X.10 presents to Boccaccio's readers. Moreover, it is only by taking seriously the extremity of Griselda's story—if only as one moment in a dialectic of irony and its reversal—that we can analyze the literary dynamics that, in Phillippy's analysis, identify the tale as "a unique locus for the development of secular literary career models" (119). Crucial here is the Christian articulation of the Book of Job as a scriptural prototype of the patient and passionate saint, a reception that in turn informs the inheritance of hagiographic motifs by the secular novella in its incarnation as *exemplum*.

The Book of Job falls into two stylistically and perhaps authorially distinct segments: the brief framing prose narrative of "a man in the land of Uz, whose name was Job," and the much longer, more difficult, and likely less ancient block of poetry, which includes the dialogue between Job and his three friends (3:1–31:40) and the speeches by the Lord and Elihu (32:1–42:6). Whereas the Job of the prose tale is characterized by legendary patience, the Job of the poetic section is a figure above all of fierce complaint. The poetic sequence, though taken up in fragments into the Christian liturgy of the dead (called "pety Job," the "little Job"), has had minimal impact on Christian narrative forms.[4] The Job of the prose tale, on the other hand, is a generative model of Christian patience in homiletics and hagiography. In his legend (a source for *Decameron* II.6) St. Eustace, like Griselda, suffers the apparent loss and eventual restoration of his children; in a vision, Christ hails the saint as "another Job," who in turn asks only for "the virtue of patience" (Voragine, *Golden Legend* 556). Compare as well the extraordinary endurance of St. Marina, who, posing as a monk in a monastery, patiently accepts slanderous charges of fornication and is only "exposed" and hence exonerated when her corpse is stripped for burial (Voragine, *Golden Legend* 317–18).

Given the divided vicissitudes of the Book of Job, it is no surprise that Boccaccio's most pointed allusion to Job comes from the prose section. Having lost his cattle, his servants, and his children,

Job says with proverbial patience, "Naked I came from my mother's womb, and naked shall I return; the Lord gave, and the Lord has taken away; blessed be the name of the Lord" (1:21). When Griselda is returned to her father's home clothed in nothing but a shift, her response recalls Job's:

> My lord, I have always known that my lowly condition was totally at odds with your nobility, and that it is to God and to yourself that I owe whatever standing I possess. Nor have I ever regarded this as a gift that I might keep and cherish as my own, but rather as something I have borrowed. . . . For it has not escaped my memory that you took me naked as on the day I was born. (E 820)[5]

For Griselda as for Job and Marina, the nakedness of the babe (or the corpse) signifies the stripping of the human to its bare essentials—in the words of Lear, the reduction of human vanity to "the thing itself: unaccommodated man" (III.iv.104–5). In Boccaccio as in Shakespeare, Job's existential nakedness, the epitome of patience, is cited in a bare, pointed, "stripped-down" form, chastely detached from the ensuing poetry of complaint. This irreducible positivity of the naked body, asserted and heightened by the confirmational mode of citation, emblematizes the poetics and thematics of Christian *imitatio* in the tale of Griselda. Whereas the religious allusions of Ser Cepperello's story operate through the ironic negation of sacred forms, the Griselda tale gains what de' Negri calls its "fixed, hammering quality" (181) through the positive isolation and citation of this key passage, its biblical message and hagiographic reverberations shining through with the haunting clarity of Job's naked body.

This positivity of the intertextual body in the tale of Griselda is itself, however, the product of two linked negations, the Christianization of Judaism and the secularization of Christianity. The interlocking dynamics of Christianization and secularization as a model for modern Western literature are programmatically set out in Boccaccio's *Trattatello in Laude di Dante*, written around the same time as the *Decameron*. In his digression in defense of poetry, Boccaccio takes the typological structure linking the Old Testament to the New in Christian exegetics as the model of (secular) poetic production. According to Boccaccio, the classical poet, like the authors of the Bible, wrote in figures: "the ancient poets have followed, as far as the human mind can, the trail of the Holy Spirit, which (we see from Divine Scripture) revealed through many mouths its profound mysteries to those who were to come, inspiring them to utter in a veiled way what in due time [*a debito tempo*] it intended to reveal through open deeds" (*Life of Dante* 37; *Opere* III: 4701). Significantly, Boccaccio chooses to emphasize not the figural hermeneutics of Christ's parables but the historical dialectic of the Old Testament, its true meaning only revealed "to those who were to come" through the later events of the New Testament.[6] Boccaccio then extends this model to "our poets," "*li nostri poeti*," a phrase that, though literally referring to the classical poets displaced by Christianity, must also include the writers of Boccaccio's era, whose world-historical role is to displace the traditional forms of Christian writing (such as hagiography) with new forms (such as the novella, the humanist biography, or the Christian epic). Such a displacement, like the testamentary logic on which it is explicitly modeled, raises what it cancels. Thus, if literature emerges in the place of the Bible, it does so by taking on the scriptural status of what it abrogates. In Boccaccio's words, "theology is nothing other than the poetry of God" (*Opere* III: 475), an early statement of that pedagogic product of secular humanism, the Bible-as-literature.[7]

Dante, "*il nostro poeta*," is the ideal case of this sublation, since the *Divine Comedy* exemplifies the modern synthesis of classical and Christian poetry (*Opere* III: 477). In relation to the *Decameron* Dante's work represents religious poetry, but in relation to the preceding tradition of Christian writing, it instantiates secular poetry. Thus Boccaccio's later commentary on the *Commedia* implicitly casts Dante's epic as a modern scripture through the labor of exegesis, and the *Trattatello*, a biographical work modeled in part on hagiography, constructs the career of the poet as a modern saint's life.[8] Boccaccio's critical writings on Dante construct a literature that displaces scripture, a literary criticism modeled on biblical hermeneutics, and a humanist biographical practice that installs itself as the afterlife of the saints.

The tale of Griselda recapitulates with exemplary clarity the paired patterns of testamentary and secular sublation within Boccaccio's own literary writing. First, the story's selective citation of the Book of Job repeats and reinforces the legendary consolidation of Christian patience out of Jewish complaint that underwrites medieval hagiography, insofar as the Hebrew Book of Job is saved for Christian prose narrative through the depreciation of Job's troubling poetry. At the same time, the relocation of virtue from the cloister to the home and the condensation of both God and Satan in the all-too-human figure of Gualtieri together effect the cancellation of hagiography by the novella, the genre of "the new" that emerges as such precisely through those secularizing revisions.[9] The medieval saint's life is at once annulled and revitalized through the exemplary narration of Griselda's patience in marriage, a process that shifts her virtue from a monastic valence to a domestic one and marks her tale as generically modern. Insofar as Griselda is a secular saint, the genre that fashions her is marked as a secular form; thus X.10, in offering for the modern wife what is called in *Lear* "the pattern of all patience" (III.ii.37), simultaneously presents the pattern of secular literature for the modern poet. Petrarch's Latin translation of Boccaccio's Griselda, taken up and vernacularized once more by Chaucer's "Clerkes Tale," should be seen, then, not simply as a moralizing misreading of the story but also as a sign of X.10's brilliant career, its ability to exemplify and push forward the ongoing dialectic of Christianization and secularization that has authorized the place of literature in the modern West.

Stories I.1 and X.10 represent two equal yet opposite programs for secular literature, the first proceeding through ironic negation and the second through selective, sublationary citation. These opposed modes are in fact linked, since, in Hegelian dialectics, sublation comes about as the negation of negation. This formula describes both the testamentary dynamic of Griselda (secularization = the negation of the Christian negation of Judaism) and the economy connecting the post-hagiographic antipodes of the *Decameron*. If Day Ten is in part a moral palinode that serves to "clean up" the irreverent bawdry of the preceding book, this retraction serves not as an apology tacked on to the work as a self-censoring afterthought, but as the recuperation and logical consequence of the text's earlier negations. Read in this way, Griselda is the grave offspring of Ser Cepperello's usurious wit, and the false saint as blasphemous notary is simply the evil twin of the secular saint of the *Trattatello*. In this sense, both I.1 and X.10 are, in Chaucer's expression, "Clerkes Tales," which cross and double-cross the notary's and the priest's senses of the clerical vocation.[10] So too, the unsettling ironies that trouble the enunciation of X.10 by Dioneo and his like-minded critics, far from disrupting the restoration of hagiography in the novella, may instead indicate the necessary copresence of affirmation and negation in the establishment of secular literature as earnest play. Petrarch and Dioneo, the historic spokesmen of the moral and the ironic readings of Griselda, agree on one point, though in different keys: namely, that Griselda's example cannot be imitated.[11] This paradoxical notion of the nonexemplary exemplum epitomizes the constitution of modern literature as the synthesis not only of the didactic and the delightful, but also of the repeatable and the unique, a determination that places Cepperello and Griselda at the mirroring ends of that dynamic continuum of repetition and innovation called the *Decameron*.

The question remains, however, as to whether any other version of the literary is left over by this relentlessly assimilative machinery, a dialectic whose Christian ethos is ultimately heightened rather than reduced by its secular cancellation. If the *Decameron*, as a self-proclaimed post-hexameral text, defines secular poetics as creation *ex nihilo*, what are the exact contours of the "nothing" around which the poetics of the novella form? Is it only the "nothing" of dialectical negation, or are there other less assimilable and assimilating forms, moods, and shapes of nothing at work in the *Decameron*? And, if the Griselda tale exemplifies the literary text as the nonexemplary example, does "something of one," an element of radical singularity, separate out from the coupling of repetition and uniqueness in order to constellate an alternate model of literary creation beyond the recycling economy of *imitatio* and allusion?

'Testa,' 'Testo,' 'Pesto'

Day Four stands out as the *Decameron*'s only sustained foray into tragic narrative, and as the section in which the relics of the martyr legends emerge most explicitly, in the repeated deformations of the human body. In Day Four, these mutilations fall into the three moments traversed in the denouement of martyrdom: the distension or rupture of the bodily envelope; the mortal blow of dismemberment; and the reliquary encryption of the body or its organs. In the *Decameron*, however, these scenes of mutilation, rather than measuring out the narrative rhythm of individual novellas in the manner of the martyr legends, are dispersed among two sequences of tragic tales in Day IV. Boccaccio breaks the death sentences of the martyrs into individual phrases that both refer the tragic tales to each other and locate Day IV in the economy of the *Decameron* as a whole. Redistributed among the tragic novellas of the *Decameron*, these three types of disfigurement map the hagiographic remnants of the testamentary dialectic of Ceperello and Griselda in the general scheme of the larger work; in this scheme, the lives of the saints both epitomize Christian typology and collect the fascinating remains of its sublationary movement.

Day IV's most famous novellas—the initial tale of Tancredi and Ghismonda, the fifth story of Lisabetta and the basil pot, and the last of the tragic tales, the story of Guillaume de Roussillon (IV.9)—all revolve around the dismemberment of the illicit lover's murdered body. In IV.1, the young widow Ghismonda, prevented from remarrying by her father Tancredi, initiates an affair with Guiscardo, a member of the noble household. When Tancredi, falling asleep in the bed-curtains of his daughter's chamber, awakes to witness their lovemaking one afternoon, he arrests Guiscardo, orders his heart torn out, and sends it in a chalice to his daughter, who then kills herself by drinking poison dissolved by tears in the cup. In the similar plot of IV.5, the scene has shifted from the country estate of the noble father to the city house of merchant brothers, who, discovering the affair of their sister Lisabetta with one Lorenzo, murder him and bury the corpse in the country. The dead man appears

in a dream to his grieving sweetheart, who then finds the body, removes its head, and places it in a pot of basil watered by her weep-
ing; when her brothers take away the basil, she dies of grief. Finally,
in IV.9 the locale of female constriction changes to marriage; the
Provençal knight Guillaume de Roussillon, discovering that his wife
has been sleeping with his best friend and namesake Guillaume de
Cabestanh, murders the rival and serves his heart to his wife; upon
learning the contents of the meal, she leaps to her death, swearing
that no other food will pass her lips.[12]

As we saw in the previous chapter, in the *Golden Legend* decapitation signals the effacement of the individual saint in the corporate
body of the Church; the saint loses her head in order to be
"crowned" by martyrdom. So too, in the *Decameron* dismemberment thematizes the alienation of the subject, but now in the order
of the family rather than the Church. These three stories share the
theme of female confinement announced in the *Decameron*'s preface, where Boccaccio writes that women "are forced to follow the
whims, fancies and dictates of their fathers, mothers, brothers and
husbands, so that they spend most of the time cooped up within
the narrow confines of their rooms [*nel piccolo circuito delle loro camere
racchiuse*]" (E 46; I 6). If the women's martyrdom is to be locked
like St. Barbara in high towers and narrow quarters by their fathers,
brothers, and husbands, the tyrannous fate suffered by each of their
lovers is murder followed by dismemberment.[13] Both the heart and
the head function as synecdoches of bodily integrity and identity; in
the threat of decapitation as displaced castration, the *testa* (head)
mirrors the *testes*. In the repeated scenario of confinement and dismemberment, participation in the order of the family and society
must be paid for with the "pound of flesh" of sexual enjoyment,
whether through the renunciation of *jouissance* itself or through the
mutilations inflicted as punishment for it. As such, the stories repeat the classical mythos of Oedipal tragedy reworked in psychoanalytic discourse, in which castration enforces the subject's submission to and internalization of the father's law in the *Untergang*, or
dissolution of, the Oedipus complex.

At the end of these stories, the protagonists are, in Donne's phrase, "*canonized* for Love"; erotically frustrated in this world, they achieve a kind of transcendence in the memories they leave behind, an inner-historical afterlife manifested above all by the retelling of their stories in the *Decameron*. These endings take up the symbolizing work of the postmortem coda to the lives of the saints. Thus, like the saints Lawrence and Stephen, the couples in IV.1 and IV.9 are buried together and mourned by the populace, who weave a memorial community around their tomb.[14] The tragedy of Lisabetta is immortalized in a ballad, becoming a "legend" in the hagiographic, historical, and fictional senses of the word. Just as these lovers die into the immortality provided by historical memory and narration, so too, hagiography dies into its *vita nuova* as romantic literature—here, the subgenre of the tragic novella that would influence prose fiction, modern tragedy, and tragicomedy.[15] Lovers' discourse both displaces and revitalizes hagiography through the shared mark of corporeal subtraction; in the intertextual repression of hagiography by romance, the motif of dismemberment itself functions as the metonymic return of martyrology within the form of the tragic novella that subsumes it.

In the *Golden Legend*, decapitation served to bring the interminable string of torturous displays to a dramatic close through the single stroke of the headsman's ax. In the *Decameron*'s Day IV, dismemberment continues to perform a punctuating function, but here its cuts break up and symbolically articulate not only the individual stories of Day IV but also the progress of Day IV as an integrated sequence of tales. The story of Ghismonda and Guiscardo that opens the tragic day establishes dismemberment as both a theme and a narrative function to be elaborated in the subsequent tales; in keeping with the function of decapitation in martyrology, IV.1's scene of dismemberment presents a "heading" or "legend" announcing a key motif. The fifth tale, that of Lisabetta and the basil pot, places decapitation at the heart of Day IV, as a cut in the body of the male lover that also marks a caesura in the tragic collection that falls into place around its central divide. Finally, in the story of Guillaume de Roussillon (IV.9), the incisive recapitulation of I.1's parallel scene of the disembodied heart brings to a close the

Decameron's tragic interlude.[16] These systematically distributed scenes of dismemberment extend the articulating function of decapitation in the denouement of martyrdom to the sequence of tragic novellas as a group, binding them together as a coherent family of tales. Moreover, insofar as Day IV is remembered as a day of dismemberments by readers of these stories, the motif of bodily subtraction establishes the function of Day IV itself as a tragic caesura in the comic fabric of the *Decameron* as a whole.[17] In the narrative continuum of Boccaccio's work, the romantic tragedies of Day IV divide and align the ironic negations of hagiography (I.1) and the positive *imitatio* of the saints (X.10) around the central cleavage of martyrological dismemberment.

Beheading and dehearting, however, though clearly belonging to the same associative chain, are not wholly homologous. Decapitation removes or truncates an external organ, and the excised heart posits a lack interior to the field of the subject. When headlessness and heartlessness are superimposed, the two types of dismemberment describe what I termed in Chapter 2 an *interior acephalism*, in which the head is not simply cut off, but is sunk into the body as an internalized void; recall the iconography of St. Dionysius, who, once decapitated, rises again, holding his head beneath his shoulders.[18] Read together, the extracted hearts of IV.1 and IV.9 pull the decapitation of IV.5 beneath the shoulders, effectively internalizing the truncation, while the upward-and-outward orientation of the head draws the interior core traditionally symbolized by the heart insistently off center, a bubble submerged just below the framework of the shoulders. Headlessness and heartlessness taken independently stage the symbolic alienation of the subject in the familial order— and the supersession of hagiography by the *dolce stil nuovo* of romantic literature. The superimposition of the two lacks points to an object that remains after the interpellative cut—not the heart or head taken in themselves as concrete entities, but rather the infolded void of interior acephalism that comes to inhabit and exacerbate the wound left by dismemberment.

Such a template of interior acephalism occurs in each of these three tales, elaborating a second martyrological deformation: namely, reliquary encryption or enclosure. In this triad of tales, the symbolizing stroke of dismemberment gives way to an act of cannibalistic incorporation, the nonsymbolizing ingestion of a traumatic alterity.[19] Ghismonda receives the dislodged heart of her lover in a golden chalice that cradles its (dis)contents like a reliquary or a communion cup. In IV.9, the quasi cannibalism of Ghismonda's deathly drink is radicalized in the scandal of the dainty meal served in a silver tureen. In IV.5, the chalice enclosing Guiscardo's heart mutates into the pot of basil, which, like the urn holding the head of John the Baptist (Voragine, *Golden Legend* 502–10), melancholically preserves a fragment of the dead lover. The void inscribed by reliquary interment takes the form of a concavity, a hollowed, depressed pocket that inters heterogeneous matter within the Cartesian plane of the symbolic order.

Interior acephalism graphs what Lacan calls "*extimité*," an "intimate exteriority" that embeds a radical otherness, a "piece of the real," within the homogeneous field of language (Miller 1988). These scenes of encryption reconstellate the account of dismemberment as castration around the traumatic immurement of *jouissance* at the heart of the symbolic order. From its opening pages, the *Decameron* locates feminine enjoyment within the *piccolo circuito*, the narrow confines of the family and society. The law of castration figures this internal perimeter as the absolute cancellation of *jouissance*, but the counter-logic of encryption posits the scandalous, unassimilated maintenance of enjoyment within the horizon of signification. Whereas the cut of dismemberment symbolizes symbolization, the interment of the objects left over by dismemberment symbolizes the limits of symbolization.

Thus Lorenzo's decapitated head (*testa*) is lovingly nestled in a pot (*testo*), its terracotta walls signaling the fundamental noncommunication between the dismembered organ and the social organization; the secret burial that Lisabetta has effected takes place outside the ordered cemetery of social and familial memory. Like a reliquary, Lisabetta's basil-pot holds a beloved body-part whose absolute nonsubstitutability materializes pure loss as a thinglike presence. Like the tombs of the saints that exude healing fluids, moreover, this funeral urn has an intrinsically open structure, with medicinal basil cascading over its uncapped rim. Whereas Lisabetta's death into the afterlife of the tale's commemorative retelling carries out the symbolizing activity of hagiography's postmortem anecdotes, this scene of encryption freezes the cultural work of elegiac substitution in the bent posture of interminable mourning. The basil does not stand for Lorenzo in an act of poetic substitution (the way that the laurel tree stands for Daphne, or the anemone for Adonis), but rather grows in the soil of his material decay, painfully literalizing the mournful metamorphoses of funeral art. The central image of the head in the basil pot implicitly casts IV.5 as the relic of the relic or the encryption of encryption, the incorporation of the topology of interment into the corpus of the *Decameron* as a moment that passes into Lisabetta's posthumous existence in legendary narration while remaining distinct from it. These images of encryption colonize the reliquary as the evacuated site for secular creation *ex nihilo*.

The image of the basil also locates this tale in a second sequence of novellas in Day IV: the "death-in-the-garden" stories that directly follow Lisabetta's. In IV.6, the young lovers Andreuola and Gabriotto, having consummated their secret marriage in her father's garden, recount two nightmares, which tragically come true when Gabriotto mysteriously dies in Andreuola's arms. In IV.7, set among urban artisans, another couple goes on a picnic with friends; the young man, Pasquino, dies suddenly after cleaning his teeth with a poisoned sage leaf, and is followed soon after by his lover when she reenacts what had happened in an attempt to exculpate herself.

This pair of stories expands the window box of Lisabetta into amorous gardens that contain *jouissance* within the city; at the same time, they replace the dismemberments of Day IV's governing sequence with increasingly insistent allusions to the plague, whose memory and effects the hundred tales are purportedly designed to quarantine. The heroine of IV.6 dreams prophetically of "a dark and terrible thing [*una cosa oscura e terribile*] issuing from [her lover's] body, the form of which she could not make out" (E 371–72; I

536). The word *oscura*—as in Dante's *selva oscura*—implies both the illegibility and the hermeneutic promise of this darkness visible in dreams; the amorphous image of the *cosa oscura* is progressively brought into signification by the young man's dream of a black greyhound, then by his sudden death, and then by the garden death of the next story, which unmistakably evokes the plague. There, Pasquino's "face and body were already covered with swellings and dark blotches [*già tutto enfiato e pieno d'oscure macchie per lo viso e per lo corpo*]" (E 380; I 550), a description that, as critics have long pointed out, recalls Boccaccio's nosography of the Black Death in the opening pages of Day I:

> its earliest symptom, in men and women alike, was the appearance of certain swellings [*certe enfiature*] in the groin or the armpit, some of which were egg-shaped whilst others were roughly the size of the common apple. Sometimes the swellings were large, sometimes not so large, and they were referred to by the populace as *gavòccioli*. From the two areas already mentioned, this deadly *gavòcciolo* would begin to spread, and within a short time it would appear at random all over the body. Later on, the symptoms of the disease changed, and many people began to find dark blotches and bruises [*macchie nere o livide*] on their arms, thighs, and other parts of the body, sometimes large and few in number, sometimes tiny and closely spaced. (E 50; I 16)

The death of Pasquino in IV.7 is linked to this passage by the swelling (*enfiato, enfiature*) of the diseased body, and both IV.6 and IV.7 are implicated in the plague description by the presence of dark blotches (*una cosa oscura, oscure macchie, macchie nere o livide*) erupting on or issuing out of the body. These paired features picture the plague as indeed a "Black Death," a disease of obscure marks that blot and stain the surface of the body.

What distinguishes these plaguelike boils and blemishes from the dismemberments dramatized in the first sequence of stories is the emphasis on the anamorphic inflating, distension, splotching, or bursting of the bodily envelope. As in the flaying, splaying, and racking of the saint before martyrdom, nothing is either amputated from or occluded into the body in these reminiscences of the plague; instead, dangerous fluctuations in tension and pressure distend or rupture corporeal surfaces. In IV.6, the *cosa oscura* of the young girl's dream realized in her lover's mysterious death is finally diagnosed as "the bursting of an abscess located in the region of his heart [*alcuna posta vicina il cuore gli s'era rotta*]" (E 376; I 543); the reference to the heart recalls the dismemberments of IV.1 and IV.9, but rewrites them in terms of an exploded pustule rather than an excised organ. The *ex nihilo* implied by the plague-sore is neither the lack created by a subtraction, nor the depression made by and for an interment, but rather a *convexity*—a boil, abscess, or carbuncle that inflates and displays the skin of representation.

In his description of the plague, Boccaccio compares the bubonic *gavòccioli* to eggs and apples [*quali crescevano come una comunal mela, altre come uno uovo*], a diagnostic metaphor that cites and inverts the Latin proverb *ab ovo usque ad mala*, from the egg to the apple, from the appetizer to the dessert (I 16). This holiday diet of snacks, this upside-down meal of sweets and savories with no main course, allows us to read IV.9's *vivandetta* and *manicaretto* (I 567)—the little dish or dainty tidbit of Guillaume de Cabastanh's heart nestled in its silver tureen—through the bloated body of Pasquino in IV.7. Across the *Decameron* and its triple logic of deformation, the cannibalistic ingestion of the excised heart hatches or ripens in the eggs and apples—the surplus value—of the symptom. In Lacanian terms, the symptom materializes the real as the *"plus de jouir,"* the little bit of enjoyment left over by the disheartening entry into language, a painful pleasure that puffs around the very cuts that constitute the signifying order.

What affiliates this final structure with the basil plant growing from Lisabetta's pot is the image of the poisonous sage bush in IV.7. The shrub of sage or *salvia* that should have helped Pasquino carry out his brief ritual of dental hygiene leads in fact to his death, due to the presence of a venomous toad later discovered beneath the sage's branches. In this miniature plague of frogs, a kind of sympathetic magic hysterically equates the warty skin and inflatable body of the toad (*botta*), the rough, bumpy texture of the sage leaf, and the bloated and blotchy corpse of Pasquino, "swollen up like a barrel [*gonfiato come una botte*]" (E 381; I 551).[20] In a proto-Boschian condensation, the sage itself seemingly sprouts from the head of the poisonous toad in a demonic crossing of the plant and animal kingdoms. The perverted grafting of toad and sage in IV.7 elaborates the striking image of the basil plant growing lushly from the decaying head of Lorenzo in IV.5, the tale initiating this second sequence of novellas. The images of the toaded sage and the headed basil recast Day IV's calendar of martyrs as an herbarium, a medicinal collection of plants for the diagnosis and treatment of those boils, inflammations, lumps, and growths that twist and pucker the body's multiple surfaces.[21]

The image of the basil sprouting from Lorenzo's severed and potted head momentarily locks the three modalities of disfigurement into place: the decapitated head or *testa*, buried in the pot or *testo*, feeds the rampant growth of the basil plant. In the dream work of Day IV, *botte* bleeds into *botta*, and *testa* into *testo*. The inflation imagined by the first and the interment performed by the second present two distinct yet interrelated responses to the narrative incision of dismemberment.

The motif of interment is internal to the first triad of tragic novellas, whose scenes of dismemberment systematically partition Day IV. In these tales the women cup the excised parts of their dead lovers into reliquary vessels, refusing all symbolic substitution in favor of cannibalistic ingestion (IV.1 and IV.9) or endless mourning (IV.5). Superimposing heartlessness and headlessness into the strange shape of an interior acephalism, the topology of interment discovers in the canonical cut of decapitation a heterogeneous, excentric void that faults symbolization. These scenes of encryption separate out and wall off the thingly product of the symbolizing stroke—not, however, as a positive object, theme, or content, but rather as an ex-timate concavity buried within the subtractions exacted by the familial order. Encryption is "internal" to the *Decameron*'s narratives of dismemberment in the sense that it draws from the wound of castration the dream of interiority as such.

The motif of bloating, on the other hand, swells around rather than plunges into the function of the narrative cut, associatively spreading into the hypertrophic gardens of the next pair of stories. Whereas the theme of reliquary interment operates on the product or remainder of symbolic castration within the tales of dismemberment (IV.1, 5, and 9), the motif of swelling projects the anamorphic distortion and inflation of the body onto an alternate sequence of stories (IV.5, 6, and 7). Just as the basil takes root in the loam cushioning Lorenzo's decaying head, the death-in-the-garden stories that follow IV.5 burgeon out of Day IV's uniformly distributed scenes of dismemberment as their excrescent symptom and strange side effect.

Encapsulating the three modes of martyrological mutilation, the decapitation of the fifth tale marks the caesura of Day IV. Not only does it divide the two halves of the tragic sequence around the truncated head of Lorenzo, but it also mobilizes the two responses to that central cut: the encryption of the severed organs internal to the tales of dismemberment, and the bloating of the textual body in the novella series that swells out of IV.5. Dismemberment, interspersed evenly throughout Day IV, thematizes the punctual function of the heading, the caesura, and the period, each of which marks a break, cut, or spacing in the text crucial to its textual and intertextual signification. Interment, internal to the series of dismemberment narratives, morbidly collects the object remainders that fall out of symbolic articulation—nonsubstitutable things-of-loss that isolate a void not subject to symbolic displacement. And swelling, a motif that clusters, multiplies, or mushrooms around the window box at the heart of Day IV, dramatizes the infectiously associative and specular relation between tales—and between the frame and its tales—in the *Decameron*, a spreading of the plague through the sympathetic magic of symptomatic likenesses.[22] Together, these three modes dislodge and reshuffle the narratological moments of martyrdom's final phase into new combinations that refer the tales of Day IV both to each other and to the lives of the saints. These motifs project the "nothing" of creation *ex nihilo* as the *lack* inscribed by dismemberment, the *void* or *vacuum* of pure loss buried within that cut, and the *jouissance* of symptomatic swelling that inflames its rim. In the post-hexa-

meral project called the *Decameron*, Boccaccio creates secular literature *ex nihilo* not simply by rejecting or reversing previous religious
traditions, but also by fashioning his own text around modes of negativity retroactively visible in the legends of the saints.

Griselda Punctured

In the dominant economy of the *Decameron*, the principle of
negation rules both the generic inversions of I.1 and the affirmative reversal of reversal performed in X.10; so too, within the tale of
Griselda, the novella's testamentary textuality enacts the principle
of symbolic castration, insofar as the biblical source text, the Book of
Job, bears a cut: the division between prose and poetry, patience
and complaint—a bifurcation repeated and introjected in the hagiographic constitution of Job's *vita* as the model of Christian prose
narrative. If the tale of Griselda repeats a cut, we are now in the
position to insist that *the text swells where it is cut*. That is, the mobi-
lization of Job's generic division in the earnest play of the literary itself spawns a dilation and torsion of received forms derived from
Boccaccio's typological model of secular literature. Such textual
"swelling" is reducible to neither the reversals performed by ironic
negation nor the inclusions mapped by Christian *imitatio*. Rather, it
hardens these very functions into relics of hagiography as a genre,
emblematic motifs that cling like pearls or barnacles to the typological significations and secular reversals that secrete them.

To return to the Book of Job: the final trial of Job is not the
reduction to nakedness cited with such candid clarity in Boccaccio's novella, but rather the move beyond nakedness, the violent de-
nuding of nakedness itself, signified by Job's traumatic affliction with
skin disease:

> And then the Lord said to Satan, "Have you considered my servant
> Job, that there is none like him on the earth, a blameless and upright
> man, who fears God and turns away from evil? He still holds fast to
> his integrity, although you have moved me against him, to destroy
> him without cause." Then Satan answered the Lord, "Skin for skin!
> All that a man has he will give for his life. But put forth thy hand

now, and touch his bone and his flesh, and he will curse thee to thy face." And the Lord said to Satan, "Behold, he is in your power; only spare his life."

So Satan went forth from the presence of the Lord, and afflicted Job with loathsome sores from the sole of his foot to the crown of his head. And he took a potsherd with which to scrape himself, and sat among the ashes. (2:3–8)

Although Job offers his wife one final sign of patience ("Shall we receive good at the hand of God, and shall we not receive evil?" he tells her), the skin disease is the last ordeal before Job lapses into complaint—and before the Book of Job breaks out in poetry. The generic and tonal division of the text is pockmarked by signs of swelling: here, the "loathsome sores" that compromise the bodily and spiritual integrity of Christianity's patient Job.

Griselda's trials stop short at nakedness, honoring the hagiographic cut in order to enunciate it as modern literature. Griselda's marital tribulations, however, are curiously named by the phrases *puntura* (I 1240, 1246)—literally, punctures, stings, bites—and *punsi e trafissi* (I 1247)—pierced and transfixed. Both phrases figure the emotional pains and humiliations inflicted by the husband on his wife as puncturings, deflationary perforations of the existential integrity represented in the story and its sources by the theme of nakedness. The word *puntura*, moreover, occurs in what is closest to a reproach in Griselda's speech; asked by Gualtieri what she thinks of his intended bride (her daughter), she replies, "I think very well of her. . . . But with all my heart I beg you not to inflict those same wounds [*puntura*] upon her that you imposed upon her predecessor" (E 822; I 1246). And, as Branca notes, Gualtieri's speech restoring his wife echoes Griselda's choice of words: "When I came to take a wife, I was greatly afraid that this peace would be denied me, and in order to prove otherwise I tormented and provoked you [*ti punsi e trafissi*] in the ways you have seen" (E 823; I 1247).[23] Finally, Dioneo's oft-noted criticism of the tale points to the limits of patience in an idiom that once more evokes the skin: "For perhaps it would have served him right if he had chanced upon a wife, who, being driven from the house in her shift, had found some other man to shake her skin-coat [*pilliccione*] for her, earning herself a fine new dress in the process" (E 824; I 1248).[24]

In these passages, the language of punctured skin staples or pierces together the moments in the text that press patience toward complaint. The repeated language of puncturing condenses the *cut* dividing the source text and the *sores* that accumulate around it. If Griselda's *puntura* manifest the cancellation of Job's boils in the Christian *stigmata*, they also function like the probing finger of Doubting Thomas, which continues to articulate and irritate the rim of Christ's wound after the fact of redemptive signification. The phrases link the *thematics* of Job's blighted skin to the *poetics* of Job's invective, and figure the intertextual transaction as itself a kind of stigmatization that binds the texts together at traumatic points or *puncta*, which exceed the field of their "proper" meaning as they enable it. Together, these phrases crystallize an empty husk, a *pillicione*, left over by the novella's dialectic of Christianization and secularization.

That remainder is literary language—language, that is, conceived apart from (or rather as the material moment of) the signifying processes of negative ironization (Ser Cepperello) and affirmative allegorization (Santa Griselda). In the *Trattatello in Laude di Dante*, Boccaccio praises "the profundity of meaning . . . hidden under the lovely cortex [*la bella corteccia*]" of Dante's words (E 49; I 483). Borrowing an ancient metaphor, Boccaccio equates the material, sensual properties of language with the bark of a tree or the rind of a fruit. This skin is coextensive with the *Decameron* itself, since there can be no signification without it. Certain moments in the *Decameron*, moreover, thematize the nonsymbolized remainder of that signification—the rind without the fruit, the bark without the tree. *La bella corteccia* encompasses not only the material properties of language (the transformation of *botte* into *botta*, *testa* into *testo*), but also the generic scenarios, literary conventions, and thematic clusters that make up a literary tradition. Key moments in the *Decameron* exhibit both the symbolic transference and the real stigmatization of the conventions transmitted between religious discourse and a secular writing constituted as such by the fact of that interchange.

The moments of stigmatization—the passionate puncturing of hagiography as a genre—are always relative to the typological dynamics that integrate the tales of the *Decameron* and situate Boccaccio's
work vis-à-vis other bodies of writing. Thus the *puntura* of Griselda
manifest the remainder of the Christianization of Job in the *Decameron*; Day IV collects the tragic leftovers that plague the comic
dialectic between I.1 and X.10; within Day IV, the scenes of encryption and swelling dramatize the impasses and side effects that
fault the canonical moves of symbolization.

In each of these localizations of biblical typology and its discontents, hagiography instates an exemplum of Christian representation (hagiography as *imitatio Christi*) and collates the aftereffects
of Christologics in the relics and realia, the hieroglyphic attributes,
of hagiography as a genre. Both moments describe the constitution
of secular literature, the first as the negation of the Christian negation, which determines the dominant ideology of literature in secular humanism; the second as the precipation of an obdurate remainder from that sublationary tactic. Thus in the Hebrew Bible,
the Book of Job, like the Book of Ruth, falls into the category of
the Ketuvim or "other writings," designated in Greek as the *hagiographa*. The accretion of Job's scripturally ex-timate position in
the cuts and punctures of Griselda indeed points to another secular
literature beyond the Christian economy of secularization, but does
so only by momentarily enunciating another hagiography, namely,
the nonsignified, unconverted *corteccia* of the saints' Jewish prehistory.

Petrarch's letter to Boccaccio suggestively yokes Griselda and
the plague as the moments of high seriousness that frame and redeem Boccaccio's dangerously superficial work:

> As usual, when one looks hastily through a book, I read somewhat
> more carefully at the beginning and at the end. At the beginning you
> have, it seems to me, accurately described and eloquently lamented
> the condition of our country during that siege of pestilence which
> forms so dark and melancholy a period in our century. At the close
> you have placed a story which differs entirely from most that precede
> it, and which so delighted and fascinated me that, in spite of cares
> which made me almost oblivious of myself, I was seized with a desire

to learn it by heart, so that I might have the pleasure of recalling it for
my own benefit, and of relating it to my friends in conversation.
(Musa and Bondanella 185)

Petrarch's comments cast Griselda and the plague as the earnest redemption of the *Decameron*'s frivolous play; at the same time, the
association of the two installments may also serve to destabilize the
logic of salvation with the swollen side effects of Day IV's *salvia*. It
would surely be an overstatement to trace Boccaccio's description of
the Black Death to the sores of Job imperfectly excised from X.10—
the book's elaboration of a mercantile *translatio imperii* governed by
a humanist-historicist impulse, for example, outlines a more obvious
though not mutually exclusive program. Nonetheless, the structural
importance of Griselda both as the hundredth story in the collection
and as Boccaccio's most crystalline model of the secular dialectic
points to the plague as a figure for a literature left over by the secular cancellation of biblical typology, a literature of old skins, fore-
skins, and plague sores realized in the *Decameron*'s deformations of
hagiography.

To borrow Lacan's formula for *extimité* as "what's in you more
than you" (*Seminar XI*: 363), this alternate model of literature is "in
the *Decameron* more than the *Decameron*." The counter-version of
the literary marked off by the recurrence of the Jewish Job within
the confines of Christian-secular literature falls out of intertextual
transactions that Boccaccio takes part in and even theorizes, but by
no means controls or initiates. Although the same might be said of
any Christian secular writer (as will be seen, for example, with
Shakespeare and Vasari), Boccaccio's distinctiveness lies in his exac-
erbation of this remainder into the expanse of Day IV, his identification of it with the relics of martyrology, and his brilliant implication of those relics in the pathology of the plague. For the plague
figures the literariness of the *Decameron* not as the *sublation* of hagiography, but as its *symptom*, as the strange growth that flourishes
like sage and basil in the cracks and crevices that articulate the passage of religious writing into its recovery as literature. Such a model
of the literary as symptom, however, cannot supplant the typologi-

cal paradigm, since its seeds are planted precisely in and by the movement of modernization. Literature as symptom must rather be, like hagiography itself, in literature more than literature, a sign of the religious paradigms that secularization intensifies rather than escapes, and also of the testamentary split on which Christian writing and its secular progeny found themselves.

CHAPTER 5

Saints on Trial

THE GENRE OF 'MEASURE FOR MEASURE'

The "saintliness" of Isabella is a topos in *Measure for Measure* criticism, whether as a rigid attribute progressively mollified by the play's humanism, or as a quality not strained by Isabella's insistence on chastity at any price.[1] Sanctity is usually invoked, however, as an unexamined content that describes and stabilizes Isabella's character in a psychological or allegorical unity. My approach differs in treating hagiography as a set of narrative practices that variously raise, frustrate, and transform audience expectations in the unfolding of Shakespeare's comedy. The confrontation between Isabella and Angelo superimposes two scenarios drawn from hagiography via the Italian conduits of the novella tradition. Isabella follows the path of the female martyr: she finds herself in the crisis of deaffiliation that marks the adolescence of many early saints, and she is subject to the trial before a corrupt and seductive magistrate that so often leads to those saints' bloody ends. If Angelo plays the tyrant to Isabella's martyr, however, he is also, in a second scenario borrowed from the *vitae* of the Fathers, hermits, and confessors, the hermit tempted by the *diable en femme*. In these stories of eremetic and institutional sanctity, woman often represents the temptations of the profane world, temptations that "prove" male sanctity in the senses of testing it and demonstrating it. The contradiction between these two tableaus, with their opposite hierarchies of gender and their distinct prehistories in two subgenres of hagiography, helps explain the status of the play as a "problem comedy" whose cold heroine has been tried and retried in the courts of Shakespearean criticism.

A generic reading of the play's hagiographic subtexts serves to redirect the critic's task from judging Isabella's action—a move that, I argue, repeats the tyrant-martyr scenario mobilized by the play—to examining the play's commentary on judgment itself, worked out in the typological debate between justice and mercy. *Measure for Measure*'s intellectual argument—that Christian mercy derives from recognizing one's own sinfulness in the other's guilt—reflects and is reinforced by the narrative movement of the play, in which Angelo and Isabella exchange positions in a process of identification and reversal. This dialectic of law and mercy is another version of the Christian typologic that underwrites the Renaissance transformation of hagiography into secular literature. The dominant movement of the play maps the opposition between Old and New Dispensations onto the breach between the Catholic Church and its Reformation in order to mark out a place for modern drama beyond the miracle and mystery plays. *Measure for Measure* also, however, isolates the Catholic and Jewish moments left over by Protestant discourse—identified with each other under the rubric of a deadening legalism—whose resistance to conversion, substitution, and reformation delimits that alternate constitution of the literary glimpsed in the *puntura* of Boccaccio's Griselda and the gleaned remnants of Chaucer's Ruth.

The Martyr and the Tyrant

A distinctively Protestant hagiography, represented most fully by the *Acts and Monuments*, John Foxe's history of the Marian persecutions, enjoys its own tradition in Shakespeare's England.[2] Yet the hagiographic discourse that flows more clearly into Shakespearean drama is that of the medieval legends of the saints, transmitted through the prose novella tradition of Boccaccio and his imitators. From its Renaissance inauguration in the *Decameron* through such practitioners as Marguerite de Navarre, Bandello, and Cinthio (the latter providing a source for *Measure for Measure*), the genre of the Renaissance novella is deeply invested in the motifs and scenarios of the late medieval legends of the saints. The Europe of Shakespeare's plays—his Venice, his Verona, and his Court of Navarre, the Paris and Florence of *All's Well*, as well as the strangely Italianate Vienna of *Measure for Measure*—is a continent of petty courts, city-states, and pilgrimage routes mapped by the literary conventions, cultural associations, and religious pretexts of the novella.

In *Measure for Measure*, Lucio's opening address to Isabella stems from the Renaissance interplay between hagiography, the novella, and drama:

> *Lucio*: Hail virgin, if you be—as those cheek-roses
> Proclaim you are no less—can you so stead me
> As bring me to the sight of Isabella,
> A novice of this place, and the fair sister
> To her unhappy brother Claudio?
> *Isabella*: Why "her unhappy brother"? Let me ask,
> The rather for I now must make you know
> I am that Isabella, and his sister.
> *Lucio*: Gentle and fair. Your brother kindly greets you.
> Not to be weary with you, he's in prison.
> *Isabella*: Woe me! For what?
> *Lucio*: For that which, if myself might be his judge,
> He should receive his punishment in thanks:
> He hath got his friend with child.
> *Isabella*: Sir, make me not your story. (I.iv.16–29)

As Robert Watson has argued, Lucio's greeting, "Hail virgin," alludes to the Annunciation (Luke 1:28), a divine reference immediately undercut by the ironic "if you be" and the displacement of "virgin" from a religious to a sexual context ("as those cheek-roses / Proclaim you are no less").[3] Like the Angel Gabriel, Lucio is a *nuncio*, a divine messenger delivering an announcement; Lucio's name echoes that of St. Luke, the one evangelist to recount the story of the Annunciation to Mary. Isabella's reference to "my cousin Juliet," moreover, recalls the second birth announcement in

Luke: "And behold, thy cousin Elizabeth, she hath conceived a son" (Luke 1:36). By extension, Lucio's lyric evocation of pregnancy recalls Elizabeth's greeting to Mary in the the Gospel of Luke a few verses later; the scriptural line, "Blessed art thou among women, and blessed is the fruit of thy womb" (Luke 1:42), burgeons into Lucio's lush simile, "As those that feed grow full, as blossoming time / That from the seedness the bare fallow brings / To teeming foison, even so her plenteous womb / Expresseth his full tilth and husbandry" (I.iv.39–44). Finally, Lucio's annunciation is brought to fruition when a virgin named Mariana, who lives at "St. Luke's" (II.1.265), becomes with the help of an Angelo a woman neither maid, wife, nor widow.

Yet I would argue that the Annunciation enters Shakespeare's text not directly from the Bible, but rather through the secular switch points that channel the legends and iconography of the saints into the prose novella. In Jacobus de Voragine's life of St. Cecilia, the saint on her wedding night is able to deflect the incipient duties of the bride into a life dedicated to chastity by drawing on the motifs of the Annunciation:

> That night, when with her spouse she sought the secret silences of the bridal chamber, she spoke to him as follows: "O sweetest and most loving youth, there is a secret that I may confess to thee . . . I have for my lover an angel of God, who guards my body with exceeding zeal! If he sees thee but lightly touch me for sordid love, he will smite thee, and thou wilt lose the fair flower of thy youth; but if he knows that thou lovest me with a pure love, he will love thee as he loves me, and show thee his glory." (690)

Cecilia is able to effect and resolve a crisis that marks the early lives of many of the martyrs, both male and female, though more consistently the latter, a crisis I term "de-fiance," in order both to evoke the modern sense of defiance as the active confrontation with authority and, through analogy with "fiancé," to designate a broken engagement or other gesture of deaffiliation. Although the wedding-night exchange between Cecilia and Valerian leads to the reconstitution of the marriage on a higher spiritual plane, similar scenes of deaffiliation often lead to the immediate persecution of the saint by a suitor-turned-tyrant (the saints Dorothea and Juliana), an angry father (the saints Barbara and Christina), or an agent of the state alerted by the spurned groom (St. Lucy). These scenes of de-fiance stage Christianity's fundamental challenge to the ancient prerogatives of the family in the first centuries C.E. In the lives of the martyrs, the replication and transmission of Christianity occurs not through the education of children in an intergenerational covenant (as in Judaism) or even through the quasi-familial structures of ecclesiastical institutions (as in the patristic and monastic *vitae*), but rather through the double spectacle of sacred testimony and suffering that creates a community of Christians who identify with its inspired speech and fascinating images. Moreover, de-fiance, often performed by a woman against her prospective spouse, narrativizes Christianity's fundamental ambivalence about marriage, a double-edged sword used in the misogynist polemics of clerical discourse and also in proto-feminist analyses of marriage as a social institution punitive to women.[4] Because of their potential for critique of domestic arrangements, such scenes of disalliance are both thematically and structurally important to the *querelle des femmes*—Christine de Pizan's extensive retelling of the legend of her namesake, St. Christina, stages her own defiance of the masculinist literary tradition (see Quilligan 212–21).

The scriptural source of the delicate scene between Cecilia and Valerian is not, however, the divisive cry of Christ's church militant ("For I have come to set a man against his father, and a daughter against her mother," Matt. 10:35) but rather the prototypical encounter between angel and woman in the Annunciation. The pictorial image nascent in Cecilia's reference to her angelic lover recurs more fully later in the legend: upon his return, Valerian "found Cecilia holding speech with the angel in their chamber [*in cubiculo*]" (691). Valerian comes upon this descent from heaven as the privileged spectator to a tableau illumined by the eerie representationality of the vision; this enunciation of the Annunciation depends upon the iconography of the scene from Luke, helping to insure its formalization and circulation in the afterlife of religious art. The allusion to the Annunciation in the legend of St. Cecilia demonstrates

the drama of de-fiance as the often feminine, generally martyrological equivalent to the scenes of vocation that characterize the typically masculine *vitae* of the apostles and Church Fathers.[5]

In *Measure for Measure*, the novice Isabella has already tried to
separate herself from the claims of marriage and family, and Lucio's
salutation calls her back to rather than away from the claims of the
family, a reversal of hagiographic de-fiance that signals the secularization of the religious paradigm. The parodic gesture links Shakespeare's play to the ironizing strategies of the novella; in the *Decameron*, Boccaccio's story of the friar who seduces a vain and silly
woman by dressing as the Angel Gabriel (*Decameron* IV.2) draws on
miracle plays, the iconography of Mary, and the hagiographic tendency to recall the Annunciation.[6] Although the gesture of parody
deaffiliates the novella from the legend, Boccaccio's reliance on the
scriptural text nonetheless indicates his continuing affinity with the
genus—the genre or family—of hagiography.

In Shakespeare's play, Lucio's mock-annunciation draws on the
iconography of the saints, but from the vantage point of their cancellation in the novella form. In *Measure for Measure*, the clerical disguise of the Duke invokes the domain of Boccaccio; the Friar-
Duke's visual presence and his behavior allude to no specific tale
but to the novella genre as an Italianate storytelling tradition with a
storehouse of monastic and hagiographic motifs.[7] And it is no accident that the Annunciation imagery of this early interchange is
eventually realized through the device of the bed trick, a conceit
crisply emblematic of the novella tradition.[8] In this set of intertextual
salutations, *Measure for Measure* reenunciates the tendency of both
hagiography and the novella to enunciate the Annunciation.

In the same scene, Lucio casts Isabella in explicitly saintly terms:

> I hold you as a thing enskied and sainted
> By your renouncement, an immortal spirit,
> And to be talk'd with in sincerity,
> As with a saint. (I.iv.34–37)

Lucio's reverence, as Isabella notes, borders on parody: "You do
blaspheme the good, in mocking me" (I.iv.38). Lucio's remark,
along with Isabella's preceding exchange with Sister Francisca, pre-

sent her in the process of withdrawal from the world, "a thing en-
skied and sainted / By your renouncement"; Isabella appears not
simply as a static exemplum of a particular attribute, but as a character "sainted" by a particular narrative trajectory.

The scene of de-fiance leads, as it does in so many martyr legends, into the trial of the saint before a magistrate, a juridical contest that elicits a peculiarly Catholic eloquence from the female saint.
Throughout the play, Isabella combines rhetorical sophistication
with a body-politics of supplication. Her forensic skills are derived
in part from the humanist source texts by Cinthio and Whetstone;
Cinthio's philosophically trained heroine Epitia, however, resembles Shakespeare's comedic cousin Portia more than Isabella herself.
Lucio counsels Isabella "to weep and kneel" (I.iv.81), and Claudio
recommends her posture as well as her eloquence:

> For in her youth
> There is a prone and speechless dialect
> Such as move men; beside, she hath prosperous art
> When she will play with reason and discourse,
> And well she can persuade. (I.ii.172–76)

Measure for Measure displaces Isabella from Cinthio's school of lib-
eral arts to the Catholic convent, which trains her in a feminine
Christian eloquence, a skill derived from the public debates between tyrant and martyr recorded in the *Acta* and forming the dramatic core of so many Catholic legends.

Exemplary here is the life of St. Catherine of Alexandria,
whose story inaugurates the hagiographic culmination ("the high
roofs of the towers") of Christine de Pizan's *City of Ladies*. In Christine's account, Catherine was "a well-lettered woman, versed in the
various branches of knowledge," who defended the faith against
"some fifty philosophers" at the behest of the pagan emperor. Her
arguments converted the philosophers, but not their ruler, who was
more enflamed by her beauty than her reasoning. St. Catherine's
combination of eloquence, virtue, and Christianity made her exemplary for Christine's feminine historiographical project; Catherine was also the patron saint of scholars for Catholic Europe.[9] While

Catherine's learning is unusual, her confrontation with a seductive tyrant is not. Flowing out of scenes of deaffiliation, the trials are often judged by a rejected suitor, an angry father, or, most commonly, an unrelated emperor or provost aroused by the saint's feminine beauty (the saints Anastasia, Margaret, Eufemia, and others). In the testimonial core of the martyr legends ("martyr" means "witness"), an extraordinary eloquence as well as a shining beauty flourish in the testamentary interval opened up by imminent death.

In *Measure for Measure* the legal setting, the attempted seduction by a magistrate, and the presentation, visual and rhetorical, of a Catholic eloquence all tally with the conventions of the female saint on trial. Some features differ: all the characters are presumably Christian, and Isabella's task before Angelo is to defend her brother, not her faith. Isabella herself, however, vividly calls up the scenario of martyrdom in her passionate desire for death in the place of shame:

> Th'impression of keen whips I'd wear as rubies,
> And strip myself to death as to a bed
> That longing have been sick for, ere I'd yield
> My body up to shame. (II.iv.101–4)

The word "impression" keys into the play's network of words concerning stamping, pressing, and minting; alluding to the moment of scourging in the denouement of martyrdom, the perforating marks projected onto the displayed screen of the mortified body imagine a hagiographics visibly attesting to chastity preserved. The image of stripping begins as an ascetic gesture, echoing Christ's flagellation, and then threatens to shift into an erotic striptease, neatly focusing the elements of mutilation and corporeal display traditionally combined in the ostensive distention of the martyrs through whipping and flaying. And, following the logical time of martyrdom, the word "strip" shifts from the scourging of the saint to the holy marriage of the martyr to Christ consummated by death.[10] Both Catholic and Protestant hagiography represent their martyrs as embracing death like brides and finding new heads in the corporate body of the Church. Isabella's lines perform a hagiographic "bed trick" combining deathbed and marriage bed as she imagines dressing herself in the jewels of martyrdom for a wedding with death.

Angelo's role as seductive magistrate extends Isabella's hypothetical image of martyrdom into a full-fledged narrative confrontation between tyrant and martyr. Although much of the play's inquisition of "tyranny" centers on the term's place in political discourse, the conjunction of the licentious judge and the chaste novice subsumes the humanist figure of the unjust ruler into the legendary confrontation between tyrant and martyr.[11] Thus Angelo threatens Claudio with gratuitous cruelty: "thy unkindness shall his death draw out / To lingering sufferance. . . . I'll prove a tyrant to him" (II.iv.165–68). Escalus's line in another context, "This would make mercy swear and play the tyrant" (III.ii.188–89), clarifies the kinship of the term "tyrant" to the specifically religious iconography of mysteries ("out-Heroding Herod") and saints' lives as well as to the political discourse of history plays and mirrors for princes. The demonization of Angelo ("Let's write good angel on the devil's horn," II.iv.16) feeds into and intensifies the buried presence of the tyrant-martyr conflict.

Yet the narrative of martyrdom is in no sense fulfilled; it functions rather as a lost scenario, a dramatic telos consistently perverted by the sexual dynamics of contemporary Vienna.[12] The pathological note in Isabella's reference to death as a bed that she "longing [has] been sick for" recalls the hagiographic understanding of illness as a modern substitute for actual martyrdom, a lived metaphor that implicitly casts the *vitae* of the modern saints as symptoms or hysterical reminiscences of the ancient martyrs.[13] Whereas Lucio's mock-Annunciation cites religious discourse as canceled by the novella tradition, Isabella's sickness for martyrdom isolates a gap or suspension within hagiography, an element of fundamental nonrealization that locates the afterlives of the saints within the domain of hagiography itself. *Measure for Measure* appropriates martyrdom not as the paradigmatic end of a fulfilled saintly narrative but as a suppressed object of nostalgia that the play itself "longing [has] been sick for."

In the central confrontations between Angelo and Isabella, the magistrate rewrites the Christian story in sexual terms, effectively impeding the text's desire for traditional martyrdom. Angelo's rhetoric of seduction twists the meaning of Christ's paradigmatic passion from death to sex in his proposition to Isabella, "to redeem [Claudio], / Give up your body to such sweet uncleanness / As she that he hath stained" (II.iv.52–54). The play's balancing of death and sex, head and maidenhead, has thus infected Angelo's interpretation of the Christian story itself.[14] Whereas the female martyr substitutes death for sex in choosing execution over defloration (and in turn transforms death into marriage with Christ), Angelo substitutes sex for death, and in the process equates them in an economy of punishment that replaces penance for a crime with repetition of it. Angelo's language rewrites Christian charity as the granting of sexual favors and reduces the holy sexuality of ancient martyrdom to the boiling corruption of modern Vienna.

Although Isabella rebels against this rewriting, insisting on the difference between "lawful mercy" and "foul redemption" (II.iv.112, 113), the sexual inflection of Christian terms infiltrates her language as well, complicating the dilemma between chastity and sexuality. Thus Isabella's response to Angelo's initial proposition, "I had rather give my body than my soul" (II.iv.54), shifts ironically between the martyr's plot (dying corporeally in order to live spiritually) and the sexual sense of "giving one's body." The possibility of this confusion already exists within martyrology, and Angelo's perverse reading of Christian redemption catalyzes the martyr's precarious spiritualization of love and death into equivocating equivalences that seductively obliterate differences between the literal and the metaphoric, the physical and the spiritual. Angelo's language, rather than being the voice of a bounded character, becomes a powerful, self-perpetuating discourse that circulates among the play's readers as well as its characters.

The Hermit and the Woman

Certain critics of *Measure for Measure* seem to ratify Angelo's prurient reading of the New Testament. Darryl Gless writes with approbation that Isabella "is being asked, in a sexual sense, to 'die' in order to 'redeem' Claudio from the 'law'" (126; see 133). According to J. W. Lever, it is reasonable that Isabella, in sleeping with Angelo, might "manifest true grace by a sacrifice made in self-oblivious charity" (lxxviii). These critics recommend and represent Isabella's defloration by the same rhetorical sleight of hand that Angelo does: they transform the Christian discourse of charity, grace, and redemption into euphemisms for sexual bargaining. I object here not simply to the content of the argument but to the way in which it reproduces, through unreflective identification with Angelo's position, a rhetoric of unholy euphemism that operates within the play as a corrupt and corrupting discourse.

Isabella, unlike her humanist forerunners in Cinthio and Whetstone, refuses Angelo's offer, and is duly condemned or defended— tried anew—by later critics. Yet the hagiographic frame of Isabella's characterization reveals the inappropriateness of such judgment in effigy. Shakespeare's deliberate staging, unparalleled in the immediate sources, of Isabella as a novice works against, at a narrative and generic level, the "charity in sin" (II.iv.63) that some critics insinuate she should have performed. The inclusion within comedy of an outdated genre with set character-types and dramatic dilemmas introduces, at the level of narrative structure rather than individual psychology, a set of motives, tendencies, and values that can cross purposes with the host genre. The potential destabilization of these tendencies through reversal, deferral, doubling, or parody is in turn inherent in hagiography's reception by the novella, exemplifying the way in which a genre, far from dictating narrative routes, multiplies them. This multiplicity, rather than indicating a series of choices or meanings subject to either adjudication or to happy coexistence, dictates a structural contradiction in the text that both elicits judgment and "illicits" it. The debates over the aesthetic and ethical integrity of *Measure for Measure* and its characters play out this ambivalent condition; the critical split between defenders of Angelo and of Isabella replicates the drama's contradictory overlay of male and female paradigms of sanctity in scenes of saintly trial.

Within *Measure for Measure*, the attributes of sanctity are applied as much to Angelo as to Isabella: his is the tragedy of the false saint, sanctimonious rather than sacred, who, like Hawthorne's Reverend Dimsdale, is broken by his own rigid principles. In relation to Isabella, he figures himself as the hermit tempted by Woman, asking, "What's this? What's this? Is this her fault, or mine? / The tempter or the tempted, who sins most, ha?" Angelo represents Isabella as a dream image come to haunt the hermit in his holy solitude: "What is't I dream on? / O cunning enemy, that, to catch a saint, / With saints dost bait thy hook" (II.ii.163–65; 179–81). Lever writes in this context that "Angelo imagines himself as an anchorite tempted in a dream by Satan disguised as a virgin saint" (50n); the soliloquy momentarily demonizes the saintly Isabella and sanctifies her persecutor, who becomes the narrative focus of a hagiographic tragedy—no longer the unjust trial of the female martyr, but the desert trials of the male hermit.

The story of St. Anthony searching for St. Paul the Hermit establishes many of the formative motifs of the eremetic paradigm. In the *Golden Legend*, Jacobus de Voragine introduces the life of St. Paul the Hermit as the inauguration of the genre:

> Paul was the first hermit: to this fact Saint Jerome, who wrote his life, bears witness. To escape the persecution of Decius, he took refuge in a boundless desert, and there, unknown to men, he dwelt for sixty years in the depths of a cave. . . . And when Saint Anthony in his turn repaired to the wilderness, thinking that he was the first hermit, he learned in a dream that another anchorite, better than himself, had a claim to his homage. (88–89)

In the continuation of the story, Anthony, led by a series of mythical beasts, eventually finds Paul the Hermit, and the two men break bread provided by Heaven. When Anthony returns with a cloak requested by the older man, he finds Paul dead, fixed in the attitude of prayer. Two lions help the living hermit bury the dead one (88–90).[15]

The acknowledged source for Jacobus de Voragine's life of St. Paul the Hermit is Jerome's *Vita S. Pauli Primi Eremitae*, written around 376 C.E. The typological structure of desert precursor to ascendant messiah that silently informs the account in the *Golden Legend* derives from Jerome's programmatic scriptural allusions. Like the *Golden Legend*, Jerome's biography opens with the question of origins: "Many have often questioned exactly who was the first monk to take up his abode in the desert. Some, indeed, searching quite deep, have gone back as far as the blessed Elias and John to find the beginning of monastic life. . . . disciples of Anthony . . . affirm even today that a certain Paul of Thebes was the originator of the practice—though not of the name [*principem istius rei fuisse, non nominis*]—of solitary living" (E 225; L 18). Jerome distinguishes between the precursor who stumbles upon a new way of life and the founder who effectively baptizes or canonizes it, giving it its name. In the typologics of Christianity, the desert is fundamentally a transitional landscape—between Egypt and Canaan, between the Old Testament and the New, between John the Baptist, last prophet and first desert saint, and the God-man who follows his wilderness path (see Matt. 4:1).[16] The event of Paul's death, which dominates Jerome's *vita* of the saint, is nothing more nor less than the encounter with Anthony, who will return to his disciples to broadcast his miraculous visit. The *vita* casts Anthony's own achievement as the establishment, fulfillment, and retroactive articulation of what Paul the Hermit, in flight from persecution, had simply found himself doing. The "Antonine" career coalesces through the example of Anthony's life as it echoes and consolidates the image of his strange double encountered like a mirage in the vast blankness of the desert. Through this sequence of doublings, the radical singularity of the eremetic life becomes open to monastic imitation.[17]

In the life of St. Paul, two exemplary scenes of martyrdom frame the saint's flight to the desert. One youth, covered with honey, suffers the stings of insects, and the other, in an oneiric transcription of the first scene, suffers the stings of desire: he "was laid upon a downy bed, in a charming place filled with soft breezes, the murmuring of water, the song of birds, and the sweet odour of flowers; and he was bound down with ropes entwined with flowers, in such a wise that he could not move hand or foot. . . . The wicked emperor then sent to him a woman as vile of soul as she was fair of form, and ordered her to pollute the flesh of the young Christian"

(*GL* 88). The concise, dramatic crossing of saint and tyrant on the public stage of trial and execution gives way to the habitual, interminable, and solitary discipline of the desert, in which the "persecution" fled by the hermit is fundamentally refigured as the pricking of a desire that will not disappear.[18] The erotic tableau of the young man caught in chains of roses associates the city with sexual temptation, imagining it as a bower of bliss perfumed with the deceptive allure of the feminine.

In *Measure for Measure*, the hermit's narrative of withdrawal and temptation had already emerged in the drama's portrayal of political study as a species of contemplation that sublimates desire; according to Lucio, Angelo "doth rebate and blunt his natural edge / With profits of the mind, study and fast" (I.iv.60–61; compare II.iv.7–9). When the Duke hands over his power to Angelo, the deputy protests, "Let there be some more test made of my metal" (I.i.49); the duty he assumes is precisely a test—a trial and a temptation. In *Measure for Measure*, the city becomes a kind of desert, a place where strict men are tempted by the *diable en femme*.[19]

This masculine paradigm of the tested hermit is reinforced in the figure of the Duke: while Angelo takes Vienna as his desert, the Duke, who has "ever loved the life removed" (I.iii.10), withdraws from the city to the monastery, where he dons his clerical disguise. He tells Friar Thomas,

> No. Holy father, throw away that thought;
> Believe not that the dribbling dart of love
> Can pierce a complete bosom. Why I desire thee
> To give me secret harbour hath a purpose
> More grave and wrinkled than the aims and ends
> Of burning youth. (I.iii.3–8)

In rejecting the prodigal world of sonnet-love, the Duke both represents himself as a sage and serious ruler, and, like the "snowbroth" Angelo, erroneously places himself beyond temptation. Distinguishing himself from the clerical seducers of Boccaccio, the Duke will nonetheless find himself at the end of the drama wooing Isabella in the place of Angelo, taking over Angelo's desire.

In Angelo's painful soliloquy of temptation, he asks himself,

"Having waste ground enough, / Shall we desire to raze the sanc-
tuary / And pitch our evils there?" (II.ii.170–72); Angelo's "waste
ground" condenses the bubbling stews of prostituted Vienna with
the loathsomely haunted desert of the anchorites. In Shakespeare's
England the Catholic sanctuaries have already been razed, but the
bare ruined choirs of hagiography continue to ground manifold narrative schemes. The transposition of the hermit/woman and
tyrant/martyr tableaus onto each other sets into motion contradictory paradigms of male and female chastity; each pair reverses the
moral hierarchy of the other, so that the tyrant is also an anchorite,
and the martyr simultaneously a devil. This conflicted overlay exemplifies the complexity and indeterminacy introduced by generic
experiment, as well as by generic criticism. But this indeterminacy
should not be seen as the polysemous cohabitation of ambiguous
meanings; it is produced by the doubling of contradictory positions
within scenes of trial. This doubling necessitates choice and, since it
doubles scenes of choice, implies a split within the possibility of
choice that infects the critical act of judgment even as it enforces it.

This condensation of complementary hagiographic scenes is a
legacy of the novella tradition. In Boccaccio's story of Alibech and
Rustico (*Decameron* III.10), for example, Alibech is an Arab girl
who goes to the desert in search of a Christian education. Turned
down by one hermit afraid of her beauty, she eventually meets
young Rustico, who teaches her a new ascetic technique called
"putting the devil back in hell"—namely, his penis in her vagina.
Like Angelo, Rustico is finally tempted not by prurience but by
virginity; both men are caught by hooks baited with saints. On the
one hand, Alibech's quest for a spiritual advisor in the desert recalls
St. Anthony's search for Paul the Hermit. On the other hand, Alibech's derailment of Rustico from his ascetic exercises replays the
specter of the male hermit tempted by the *diable en femme*, a phrase
comically literalized in the activity of "putting the devil back in
hell," a game in which the devil is quite literally in woman. Boccaccio's transposition of the two scenarios, which effectively doubles
the desert *vita* back on itself, brilliantly folds the hagiographic subgenre into the new form of the comic novella.

Whereas the tale of Alibech and Rustico crosses two scenarios within the eremetic strand of hagiography, the Isabella and Rodomonte episode of *Orlando Furioso* superimposes scenes from two different hagiographic subgenres, the martyr legends and the desert *vitae*. Isabella, on her way to a convent with the corpse of her lover Zerbino, comes across the lovesick Saracen Rodomonte, who has ensconced himself in the church of a deserted French village. Isabella preserves her virginity by promising the pagan immortality with an herbal potion; offering her own neck as proof of the drug's potency, she orchestrates her decapitation at his hands. She thus places herself in the tradition of St. Barbara and the host of other headless female saints; schooled by a monk in "good examples" of "women from the Old and New Testaments" (*Orlando Furioso* 24.28), Ariosto's Isabella sacramentally returns to the arms of her dead lover, a headless saint reheaded by her heavenly husband (29:30). If the dominant paradigm in Ariosto's tale is the confrontation between the female saint and a seductive pagan tyrant, however, Rodomonte's quasi-monastic withdrawal to an abandoned church activates the plight of the hermit tempted by woman, a motif likely borrowed from the *vitae* of the desert fathers through its parody in the Alibech and Rustico novella.[20]

The episode in *Orlando Furioso*, novellalike in its brevity and detachability from the framing epic as well as from its source in the *Decameron*, comes just after a brief tale against women, to which the Isabella and Rodomonte episode is framed as a response. Through its martyrological resonances, *Orlando's* Isabella episode serves as a defense of female virtue, not unlike Christine de Pizan's use of the saints of the *Golden Legend* and the heroines of the *Decameron* for feminist purposes. At the same time, the embedding of the misogynist topos of the *diable en femme* within the martyr legend emphasizes the *querelle's* rhetorical character as a courtly game in which the two sides, ultimately interchangeable, use the resources of wit and hyperbole in order to make their points. The Isabellas of both Ariosto and Shakespeare emerge, then, from the juncture of eremetic and martyrological paradigms of sanctity, though to different purposes. Whereas Ariosto's primary interests in playing off the two genres are rhetorical, Shakespeare's are dramatic insofar as he emphasizes different kinds of dramatic conflict. The plot of *Measure for Measure*, unlike the parallel story in *Orlando Furioso*, develops the verbal and sexual confrontation of the saint with the tyrant that forms the dramatic juridical nucleus of the martyr legends.

The motif of saints-on-trial in the play also rests on the plotting of critical positions by those juridical scenes for the viewers of the play, who sit in judgment over the actions witnessed. Angelo's evocation of Isabella as the *diable en femme* predicts the critical demonization of Isabella; according to G. Wilson Knight, Isabella initially "stands for sainted purity," but then "behaves to Claudio . . . like a fiend" (74, 92), a demonization repeated in a psychologizing key by critics who accuse Isabella of "hysteria."[21] Isabella's sanctity and her "fiendishness" should be seen as derivations of alternate hagiographic plots whose subterranean interaction can affect critical narratives that appear to master the text and its characters as well as the drama's movement as a whole. Although the language of demonization is increasingly attached to the devilish Angelo within the play, that rhetoric contaminates Isabella at the level of criticism, and replicates on that level Angelo's anchorite fantasy. The tyrant-martyr scenario sets up and anticipates the scene of judgment staged by critics who insist on condemning Isabella all over again, rather than recovering the play's generic, thematic, and dramatic account of the conditions and prototypes of judgment as such. In her essay on *Measure for Measure*, Kathleen McLuskie calls for a shift in critical attention "from judging the action to analysing the process by which the action presents itself to be judged" (95). It is precisely this shift that a hagiographic analysis of *Measure for Measure* promotes. The critical trial of Isabella is itself anticipated and staged in martyrology, which centers repeatedly on scenes of judgment. By looking at the saint's life as a narrative form, we can examine the conditions of ethical choice and the narrative foundations of literary character rather than repeat a spectacle of judgment whose terms lock us into the illusion of mastery.

A Kind of Incest

The drama's narrative and philosophical debate between justice and mercy present an obvious focus for an examination of judgment within and about the play. Allegorical and thematic readings of *Measure for Measure* tend to gravitate between two poles: Isabella as the representative of mercy (M. C. Bradbrook, Roy Battenhouse, Nevill Coghill) or of law (Darryl Gless). I would argue, however, that Isabella's character represents neither law nor mercy as exclusive opposites, but rather takes shape in and as the conflicted movement between the two, a process of reversal and internalization.[22] Whereas the logic and momentum of the first interview urges her more and more univocally into the defense of mercy, the second turns her into the representative of the law against Angelo's perverse espousal of "charity in sin." This pattern of reversal enacts Isabella's argument that Christian mercy stems from identification with the guilt of the accused. Thus the theme of the law, as the theme of structure per se, does not operate as one content among others but itself describes and informs the narrative operations of the play.

Isabella begins the first interview with Angelo by describing her self-division between justice and mercy:[23]

> There is a vice that most I do abhor,
> And most desire should meet the blow of justice;
> For which I would not plead, but that I must;
> For which I must not plead, but that I am
> At war 'twixt will and will not. (II.ii.29–33)

The debate *between* Angelo and Isabella is thus repeated *within* Isabella's own position; throughout the play, mercy systematically appears as a function of justice—as its complement and as its contradiction. Thus Isabella's New Testament appeal for mercy is founded on an exchange of places. She asks Angelo to put himself in Claudio's position:

> If he had been as you, and you as he,
> You would have slipp'd like him, but he like you
> Would not have been so stern. (II.ii.64–66)

This plea for sympathetic identification with the position of the judged echoes the Sermon on the Mount, in which Christ represents himself as the new Moses fulfilling the Old Law by turning it inward. Christ says, "And why beholdest thou the mote that is in thy brother's eye, but considerest not the beam that is in thine own eye?" (Matt. 7:4).[24] The Sermon conditions judgment by interiorizing the law, both by insisting that the magistrate examine himself before judging others and by extending the jurisdiction of the law from external acts to internal desires. As Gless interprets the Sermon, "Christ internalizes what had been, or had been misinterpreted to be, an ordinance governing external acts" (46).

In this internalizing intensification of law, anger against one's brother is thus equivalent to fratricide: "Ye have heard that it was said by them of old time, Thou shalt not kill. . . . But I say unto you, That whosoever is angry with his brother without a cause shall be in danger of the judgment" (Matt. 5:21–22). Freud analyzes this inward turning of the Decalogue in his account of the child who internalizes parental law by redirecting its infantile rage against the parents onto its own ego. As in Christ's equation of anger and murder, the superego finds thoughts and deeds equally culpable; mercy and forgiveness toward others is thus a consequence of acknowledging one's own guilt, a conscience of sin as much inherited as performed, and directed against desires as well as deeds.

The exercise of mercy, then, stems from the judge's acknowledged affinity with the criminal's guilt, a connection that Isabella makes explicit in her injunction to Angelo at the end of the first interview:

> Go to your bosom,
> Knock there, and ask your heart what it doth know
> That's like my brother's fault. If it confess
> A natural guiltiness, such as is his,
> Let it not sound a thought upon your tongue
> Against my brother's life. (II.ii.137–42)

By changing places with Claudio, Isabella suggests, Angelo will discover the applicability of the law to his own guilty desires, and thus be drawn to mercy. This program of internalizing the law through change of positions is not simply a topic in *Measure for Measure*'s intellectual debate; rather, it describes the formal movement of the two interviews, in which Angelo, with unintended effect, takes the position of "natural guiltiness" offered him by Isabella and adapts her language of mercy to his erotic ends. Similarly, Isabella's initial plea, "I would to heaven I had your potency, / And you were Isabel!" (II.ii.68–69), becomes a principle of dramatic irony as she increasingly takes over the voice of the law in the second interview.

Because mercy only qualifies law by doubling it, it threatens either to decay into licentiousness or to ossify into an obsessively rigid conscience. Angelo, surprised by sin, discovers the tyranny of desire rather than the self-judgment of guilt, and Isabella must subject herself (and her brother) to the rigors of the law before she can perform an act of mercy. The dramatic irony of these deflections reveals the chronic instability, the dangerous drifting between figurative and factual registers attendant on the equivalence of deed and desire, that faults the ethical internalization of law. In *Measure for Measure*, mercy can be reached only across the shifting sands of acknowledged desire and enforced law, positions assumed by Isabella and Angelo in the movement from the first interview to the second.

Isabella's most notorious speech exemplifies the intensity of her identification with the law. When Claudio pleads with Isabella, "Sweet sister, let me live," she reacts violently:

> O, you beast!
> O faithless coward! O dishonest wretch!
> Wilt thou be made a man out of my vice?
> Is't not a kind of incest, to take life
> From thine own sister's shame? What should I think?
> Heaven shield my mother play'd my father fair:
> For such a warped slip of wilderness
> Ne'er issued from his blood. Take my defiance,
> Die, perish! Might but my bending down
> Reprieve thee from thy fate, it should proceed.
> I'll pray a thousand prayers for thy death;
> No word to save thee. (III.i.135–46)

This passage has been read as ample proof of Isabella's excessive, un-natural attachment to chastity; J. W. Lever labels Isabella's incest analogy a "hysterical conceit . . . in keeping with the speech as a whole" (75).[25] Such readings ignore, however, the way in which the speech repeats basic motifs from the play concerning the law; far from being an irrational diatribe, the passage is a hyperrational replay of *Measure for Measure*'s commentary on the law.

Isabella's shift from incest to her mother's cuckoldry of her fa-ther repeats and undoes an earlier interchange in the same scene:

> *Claudio*: If I must die
> I will encounter darkness as a bride
> And hug it in my arms.
> *Isabella*: There spake my brother: there my father's
>   grave
> Did utter forth a voice. Yes, thou must die. (III.i.82–86)

The interchange plots a pattern of identifications with and through the dead father. Claudio's embrace with darkness echoes Isabella's earlier desire to "strip myself to death as to a bed / That longing have been sick for"; at the moment when the brother's language approximates the sister's, she hears her father speak, or rather his grave.[26] In *Measure for Measure*, as in psychoanalytic theory, the law derives its massive authority from the father, and its quality of ab-straction from the father's fundamental nonpresence. In *Totem and Taboo*'s myth of primal father-killing, the band of brothers kills the tyrannous father only to legislate against further murder and against incest, the original goal of their usurpation; the dead father speaks his law through them. Isabella ends her avowal of kinship with a death sentence ventriloquizing the father's grave: "Yes, thou must die." So too, in the "kind of incest" speech, she traces her moral righteousness to her dead father, and repeats the death sentence against Claudio ("Take my defiance, / Die, perish!"). Isabella be-comes, in the reiterated term of the play, the "substitute" of her dead father, and the spokeswoman of the law (see V.i.136).

Angelo too stands in for an absent lawgiver, since the Duke has "elected him our absence to supply" (I.i.18). The law that Angelo enforces is associated not so much with a dead father as with an impotent one; although severe in its letter ("strict statutes and most biting laws" I.iii.19), the law has grown weak in practice. The Duke chooses a domestic analogy:

> Now, as fond fathers,
> Having bound up the threatening twigs of birch,
> Only to stick it in their children's sight
> For terror, not to use, in time the rod
> Becomes more mocked than feared: so our decrees,
> Dead to infliction, to themselves are dead (I.iii.23–28)

The father's "rod" is the object of mockery, of symbolic castration, leaving the law itself dead or asleep ("The law hath not been dead, though it hath slept" II.ii.91). If law is founded on the death or absence of the father, who then speaks through the inheriting magistrates from the grave, it is also constitutionally subject to an impotence or castration, insofar as its founder and referent is never present, a state that permits his rod to "become more mocked than feared." The dead father is at once castrated and castrating; Lucio represents Angelo as an "ungenitured agent" who will "unpeople the province with continency" (III.ii.167–68).[27] From the very first scene, *Measure for Measure* dramatizes the consequences (licentiousness from below, tyranny from above) of the father's crippling absence from the law, an absence that precedes the Duke's departure from Vienna (" 'twas my fault to give the people scope" I.iii.35).

In Isabella's "a kind of incest" speech, her father remains the moral force behind her convictions. The imputation of his cuckoldry, however ("Heaven shield my mother played my father fair") emasculates him. Here as elsewhere in the play, the death of the father in and behind the law has two contradictory meanings: his absence enables the articulation and severity of the law (as in the psychoanalytic aphorism that fathers are most powerful when dead).[28] At the same time, the father's absence, founded on his ritual humiliation, leaves the law open to incapacitation and abuse. Thus the superego, far from being an abstract regulator of moral conscience, can enforce the most obscene and sadistic of fantasies. More than a personal aberration, then, Isabella's cuckolding reference to her dead father reiterates the account of law as expressed elsewhere in the play.

In its Christian figuration as the Old Dispensation, the law appears as typologically overshadowed, a law of the past. The Old Law continues to live in the New, in intensified because internalized form; at the same time, it is constitutionally disqualified by the epochal event that negates and subsumes it. The law in Christian discourse, too, is both castrating (the severe law of fear, judgment, and circumcision) and castrated (outdated by the new law of love, mercy, and circumcision "of the heart" [Rom. 2:29]). In the psychoanalytic account of the Judeo-Christian tradition, Jesus's death at once articulates, redeems, and repeats a primal crime against God the father. The Christian story exemplifies the power of the dead father in the law, since through death Christ becomes all-powerful (law as Christian law), and the castrating abrogration of the law that transforms it into a dead letter (law as Mosaic law).

The New Law's over- and inward-turning of the Old is a historiographical rhythm inherited from the Jewish tradition of the Prophets and then imposed onto it in an act of Christian self-differentiation; it is a rhythm, moreover, repeated throughout Christian history, both within the Catholic church and in the Reformation of it.[29] The "old" or "external" law is always an ideal moment recreated in relation to a movement of reform that defines itself against that which it repeats. Thus Isabella in clerical garb can represent (in the legal sense) simultaneously the New Dispensation in relation to Judaism, and the Old Law in relation to Protestantism, a double reading unfolded in the two interviews, which shuttle her from the discourse of mercy to the discourse of justice, and, finally, to a realization of charity that continues to manifest its unstable origin in the abrogated rigor of the law.

Isabella's "kind of incest" speech moves from the cuckolding of her father to the damning of her brother: "Take my defiance, / Die, perish!" Once again, the speech reiterates and undoes her earlier claim to kinship with her brother; the line echoes her prior death sentence, "Yes, thou must die," but now in a gesture not of affinity or "affiance" but of disinheritance or "de-fiance." For "de-fiance" here means not resistance to her brother's authority but rather a renunciation of family ties; the speech renders explicit the muted allusion to the de-fiance of the martyrs already intimated in Lucio's enunciation of the Annunciation. Like the young women of the *Golden Legend*, Isabella renounces her ties to her brother in order to preserve her new allegiance to the Church. It is in this tradition of radical de-affiliation that Isabella declares, in a statement that has condemned her in the eyes of many readers, "More than our brother is our chastity" (II.iv.184).

Isabella's symbolic act of fratricide, moreover, like her memorial cuckolding of her father, links her to Angelo and the procedures of the law: Angelo tells her in the first interview, "It is the law, not I, condemn your brother; / Were he my kinsman, brother, or my son, / It should be thus with him" (II.ii.80–82).[30] Here Shakespeare deploys a common topos of justice in which the magistrate's ability to execute his own brother guarantees the objectivity of the law, in order to show that every act of execution is by extension a kind of fratricide. Throughout the play, Claudio takes on the role of an archetypal brother akin to both "high" and "low" characters; in the words of the Duke, "He is my brother too" (V.i.491). His pending execution looms as an act of communal fratricide involving the entire city. In *Measure for Measure*, brothers act as weak fathers: Mariana's dead brother Frederick leaves her without dowry; the orphaned Isabella's brother is imprisoned; the Duke, addressed as "good father friar" (III.ii.11), seems dangerously unable to govern the city. Fratricide rewrites patricide as the mythic founding crime, inflecting the impotence of the dead father over his posthumous power and moving from vertical relations of hierarchy to lateral relations of equality differentiated by violence. In the psychoanalysis of religious typology, the death of Christ repeats and redeems the crime against the father by restaging the founding murder at the level of son and brother rather than parent.[31] The Christian movement from patricide to what Juliet Flower MacCannell has called "the Regime of the Brother" coincides with the transition from law to mercy, whether the individual doubling over of external law as internal guilt, or the epochal re-form of the Old Dispensation into the New through self-differentiating rehearsal.

Isabella's rejection of incest, her alignment of law with her dead and cuckolded father, and her ritual fratricide all repeat basic mechanisms of the law articulated elsewhere in the drama.[32] Her positioning as spokeswoman of the law occurs through the pattern of reversal and identification that aligns her with Angelo as the Duke's substitute. J. W. Lever notes Angelo's adoption of Isabella's ethical language in the second interview, but he argues that Isabella's "stance is occasioned by no true principle" (lxxvii–viii). I would insist to the contrary that Isabella has come to represent principle as such, since she has entered the position of the law abandoned by Angelo. Her violent rejection of Claudio's plea for life is not an eccentric, irrational reaction, but the consummation of her identification with the law in its dead and killing letter. It is a law typologically both fulfilled and undercut by the advent of mercy, a law associated in her own speech with a dead and cuckolded father mortified by the weaknesses of his heirs.

'Measure for Measure' and Secular Literature

So far I have discussed the interviews between Angelo and Isabella according to two different though related registers: the genre of the saint's life, and the typological relation between law and mercy. The final act of the play is the proper site for the graphing of these two topics onto each other, for it is in this extended trial scene that the ends of hagiography most clearly oppose those of secular comedy and that Isabella becomes, through her detour into the law, the spokeswoman of a kind of mercy. In the final scene of *Measure for Measure*, Isabella's kneeling for Angelo and the Duke's marriage proposal are "decisive" moments—cruxes in which the play determines itself in favor of particular generic and epochal solutions. By adjudicating in favor of both marriage and mercy—the progressive halves of the two oppositions in which these terms appear—the play also decides in favor of literary secularization, at the expense of the Catholic forms it borrows. In a tactic by now familiar, *Measure for*

Measure uses the dialectic of the Old and New Dispensations in order to stage the founding of secular literature on the supersedure of Christian forms. In the play the figure of Barnardine focuses the remainder of that dialectic, insofar as he presents the material obstacle, at once resistant and residual, that stalls the symbolic exchanges structuring both the plot of *Measure for Measure* and its staging of Christian secularization.

Throughout the play, the Catholic feminine rhetoric of supplication is associated with the body language of kneeling, from Isabella's "prone and speechless dialect" (I.ii.173) to Mariana's oath in Act V, "As this is true / Let me in safety raise me from my knees, / Or else for ever be confixed here, / A marble monument" (V.1.229–32). Finally, Mariana begs Isabella, "do yet but kneel by me; / Hold up your hands, say nothing: I'll speak all" (V.1.435–36). This request splits language and gesture and word and deed in emblematic fashion, fixing Isabella as a paradigmatic hagiographic icon, a "marble monument" of a saint kneeling in intercession and, more distantly, in martyrdom.[33] Isabella responds by both kneeling and speaking, becoming picture and gloss in a tableau vivant of sanctity.

This tense trial of Isabella's charity is emotionally and intellectually charged by the play's earlier exchange of law and mercy. Whereas the second interview with Angelo had transferred Isabella to the place of the law, her final intercession returns her to the role of mercy, the entire circle enacting the dialectical internalization of law. Yet her arguments for clemency at both beginning and end undo Christ's elevation of evil intent to the culpability of an executed deed, the equation that had led from judicial righteousness to "natural guiltiness," and from there to the exercise of mercy. Contrary to the Sermon on the Mount, Isabella defends Angelo by separating deed and intent:

> His act did not o'ertake his bad intent,
> And must be buried but as an intent
> That perished by the way. (V.i.459–61)[34]

The contradiction here between legalistic content and merciful intention, which repeats Mariana's emblematic division of word and gesture, is one point in the play's ongoing crossing and uncrossing of the discourses of justice and mercy. Although it is an undeniably stabilizing, climactic moment in which the play "settles" in favor of mercy, this adjudication nonetheless occurs at a point when mercy appears in a split relation, disjunct rather than complementary, with the law. Isabella's plea is "ironic" in the broadest dramatic sense: while she *speaks* the old law, she *means* Christian mercy.

In this ironic structure of split signification, the bar between legalistic signifier and merciful signified is the line produced when external law is doubled over into internal guilt, the bar that both differentiates law and mercy, Old Dispensation and New, and attests to their precarious affinity, their incestuous etiology. In this sense, Isabella becomes an "allegory" of mercy: not a static, abstract exemplum, but rather a figure of disjunct signification that displays mercy *as* allegory in relation to the law from which it epochally separates itself.[35] The split between her legal language and her merciful intent is underwritten by the narrative reversals that have shifted her from a shallowly voiced mercy to a "hysterically" asserted law to a mercy bifurcated by the law that has helped produce it.

Isabella's argument takes on further dramatic irony: her very failure to argue for mercy in terms of "natural guiltiness," which would mean imputing Angelo's desires to the Duke, anticipates by default the Duke's adoption of Angelo's suit in the same scene. The Duke's proposal to Isabella repeats the genetic and generic coupling of law and mercy by crossing from hagiography to secular comedy. Both the Duke and Angelo, placing themselves outside of love, are caught within it; in this, the two men are not simply "foils" following parallel paths, but, in the language of the play, "substitutes" for one another who, in exchanging places, also transfer their desires. The Duke's sudden proposal double-crosses the ends of male and female renunciation set off by the drama's gendered paradigms of hermit and martyr; moreover, it does so by counterfeiting Angelo's desire. Like Isabella's plea for mercy conducted in the language of law, the Duke's proposal is a climactic and defining moment that determines the play in favor of secular comedy while exposing the arbitrariness implicit in arbitration. The continuing force of hagiography is mutely evident in Isabella's enigmatic silence, which assures the play's readers that the case is not closed. By casting Isabella as a saintly nun, *Measure for Measure* creates a palpable tension between marriage and renunciation, in which Isabella's chastity functions as a *narrative* virtue as well as a moral one, in the classical sense of an active power or operative influence. Moreover, much of hagiography's power in the play derives from its repressed status, which grants its return a disruptive, unsettling force in contrast with the more institutional claims of comic closure. Hagiography survives in the very act of the play's decision against it. In *Measure for Measure*, secular comedy, rather than unrepressing desire, represses repression as a defining feature of sanctity, and, in negating that feature, forever preserves it.

Marriage in *Measure for Measure* has the power to deflect the telos of renunciation. It does so by appropriating—by making its own, but also by making *proper*—Vienna's forces of seduction. While the play ends with weddings designed to contain and resolve the drama's manifold tensions, marriage continues to manifest its affinities with both renunciation and prostitution. The Duke's final act of clemency—his injunction that Lucio marry the woman he has both pimped for and impregnated—implicates wedlock in the competing tyrannies of prostitution and martyrdom. As Lucio protests, "Marrying a punk, my lord, is pressing to death, / Whipping, and hanging" (V.i.520–21). If hagiographic chastity is the law of the play, comedic marriage is its mercy: both its double and its other, its internalization and its abrogation.

The overlay and interplay of theme and position, intellectual content and narrative progression, exemplify the play's thematization of structure and structuration by theme. The ethics of the Sermon on the Mount describe not only the play's philosophical "position" on the status of mercy, but the play's *positioning* of characters in changing relations of justice and mercy, moral authority and illicit desire. The figure of Isabella does not "represent" law or mercy as fixed allegorical contents but rather is represented by them insofar as the principle of guilty identification helps constitute the action as well as the argument of the play. Moreover, these procedures, founded on biblical typology, describe the play's constitution of itself as secular literature through the renovation of hagiographic conventions, which speak from beyond the grave of their Protestant anullment. Spiritualized into the pure structure of a renovated Christian law stripped of mere (Judaic and Catholic) legalisms, the forms of hagiography take on new life in the Christian-secular alchemy of Shakespeare's tragicomedy.

Is there a remainder to this dialectic? The striking affinities between Shakespeare's Vienna and his Venice, each governed by the typological internalization of law into mercy, isolate once more the figure of the unconverted Jew as one limit point of Christian secularization. In *Measure for Measure*, the place of failed conversion is held by Barnardine, the one head in the whole system of the play that will not and cannot be exchanged, the head whose obdurate, thinglike intransigence resists the redemptive substitutions required of it by the narrative and moral exigencies of the plot.

In this, *Barnardine* is the distant cousin of *Barabbas*, the criminal in the Gospels whom the Jews refuse to switch for Christ in the assembly before Pilate:

> Now at the feast the governor was accustomed to release for the crowd any one prisoner whom they wanted. And they had then a notorious prisoner, called Barabbas. So when they had gathered, Pilate said onto them, "Whom do you want me to release for you, Barabbas or Jesus who is called Christ?" . . . Now the chief priests and the elders persuaded the people to ask for Barabbas and destroy Jesus. . . . Then he released for them Barabbas, and having scourged Jesus, delivered him to be crucified. (Matt. 27:15–26)

In the Gospels, Barabbas, released from his death sentence by Pilate at the request of the Jews, is the true criminal who does not die in the place of the innocent Christ. In *Measure for Measure*, Barnardine is the unregenerate prisoner who refuses to be executed in the stead of the less blemished Claudio. In the face of all demands to go to his death willingly, Barnardine, anticipating Melville's Bartleby, simply "prefers not to."[36] The names "Barabas" and "Barnardine" were already associated with each other in Marlowe's

The Jew of Malta, a primal text in Shakespeare's typological consciousness. Whereas "Barabas" names the Jew of Marlowe's play, "Barnardine" is a corrupt friar whom the converted Abigail, daughter of Barabas, calls her "ghostly father" (III.vi.13); the contiguity of the names in the world of Marlowe's play allows Shakespeare to Judaize the unrepentant criminal languishing in his Viennese prison. Like the biblical Barabbas, Shakespeare's Barnardine has the sole narrative purpose of not-taking-the-place-of another—a more innocent—man, and is thus a figure of resistance to the play's substitutional logic of redemption, in which Mariana stands in for Isabella in the bed trick's exchange of maidenheads, Isabella takes the place of Angelo in the dialectic of law and mercy, and marriage supplants virginity in the play's adjudication of genres.

In *Measure for Measure*, the relentless circulation of severed heads and their punning equivalences—heads of coins, heads of state, maidenheads, and so on—converts the parochial coinage of martyrological beheading into the common currency of sex and politics. The exchange of heads and maidenheads in particular emblematizes the play's climactic substitution of the martyred saints of hagiography for the married heroines of romantic comedy, a generic transaction that installs Shakespeare's play as the afterlife of the Catholic saints. This use of decapitation as a principle of secularization is itself borrowed from the dominant logic of beheading in the legends of the martyrs, in which the incisive stroke of decollation serves to canonize the dead saint in the calendar of the Church. In such scenes, decapitation—like castration in psychoanalytic theory—represents the gesture of symbolization *par excellence*, combining as it does both the absolute alienation of the individual through the loss of the singular head, and the reward of a place in the order of history and memory through this sacrifice. The play uses the hagiographic motif of decapitation in order to decapitate hagiography itself, transferring canonization from the order of the saints to the order of literature.

Recall, however, that the legends of the martyrs sometimes aggravate the symbolic cut of decapitation into a real wound by separating the severed head out from the intercalating procedure of decollation. These miraculous remnants of decapitation extend the trials of martyrdom beyond the closure so decisively marked, stilling and distilling the sublationary movement of the Christian mythos around the material accretion of its own narrative structure. So too, in *Measure for Measure*, the nonsubstitutable head of Barnardine, uncut and unshaven (like a Nazirite dedicated to the Temple), refuses to submit to the alienating stroke of execution, putting a temporary stop to the play's progressive march of sexual, typological, and generic settlements.

The lumpenproletarian Barnardine thus represents the dregs of secularization in the economy of *Measure for Measure*, insofar as he encapsulates or brings to a head several epochal remainders. Through the scriptural ties between Barabbas and Barnardine, as well as the strange passageways linking Shakespeare's Vienna to his Venice, the unregenerate Barnardine distantly activates the type of the unconverted Jew whom we have repeatedly encountered at the far reaches of biblical typology. In addition, the hagiographic provenance of the decapitational motif isolates Barnardine's head as a nonexhangeable coin within the play's generic economy. The head of Barnardine emblematizes the relics of hagiography in Shakespearean drama, taken now not as a progressively *Christian* model and object of secular conversion, but as a residually *Catholic* discourse not fully subject to its Reformation into secular literature. As Isabella says to the Lucio who hails her, "Make me not your story" (I.iv.29). This is the answer of Barnardine as well.

PART III

Iconographies of Secular Literature

CHAPTER 6

Typological Designs

CREATION, ICONOCLASM, AND NATURE IN

VASARI'S 'LIVES OF THE ARTISTS'

Giorgio Vasari's *Lives of the Artists*, first published in 1550 and then revised and expanded in 1568, borrows motifs, narrative turns, and historiographical rhythms from Christian discourse in order to institute a theoretical and historical mythos for what Jacob Burckhardt has christened, in a phrase designed to celebrate the triumph of secular aesthetics, "the culture of the Renaissance in Italy."[1] The scheme of the *Lives*, most clearly evident in the 1550 edition, which culminates in the life of Michelangelo, begins by rewriting the doctrine of creation *ex nihilo* as the inauguration of the opposition between *disegno* and *colore* that regulates the course of Italian art. The dynamic of that progression, moreover, is fashioned on the typological relation between the Old and New Testaments. Vasari's appropriation of Christian paradigms, far from marking a lingering medievalism that constrains his generally humanist project, is in fact fundamental to the invention of the secular art historiography from within which current historians both receive and critique the contributions of the *Lives* to their discipline. The alliance between medieval hagiography and classical biography in the *Lives* is not a naively unhistorical failing readily corrected by more critical methods, but rather a new covenant between narrative genres that forever weds Vasari's art history to the medieval forms it subsumes.

Just as Boccaccio's exemplary hagiographic maneuvers constitute secular literature on the model of the Christian sublation of Judaism, Vasari's *Lives of the Artists* establishes the narrative of a classical rebirth by using the historical and hermeneutic apparatus of biblical typology. In the series of equations already at work in Augustine's typological defense of Christian humanism, Greco-Roman antiquity is to the Renaissance as the Old Testament is to Christianity, and the negated middle named by the "Middle Ages" takes as its exegetical analogue the survival of Judaism into the common era. Vasari's typological identification of antiquity with the Old Testament, however, comes up against a problem of particular concern to the theorist of art—namely, the stance of iconoclasm, which functions as the necessary negative moment in the dialectic of cultural conversion and as a posture of active resistance to the classical ideal of the plastic symbol resurrected by typology. As such, iconoclasm is both interior to and in excess of the Christian-secular dynamic. Whereas typology equates Judaism and antiquity as twinned foundations of Christian modernity, the trauma of iconoclasm sunders monotheism from polytheism as an irreconcilable worldview with an absolutely distinct representational mandate, a breach overcome in incarnational aesthetics but reasserted by both Jewish and radical Protestant repetitions of iconoclasm.

In the *Lives'* devolving hierarchy of historiographical patterns, the text's central narrative of classical rebirth comes up against the obstacles posed by the remainders of its own logic—the figure of the modern Jew as a metaphor for the persistence of medievalism, for example. It also faces the imperatives of the competing theologico-historical scheme that it takes as its originating myth—the iconoclasm/idolatry dialectic that periodically if impossibly insists on the unrecuperated negation of mimesis. Vasari's aesthetic history proceeds by folding the trauma of the Jewish creation story into the typological progress of Western mimesis, which absorbs but never fully neutralizes the iconoclastic thrust of Judaism. Vasari's account of artistic innovation—the event that keeps the historical narrative going forward—is the key locus for this logic, where *natura* functions as the normative object of mimesis and as a recurrent disruption of mimetic conventions.

First Things

Giorgio Vasari's Preface to the *Lives of the Artists* begins with the question of beginnings:

> I am fully aware that all who have written on the subject firmly and unanimously assert that the arts of sculpture and painting were first derived from nature by the people of Egypt. I also realize that there are some who attribute the first rough pieces in marble and the first reliefs to the Chaldeans, just as they give the Greeks credit for discovering the brush and the use of colors. Design, however, is the foundation of both these arts, or rather the animating principle that conceives and nourishes all creative processes: and surely design existed in absolute perfection before the Creation when Almighty God, having made the vast expanse of the universe [*il gran corpo del mondo*] and adorned the heavens with his shining lights, directed His creative intellect further, to the clear air and the solid earth. And then, in the act of creating humans, He fashioned the first forms of sculpture and painting in the sublime grace of created things [*con la vaga invenzione delle cose*]. (Bull I: 25; Ragghianti I: 227; trans. mod.)[2]

As we have seen in earlier chapters, the topos of creation *ex nihilo* recurs throughout the literary afterlives of the saints, marking the divide between hagiography and secular literature: as the epochal negation of the first discourse by the second, and as the retroactive isolation of a dormant negativity that will have already faulted the prior genre. It is no accident, then, that Vasari's *Lives*, a text that decisively supplants the lives of the saints with the lives of the artists, begins by retelling the biblical myth of creation.

The first lines of the Bible establish the creative capacity of the single God through the work of the word, the story of creation that distinguishes Jewish monotheism from both classical physics of eternal matter and from pagan theogonies of multiple gods:

> In the beginning God created the heaven [*shamayim*] and the earth. Now the earth was unformed and void, and darkness was upon the face of the deep [*tehom*]; and the spirit of God hovered over the face of the waters [*mayim*]. And God said: "Let there be light." And there was light. (Gen. 1:1–3)

The image of God hovering over the face of the waters figures the moment before creation as a scene of primal lovemaking, like that between Uranus and Rhea in Greek mythology, or Apsu and Ti'amat (echoed in the Hebrew *tehom*, "deep") in the Babylonian theogony.[3] Yet such polytheistic tableaus only remain in the biblical text in the form of metaphor, as watery memories that inhere in the anthropomorphism of the word "face." In the Hebrew text, the *mayim* (waters) of verse 1:2 echoes the *shamayim* (heavens) of verse 1:1; the use of linguistic repetition and variation here anticipates and syntactically enacts God's signification of the radical negativity of the void into the positivity of the divinely crafted world. The parallelism of the Hebrew verse iteratively builds from "darkness . . . upon the face of the deep" to "the spirit of God . . . over the face of the waters." This doubling of the "face of the deep" into the "face of the waters" folds and flattens the anthropomorphic face of a forgotten mother goddess into the reflective sur-face of the waters. The transformative repetition of the word "face" drains off and dams up the polytheistic fertility of the ancient cults, teeming like Shakespeare's Nile with an infinite variety, into the reflective abstraction of the *logos*, whose creative metaphorizations at once recall and repress pagan myths of a sexually generated world. The single stroke of the divine Word cancels the scene of pagan copulation, forever marking it as lacking; in the process, the *Abgrund* or abyss of the unformed and voided deep becomes the *Grund* or ground for the designs of the Creator.[4]

Insofar as the *nihil* of creation *ex nihilo* names not only the void that preceded the making of the world but also the active annihilation of pagan mimesis, then the act of *creation* is also paradoxically an act of *iconoclasm*. Calum Carmichael has argued that the entire first tablet of the Decalogue (which includes the prohibition against polytheism) was composed by the Priestly author as a legal rewriting of the narrative scene of the Golden Calf, and he suggests that the same writer's creation story was composed specifically as a refutation of idolatry (*Origins of Biblical Law* 46). The wording of the Second Commandment, "Thou shalt have no other gods *before Me*," literally reads, "Thou shalt have no other gods *before my face* ['al *panay*]," the same word used in the Genesis expressions "face of the deep" and "face of the waters." To appropriate Lévinas, the singular face of the God of Creation and Revelation, unlike the multiple faces of the pagan gods, delivers itself as speech rather than icon: "If the transcendent cuts across sensibility . . . it cuts across the vision of forms . . . It is the face; its revelation is speech" (*Totality and Infinity* 193). The cut of the creative word that divides the light and the dark, introducing what Lacan calls in his gloss of creation *ex nihilo* "oppositional structures whose emergence profoundly modifies the human world" (*Seminar VII* 119), makes visibility possible while calling its rule into question.

In Vasari's text, the governing function of the rewriting of Genesis is to establish the authority of art on the model of God's creative Word, a move that depends on the equation of *disegno* with the *logos*. In the *alpha* and *omega* of the *Lives*, the origin of sculpture and painting and of *disegno* and *colore* in God's creative acts will have met its finest representation and confirmation in the virtuosity of Michelangelo, whose life crowns the first edition of the *Lives* and whose Sistine frescoes suffuse Vasari's recollection of Creation here.[5] *Disegno*—design, drawing, draftsmanship—encompasses both the use of lines by the artist and the conception, plan, or idea of something. By extension, *disegno* designates the consummate value of compositional and narrative unity that Vasari attributes both to works of art and to the text of history. Insofar as the *disegno* of the artist-historian functions as the secular repetition of Creation, his products displace and extend the authority of God's work through the act of emulation.

At the same time, however, Vasari's inaugural analogy of *disegno* with creation *ex nihilo* mobilizes the role of "nothing" in acts of making—that is, it makes plain the function of a lack at once discovered and introduced into a prior order of signification. In the *Ethics of Psychoanalysis*, Lacan identifies himself as a "creationist" rather than an "evolutionist"—not in the narrow sense of preferring biblical to scientific explanation but rather in the sense of eschewing developmental schemes in favor of structural paradigms, and of attributing to key signifiers an originary, even catastrophic power to constellate new worlds around their cut. Vasari's allusion to the Genesis myth identifies him as a "creationist" in both these senses. Vasari's recreation of creation pushes aside the question of art's historical origin—was it in Greece, Egypt, or Chaldea that painting and sculpture first began?—in favor of God's design of the world and humanity as the true beginning of art. The strategy here is not so much to find the earliest possible historical moment along an incremental continuum of dates, but rather to substitute a logical, theoretical account of artistic genesis for a chronological, historical one. It is a "creationist" theory insofar as it eschews an evolutionary or historicist model for one that emphasizes both *structure* (the logical priority of design in any artistic act, even when that design is only retroactively visible) and *trauma* (the cut introduced by the divine *logos* in the preexisting order of things). The latter is visible in the sequence of classical oppositions that God's design installs: God's fashioning of the *gran corpo* of the world followed by His ornamentation of the heavens with light is repeated and drawn out in the hierarchical pairing of "sculpture and painting" born with the creation of man and, implicitly, of woman, whose sexual difference becomes a model of the *disegno-colore* opposition that governs Italian art theory.[6] The binaries that found the aesthetics of the high Italian tradition bring into signification the pure difference of the creative/iconoclastic stroke, just as the six days of creation build an entire world out of the division between light and dark introduced by and as the first day.

Moreover, the shift from a historical to a theological framework allows Vasari to bypass the idolatrous origins of art with which the historical record necessarily confronts him. Thus Vasari's subsequent list of early artists includes "Belos, son of the proud Nimrod," "Semiramis, queen of Babylon," and Laban, his idols stolen by his daughter Rachel (Bull I: 26). By finding and founding art in the image of God's creation, Vasari cuts through and conceptually unifies the bewildering multiplicity and idolatrous promiscuity of historical beginnings within the unifying symbolic framework of *disegno*. Vasari's grafting of *disegno* onto the *logos* approximates the world-creating power of the divine word to the compositional func-

tion of the line in order to identify genuine creativity *not* with idolatry (where one might expect it) but rather with a kind of iconoclasm, a *nihil*-ization of polytheistic representation. For Vasari, following the author of Genesis 1, the great artist is like God insofar as
he creates a uni-verse that turns around the singularity and signature
of his line. The single cut of the line blossoms immediately into the
composition of a coherent likeness, supported by the verisimilar addition of color; the iconoclastic force of the *logos* as sheer difference
disappears into the order of a new mimesis, the freshly intricated
network of signifiers that organize the high Italian tradition. In the
Lives of the Artists, *disegno*, the annihilating mark that allows for the
advent of a new epoch of symbolization, functions as a key word
or master signifier that pierces together theological, historiographical, and artistic discourses, a punctual joining of genres that in turn
composes the network of correspondences, valuations, and kinds of
facts that relate the lives both to each other and to their hagiographic prototypes.

Typology and Hagiography in Vasari's 'Rinascita'

Vasari's prefatory reworking of Genesis programmatically installs the ideals and ideology, the methods and materials, of his art-
historical project, which uses Judeo-Christian paradigms to narrate,
explain, and evaluate the central thrust and dynamic of Italian art.
Whereas creation *ex nihilo* offers Vasari a structural rather than historical model for the genesis of art, biblical typology establishes the
temporal rhythm of Western (Greco-Roman-Italian) art history
charted by the *Lives*. In Vasari's narrative, the inaugural cut of *disegno*
ex nihilo disappears into the Christological unfolding of the *logos* in
time, which, already intimated in Vasari's initial projection of Michelangelo's Sistine ceiling onto the vaulted heavens of Creation,
determines the symbolic relationship between key artists in the *Lives'*
design of history.

In the theoretical prefaces to the different sections of the *Lives*,
Vasari combines cyclical and linear paradigms of history by comparing the arts to the progress of a human life:

For from the smallest beginnings art attained the greatest heights, only
to decline from its noble position to the most degraded status. Seeing
this, artists can also realize the nature of the arts we have been dis-
cussing: these, like the other arts and like human beings themselves,
are born, grow up, become old, and die. And they will be able to
understand more readily the process by which art has been reborn [*il
progresso della sua rinascita*] and reached perfection in our own times.
(Bull I: 46–47; Bellosi and Rossi 101)

The human life, the basic unit of Vasari's collection of biographies,
also provides a model of historical development and decline; just as
a human being goes from infancy to adulthood to old age, so too,
Vasari suggests, the arts advance, mature, then fall off. Thus the three
parts of the *Lives*, beginning with Cimabue and ending with Michelangelo, narrate the childhood, adolescence, and maturity of Italian art—with old age implicated in the retrospective vantage point
of Vasari's composition. Moreover, the model of the individual life
always implies for Vasari the dynamic relationship between generations, whose bonds of filiation help give his historiography its dialectical character. The decline of one period promises the birth of
another; further, the positive appearance of incremental growth
within the progress of a single epoch only occurs through the negative maneuvers of emulative displacement.[7] Thus Vasari aims to
"deal with artists according to schools and styles rather than chronologically" (Bull I: 47), for the proper object of his history is not a
series of discrete lives taken as independent and detachable entries
but rather those significant relationships of artistic instruction, competition, and conversation that constitute a period and a tradition.
Thus one tends to remember Vasari's *Lives* in significant clusters of
relationship: the model apprenticeship of Cimabue and Giotto; the
confraternity of artists formed by Masaccio, Brunelleschi, and Do-
natello; or that transcendent triumvirate of the high Renaissance,
Leonardo, Raphael, and Michelangelo.

And the critic could easily find all of this in Vasari's classical
models, from Plutarch's *Parallel Lives*, with its canny intuitions into
the significant correlations between brilliant careers, to the cyclical
historiography of Polybius appropriated so effectively by Vasari's

compatriate Machiavelli, to the Aristotelian valuation of plot rediscovered by the Italian critics of the sixteenth century. Vasari, however, reinforces the humanist scaffolding of his text through a series of biblical allusions that charge his narrative of classical rebirth with the specific gravity of Christian providence. His adaptation of scriptural and hagiographic patterning takes religious motifs as logics rather than contents, as powerful formulas ready to be animated by the heroic characters of his artistic epic. Indeed, we could say that this paradigmatic use of religious discourse to narrate classical rebirth—a *mythological* use in the strongest Aristotelian sense of a governing plot or story—characterizes the secularism of Vasari's foundational project. Or, in the language of Renaissance Italian art theory, the plots of Christianity "design" or "compose" the *istoria*, the dramatic narrative, of Vasari's text. Whereas the story that Vasari relates is not religious in subject matter, the generic models that inform it are, giving the *Lives* both their hermeneutic flexiblity and their philosophical cohesion.

Part I begins with the life of Cimabue, the last of the medievalists and the first of the Renaissance men:

> The flood of misfortunes [*l'infinito diluvio de' mali*] which continuously swept over and submerged the unhappy country of Italy not only destroyed everything worthy to be called a building but also, and this was of far greater consequence, completely wiped out the artists who lived there. Eventually, however, by God's providence, Giovanni Cimabue, who was destined to take the first steps in restoring the art of painting to its earlier stature, was born in the city of Florence, in the year 1240. (Bull I: 49; Ragghianti I: 265)

Like the *Heptameron* of Marguerite de Navarre, Vasari's life of Cimabue begins with an epochal allusion to the Flood, God's effective de-creation of His six days' work in order to start humanity over again.[8] In the historical allegory imagined by Vasari's allusion, the first flowering of the arts achieved by the generations closest to Paradise fell with Rome and the onset of the medieval period. The career of Cimabue, schooled in the Byzantine (or, in Vasari's vocabulary, "Greek") manner yet working toward the rebirth of an tiquity, is thus comparable to that of Noah, survivor of the Flood; Abraham, first of the patriarchs to enter into a special covenant with God; or Moses, who only saw the Promised Land from a distance. These proto-historical forefathers of the Israelites bespeak both a sublime archaism and the promise of a new beginning, and thus provide compelling analogues to the epochal function of Cimabue at the threshold of the *Lives*.

The life of Giotto, falling a few chapters after the *vita* of Cimabue, is clearly linked to that of the earlier master through the scenes of vocation and discipleship that cross their careers. Giotto is a young shepherd who, "drawn instinctively to the arts of design [*l'arte del disegno*], was always sketching [*disegnava*] what he saw in nature, or imagined in his own mind, on stones or on the ground or the sand." Cimabue stumbles onto this pastoral scene of natural art on his way between two cities: "One day Cimabue was on his way from Florence to Vespignano, where he had some business to attend to, when he came across Giotto who, while the sheep were grazing near by, was drawing one of them by scratching with a slightly pointed stone on a smooth clean piece of rock" (57). Giotto becomes, in a word used frequently by Vasari to describe the relationship between teacher and student, the *discepolo* of Cimabue; whereas the disciples of Christ were called from being fishers of fish to fishers of men, Giotto is called from being a draftsman of sheep— an intuitive pastoral artist—to a painter of men—the first great depicter of significant human interaction in Vasari's history of Italian art.

In the apprenticeship that follows this scene of vocation, the student rapidly eclipses the master: "In a very short space of time Giotto not only captured his master's own style but also began to draw so ably from life that he made a decisive break with the crude traditional Byzantine style and brought to life [*risuscitò*] the great art of painting as we know it today" (Bull I: 57–58; Ragghianti I: 358). The initial scene of vocation leads to the effective displacement of the teacher by the student: thus Vasari is able to claim later in the biography that "it was indeed miraculous [*fu in que' tempi un miracolo*] that in those days Giotto could paint with such sublime grace, especially when we consider that he learned his art, so as to speak, without any instructor [*senza maestro*]" (Bull I: 73; Ragghianti I: 382). Here, Cimabue has vanished from the scene of art's rebirth, a "miraculous" erasure that recasts the older artist as teacher and precursor rather than as innovator, part of the prehistory of modern art rather than its beginning.

Yet if Giotto's life institutes a *new* beginning, it is *only* a beginning, an inaugural moment that sets the stage for the action proper. Whereas the figure of Cimabue takes shape as a mythic composite of Noah, Abraham, and Moses, a patriarch of Italian art who nonetheless remains outside the golden circle of its full dispensation, Giotto plays the world-historical role of John the Baptist, the last of the Old Testament prophets born within the confines of the New Testament. Such a role accommodates both Giotto's cancellation of Cimabue's medievalism and his own supersedure by each subsequent artist, especially, in the deeper providential scheme of the *Lives*, by the divine Michelangelo, the man whose work "transcends and eclipses [*trascende e ricuopre*] that of every other artist, living and dead" (Bull I: 253; Ragghianti II: 591).

For, in the iconography of the saints, John the Baptist is a precursor figure with the fundamental role of pointing forward to the coming of Christ. In paintings of the *sacra conversazione*, in which a company of saints gathers around the heavenly throne of the Mother and Child, John the Baptist often plays the role of explicator, directing the viewer's eyes toward the central vision.[9] In the *istoria* that unifies the *Lives of the Artists*, the life of Giotto serves to point forward to the central drama of the text by recapitulating and advancing the testamentary cadence instated by the patriarch Cimabue. In the larger narrative of the book, Giotto functions as the demonstrative herald of a miracle far greater than himself in the *sacra conversazione* constituted by the community of artists who congregate around the œuvre of Michelangelo. The Johanine model permits Vasari both to praise Giotto's natural artistry as a man ahead of his times in Part I, and to relegate his art to a voice in the wilderness, predicting the time of another, in Parts II and III. The emplotting power of typology, moreover, lies not in the binding of each artist to a particular scriptural type, but rather in the ability of biblical pairings and formulas to be shifted from one constellation of artists to another, recalibrating their achievements in relation to the dialectically renovated coordinates of future periods. Thus in the book's unfolding series of retroactive inscriptions, Giotto can be Christ to Cimabue's Baptist, but John the Baptist to Michelangelo's Christ, allowing Vasari to evaluate the work of each artist in relation to both the painter's own time and to the future his work helps make possible.[10]

Biblical typology accounts for the scriptural proto-saints and super-saints that undergird the *Lives of the Artists*, and informs Vasari's hagiographic borrowings from the heroes of the postbiblical Church as well. Here the key text is not the *Golden Legend* but rather Boccaccio's reworking of the medieval legends into the forms of the novella, a generic overhaul that, as I argued in Chapter 3, uses the mechanism of typology in order to construct secular literature on the model of the Bible.[11] In the lives of Fra Angelico and Fra Lippi—tales respectively of the painter as good and bad priest— Vasari draws on the hagiographic resources of the novella. Fra Angelico exemplifies the principle that "artists who devote themselves to work of a religious or holy kind ought themselves to be genuinely holy and religious" (Bull I: 204); the life of Fra Angelico functions as the Griselda tale of Vasari's artistic *Decameron*, since it places the artist's biography in a continuous, affirmative relation with the genre of hagiography. By casting Griselda as a modern Job—"modern" in the sense of both Christian and secular—Boccaccio constitutes literature as a new scripture. Vasari, following Boccaccio's initiative, uses the life of Fra Angelico to validate the artist as the new saint, at once authorizing the artist through his sacred prototype and effectively replacing the prior form by aligning the artist's biography with the secular novella.

In the *Decameron*, the palinodic affirmation of hagiography performed by the exemplum of Griselda (*Decameron* X.10), the hundredth tale of the collection, is itself the negation of the ironizing procedures of the very first story of the collection, the mock-legend of Ser Ciappelletto (I.1). So too, Vasari's life of Fra Angelico must be read against his *vita* of Fra Filippo Lippi, a portrait of the artist as a false saint. Lippi, raised in a Carmelite convent to be a friar, falls in love with a young novice named Lucrezia, who poses as the Madonna for one of his paintings; enraptured by her beauty, he steals her away from the convent on the Feast of the Girdle of Our Lady (Bull I: 217–18). Colored by recollections of Ovid's Pygmalion, Livy's Lucretia, and Dante's Paolo and Francesca, the erotic episode narrates the debasement of religious imagery by the eros that infuses its production, and hence thematizes the fall of hagiography into secular romance, as the friar-painter is literally defrocked by the forces of passion.

In Vasari's account, Fra Lippi appears as a consummate painter of the Annunciation.[12] Lippi's sexual exploits travesty the religious subject matter of his paintings, such that the young artist positioned before the novice Lucrezia becomes a Gabrielesque St. Luke painting a vision of the Virgin, but now in an act of devilish seduction rather than divine inspiration. In this, Vasari's Fra Lippi resembles Friar Alberto in the *Decameron* IV.2, who seduces the insipid Monna Lisetta by pretending to be the Angel Gabriel. In Boccaccio's tale, Alberto's seduction succeeds in part through the currency of Annunciate iconography; Monna Lisetta believes that Gabriel is the secret lover of Mary, since "in all the paintings she had seen of him, he was invariably shown kneeling in front of the Virgin" (*Decameron* E 347). Like the mock-Annunciation in *Measure for Measure*, Vasari's tale of Lucrezia's seduction borrows the tendency to enunciate the Annunciation from hagiography (for instance, the legend of St. Cecilia) via the novella, here locating the perverse reading of Marian iconography in the very scene of its artistic production.

Vasari negatively keys the life of Lippi to that of Fra Angelico through the ironic divide he inserts between Lippi's personal conduct and the holy subjects of his work, and through the figuration of Lippi as a bad Gabriel, the un-Angelico. By balancing the affirmation of hagiography found in novellas with its equally novellalike ironization, Vasari's text borrows the secular logic of the *Decameron*, in which the inverse tales of Griselda and Ciappelletto generate secular literature as the renovation of the lives of the saints. In his double transaction with hagiography and the novella, Vasari restores the motifs of the saints to their originally biographical project, but within the new context of humanist historiography. By reappropriating hagiography to biography through the intermediary of the novella, Vasari's identification of the artist and the saint, far from manifesting a retrograde historical primitivism, becomes a self-conscious act of secular modernization.

Typology Short-Circuited

In his life of Michelangelo, Vasari transfers the great scriptural themes of the Creation, the prophets, and the Last Judgment depicted in Michelangelo's art to the world-historical significance of the artist himself, taken as the Christological incarnation of the book's opening fable of *disegno ex nihilo*. Vasari writes of Michelangelo's Moses:

> For, through the skill of Michelangelo, God has wanted to restore and prepare the body of Moses for the Resurrection before that of anyone else. And well may the Jews continue to go there (as they do every Sabbath, both men and women, like flocks of starlings) to visit and adore the statue, since they will be adoring something that is divine rather than human. (Bull I: 345; Ragghianti IV: 335–36)

In the original scheme for the tomb of Julius II, the statue of Moses was to be paired with one of St. Paul; as Paul Barolsky argues, "The relation of the two statues would have suggested to Vasari the spiritual progress from law to grace and thus to the resurrection of the perfect body" (*Michelangelo's Nose* 43). Vasari uses the typological content of Michelangelo's religious sculpture to characterize the artist's own messianic role in the Renaissance redemption of art; Michelangelo, like Christ, is a second Moses, the bringer of a new law that at once resurrects and subsumes the first.

Yet Michelangelo's Moses sits without Paul, a solitude foregrounded by the strange image of the Roman Jews adoring his statue. Barolsky takes this anecdote as a further sign of the conversionary dynamic mobilized in Vasari's association of Michelangelo with a Moses-turned-Paul.[13] I would argue to the contrary that the appearance of contemporary Jews on the site of Christian typology signals the limits of Pauline exegesis. After all, these are not the Chosen People of the Old Testament who happily prefigure the order that will have superseded them, but rather Jews of modern Rome, who, like Shakespeare's Venetian Shylock or the Barnardine of his Italianate Vienna, decidedly prefer not to convert. Unlike the *istoria* that governs the *Lives*, in which the heroes of art history congregate around the throne of Michelangelo, this picture is a genre piece rather than a history painting, a scene of everyday life in contemporary Rome. Vasari represents the contemporary Jews as a "flock of starlings"—not a group of typologically differentiated human figures, but an indiscriminate swarm of circling birds. Vasari has tellingly borrowed the simile from Dante's description of the crowd of carnal sinners in the *Inferno*, Canto V, the circle in which the adulterous lovers Paolo and Francesca per-vert Augustinian conversion through their illicit reading of romance literature.[14] Whereas in Vasari's *sacra conversazione* of great artists, scriptural types regulate the intervals and interchanges between historical figures in a dialectical succession, in this scene, the unexpected appearance of the modern Jews short-circuits typology by separating out Moses as the nonsublated ground of St. Paul's exegesis.

This symptom of curtailed typology inhabits the very terms of Vasari's historical periodization. Vasari divides the art of the Italian peninsula into the *antico*, the *vecchio*, and the *moderno*; in the cultural myth of Renaissance, the *moderno* is constituted by the rejection of the *vecchio*—the merely old—in favor of the *antico*—the authentically classical, which the *moderno* renews within a new (that is, Christian) historical plane.[15] That much is commonplace. Perhaps less obvious, however, is the recurrence of the word *vecchio* in a parallel opposition, namely, the *Vecchio e Nuovo Testamento* (for instance, Ragghianti I: 371, 375). In Vasari's historical ratio, the Old Testament is to the New Testament as the ancient is to the modern. That is, insofar as the Hebrew Bible dies in order to be reborn as the Gospels, it carries the weight of the antique, at once sublimely authoritative and profoundly displaced by the new order modeled on it; this is the position of the Jewish patriarchs and prophets in the gallery of the Christian saints, and of Cimabue in the school of Vasari.

When the Jews decline entry into that dialectic, however, the *Vecchio Testamento* approaches *le maniere vecchie* of Gothic art: it enters an old age devoid of wisdom or authority, calcified rather than classical, that is thoroughly lacking in both artistic and providential grace. The sublimely unsublimated elements of the Hebrew Bible, old rather than ancient, come to figure the resistant strains of medievalism that continue to infect contemporary art. These elements of nonconversion, of aborted renaissance, include the Gothic mannerisms, descriptive concerns, and miniaturist tendencies found in the art of Northern Europe and also in the works of such Italian figures as Masolino, Pisanello, and Crivelli. The generic predilections and pictorial conceptions of such art are difficult to comprehend and evaluate within the criteria of narrative significance and compositional clarity, of Alberti's *istoria* and Vasari's *disegno*, that dominate Italian art theory. These artistic phenomena suggest the points of strain and ideological exertion in the Tuscan conception of the Renaissance. It is not simply that Vasari's system requires a subordinate, negative element—*vecchio* as the degraded middle term that serves at once to distinguish and equate the ancient and the modern—but that the *vecchio* unexpectedly, even embarrassingly, persists beyond the point of its world-historical abrogation. It is this intractable residualism of apparently superseded positions—exemplified, for example, in the "legalism" that will identify Catholicism with Judaism in the eyes of the Reformation—that threatens the contract between classical humanism and Christianity brought off by *disegno* and typology in Vasari's text.[16]

Yet the typological figure of the remnant does not exhaust the effects of a sublated Judaism in Vasari's secular history. The moment depicted in Michelangelo's statue, as Freud laboriously reconstructs it in his essay "The Moses of Michelangelo," may be the instant when Moses, descending from Sinai with the two tablets, sees the Israelites worshipping the Golden Calf.[17] Whereas Vasari's description of Moses captures the majesty of the sublime Law-Giver, the unexpected vision of the Jews adoring his statue uncannily locates the threat of idolatry within the historic moment of its prohibition (namely, in the second commandment of the first tablet). Adored by the Jews, the oddly horned statue—in Freud's phrase a "Moses with the head of Pan"—begins to shimmer with the memory of the Golden Calf.[18] The scene reinstates the dialectic of idolatry and iconoclasm, this time not as the moment that sets the typological vision of world history into motion but rather as a counter-rhythm that threatens to negate its progressive translations. Recall Augustine's typological image of the Israelite women transporting "vases and ornaments" out of Egypt, "taken . . . as from unjust possessors and converted to [their] use," a figure for the Christian recuperation of classical civilization (*On Christian Doctrine* 75). Yet the conversion is apparently incomplete, since the Golden Calf is made out of the "golden rings . . . in the ears of your wives" (Ex. 32:2), likely the same jewelry that the women had stolen from their Egyptian mistresses. As such, the Golden Calf emblematizes the pagan possibilities remaining in the sublation of classical culture, and thus triggers the reassertion of the law against idolatry. In this scenario, iconoclasm names both the negative moment inherent in the conversion of polytheistic civilization to monotheistic ends (Augustine's rejection of pagan content) and the secondary reaction to the carrying over of a sublated idolatry into the forms of the new order.

The tableau of the modern Jews stationed before an iconoclastic Moses separated from his Pauline twin brings into play both the homologies and the contradictions between the historical patterns of typology and iconoclasm. First and foremost, the Jews of Counter-Reformation Rome represent the remainder of the typological rereading of the Old Testament by the New. The scene's intimation of the Golden Calf, however, activates the iconoclasm commanded by the Decalogue in relation to pagan representation. In Vasari's typological staging of the Renaissance as a historical epoch, the hermeneutic vicissitudes of the Jews in the Christian canon lay out the spaces for three distinct analogues in secular history. First, the type of the patriarch figures antiquity as the heroic yet supplanted ground of modernity. Second, as the product of that typological transaction, the specter of the modern, unconverted Jew represents the negated yet residual middle ground of medievalism. Finally, the Mosaic prohibition against idolatry insists on the moment of pure negation that both refuses and revitalizes the modern mimetic project. The failures of historico-religious transcription embodied by the modern Jews in front of Michelangelo's Moses introduce two discontinuities into the dynamic of Christian secularization that governs Vasari's text. The Jew represents the persistence of the *vecchio*—of "medieval" nonmimetic tendencies—as the residual symptom that gives the lie to the story of art history as the progress of mimesis. The Jew also introduces the cut of iconoclasm that refuses the historical steps of imitation, in the process pushing them forward; in this scheme, the Jew is no longer the sign of historical atavism, becoming instead the dialectical instigator of mimetic innovation through its radical negation. The cut of iconoclasm, as we will see in the next section, repeats the creative annihilation of *disegno ex nihilo*, and thus articulates the void at the incarnational heart of Vasari's historical narrative.

The 'Natura' of Creation

In Benjamin's writings on the Baroque, the archaeological stratifications of natural history presented an antidote to the typologically driven dialectic of the German philosophy of history. Vasari's *Lives* offers a sixteenth-century sampling of the dynamic isolated by Benjamin, since Vasari's art history is a discourse carved out of the much larger field of natural history, represented for Renaissance art theory above all by the work of Pliny. Vasari's account of artistic innovation, oriented toward the progressive stages of the mimesis of nature, confronts the *natura* shared with natural history as both the normative object of mimesis and as the heterogeneous exception to the mimetic rule. Innovation, as a secular repetition of creation *ex nihilo*, inserts the dialectic of iconoclasm into the typological unfolding of the Renaissance.

Books XXXIV and XXXV of Pliny's massive *Naturalis Historia*, an encyclopedia in thirty-seven books written in the first century

C.E., form the major extant source on artists of antiquity; hence practically every Renaissance commentator on the visual arts draws on Pliny's stories, ecphrases, and catalogues of such artists as Phidias, Zeuxis, Appelles, and Praxiteles.[19] Vasari, too, borrows much from the *Naturalis Historia*, including Pliny's attention to patterns of apprenticeship and competition, his valorization of line over color (see XXXV.67–68), his taste for the telling anecdote, and his critical investment in the possibility of artistic progress. And yet Pliny's natural history diverges greatly in organization and governing conception from the art history founded by Vasari. A systematic description of engineering more than what we would think of as pure science, natural history catalogues man's interactive manipulations of nature; thus Pliny's discussion of botany is divided between the practical fields of horticulture and medicine. Pliny's histories of sculpture (Book XXXIV) and painting (Book XXXV) appear under the general topic of "minerals," with sculpture explored under metallurgy, and the discussion of painting introducing his treatment of dyes. Far from forming a continuous history, Pliny interrupts his accounts of sculpture and painting with a lengthy digression on the pharmaceutical uses of metals. Art can be part of natural history insofar as nature itself is conceived as the object of human intervention, transformation, and use.[20]

Natural history à la Pliny represents the classical substratum for much collecting and thought about art in both Vasari's Italy and Northern Europe. As Adalgisa Lugli has demonstrated, the humanist and princely museums of the sixteenth century assembled their objects on either side of the structuring divide between the *naturalia*— shells, plants, rocks, stuffed animals, insects—and the *artificialia*— clocks, exotic costumes, and the instruments of music and math as well as antiquities and paintings. Samuel Quiccheberg's *Inscriptiones vel tituli theatri amplissimi*, a text that would become the "standard of reference" for two centuries of curators in the natural-history mode, was published in 1565, falling between the two editions of Vasari's *Lives* (Lugli 115). The dominant line of Vasari's project, however, already carves a distinct space for art history and its museum out of the vast field authorized by natural history. Far from

taking the history of art as simply one in a set of contiguous mi-
crohistories investigating the diverse practices that make up human
culture, Vasari isolates Pliny's paradigms of artistic virtuosity and
competition from their natural-historical framework in order to free
modern sculptors and painters for the heroic task of representing
significant human action, and thus themselves taking a place in the
story of history.

The word *natura* appears to be the switch-point between Pliny
and Vasari, as the object of technological manipulation in the earlier
author and of mimesis in the latter. I would argue to the contrary,
however, that the fundamental non-commutativity of the word between Pliny and Vasari deposits the disciplinary framework of natural history as an objectal remnant in the discourse of the *Lives*. It is
not simply that "nature," a concept apparently shared by the two
authors, in fact means different things to each of them, but that the
very divergence of the two discourses implies a third valence of
natura excluded by both. Whereas for Pliny, "nature" encompasses
the sum of resources available to human engineering, including the
various minerals used to make paint or the types of stone and metal
worked by the sculptor, for Vasari, "nature" usually names the object of mimesis, understood above all as a cognitive rather than a
manual process. The question of innovation, however, of creating
something new, points once again to the operation of a *nihil*, of a
lack introduced into the fabric of representation as an iconoclastic
affront to its mimetic claims; it is precisely as this *nihil* of creation
that a third function of nature, taken as the difference between natural history and art history, operates in Vasari's text.

For Vasari, imitation encompasses both the student's study of
great works of art and the exercise of drawing from life. These two
activities, moreover, confirm and depend on each other: the artist
only learns to imitate nature by studying the examples of the masters, while drawing (*disegno*) from life generally means figuring out
the underlying design of the Master, God. Thus in Vasari's program
for an aesthetic education, objects of art and nature are practically
interchangeable, since both offer models of design to be drawn upon
by the student.[21] The *discepolo* moves between the works of the *mae-*

stro and *natura* in order to learn the techniques of mimesis, for the art of the master helps the student comprehend nature as *already art*, the creation of God.

The subsumption of *natura* within the symbolic mandate of *disegno*, however, cannot effectively account for artistic change, since the new painter displaces his teachers only by being able to perceive and represent nature differently—paradoxically, he must somehow get outside the art-nature loop if he is to imitate differently, and thus become a *maestro* himself. In the scene of mimetic innovation, "nature" must function not only as an object of imitation within a system of representation shared by *maestro* and *discepolo* alike, but also as a foreign element that disequilibrates the established isomorphism between natural forms and their artistic imitation. Thus Vasari criticizes the Byzantine painters in the time of Cimabue for "blindly following what had been handed on year after year by painters who never thought of trying to improve their drawing" (Bull I: 50–51). Giotto avoided the blind repetitions of a pure traditionality by turning to nature: "Giotto not only captured his master's style but also began to draw so ably from life that he made a decisive break with the crude traditional Byzantine style" (Bull I: 58; Ragghianti I: 358). Giotto, writes Vasari further on, "could rightly claim to have had nature, rather than any human master, as his teacher [*meritò d'esser chiamato discepolo della natura, e non d'altri*]" (Bull I: 61; Ragghianti I: 364). The formulation effectively substitutes "nature" in the place of "Cimabue" in the scene of artistic vocation, a *second nature*, however, that reinstalls the initial pastoral image of Giotto in his meadow from the vantage point of his discipleship in the city.

In Vasari's scheme, artistic innovation requires that the painter detour through the techniques of the master in order to see nature otherwise, effecting a kind of trauma or perceptual shock that shakes up and reshuffles the representational conventions that constitute reality for a subject at a particular moment. Innovations in mimesis demand a moment of creation *ex nihilo*—the discovery of a lack in the reigning tradition that marks the tradition's horizon and simultaneously expands it. Such creation *ex nihilo* implies an element of iconoclasm, insofar as it challenges the current regime of mimesis by revealing its conventionality and breaking up the naturalization of the signifier/signified relationship. In this regard, Vasari frequently refers to innovative art as *miracoloso*, a phrase that we should take not as pious platitude or aesthetic hyperbole, but rather as a succint registration of the role of an *unnatural nature*, aberrant and erratic, in the normalization of a *naturalized nature* working according to predictable laws. Recall here Carl Schmitt's identification of the "state of emergency" and the cut of the juridical decision with the theological structure of the miracle, which he also associates with a "creationist" rather than evolutionist view of the state (*Political Theology* 36). In Vasari's brand of creationism, the order of the *miracoloso*—in Lacan's terms, the Real as opposed to reality—is itself never a purely external ground or force, but rather a second nature, a residual nature produced through the iconoclastic interference, redoubling, or creasing of representational conventions. Momentarily directed against the current mimetic regime, *disegno* as iconoclastic cut is also a creative act that furthers the renovation of mimesis.

In the life of Giotto, Vasari narrates a brief tale of mimetic virtuosity that relays the shock value of such an encounter with the real:

> There is a story that when Giotto was still a young man in Cimabue's workshop, he once painted on the nose of one of the figures Cimabue had executed a fly that was so lifelike [*una mosca tanto naturale*] that when Cimabue returned to carry on with his work he tried several times to brush it off with his hand, under the impression that it was real, before he realized his mistake. (Bull I: 80; Ragghianti I: 393–94)

The story derives from a similar incident in Pliny, much cited in Renaissance writings on art:

> [Parrhasius] entered into a competition with Zeuxis, who produced a picture of grapes so successfully represented that birds flew up to the stage-buildings; whereupon Parrhasius himself produced such a realistic picture of a curtain that Zeuxis, proud of the verdict of the birds, requested that the curtain should now be drawn and the picture dis-

played; and when he realized his mistake, with a modesty that did him honour he yielded up the prize, saying that whereas he had deceived birds Parrhasius had deceived him, an artist. (XXXV.65)

Lacan, taking up the tale from Pliny, distinguishes the ethological effects of the first exercise from the hermeneutic and significatory structure of the second:

> In the opposition of the works of Zeuxis and Parrhasios, [there is] the ambiguity of two levels, that of the natural function of the lure and that of *trompe-l'œil*.
>
> If the birds rushed to the surface on which Zeuxis had deposited his dabs of colour, taking the picture for edible grapes, let us observe that the success of such an undertaking does not imply in the least that the grapes were admirably reproduced. . . . There would have to be something more reduced, something closer to the sign, in something representing grapes for the birds. But the opposite example of Parrhasios makes it clear that if one wishes to deceive a man, what one presents to him is the painting of a veil, that is to say, something that incites him to ask what is behind it. (*Seminar XI*, 112)

The painted grapes materialize the knotting of the imaginary and the real, insofar as a particular visual formation emerges out of representation with the force of something actual—not, moreover, as an object of cognition but as a stimulus of hunger, flight, or arousal, symptomatically registered at the level of the organism as an instinctual response. Rather than simply viewing the grapes, the birds become part of the picture of the grapes, inscribed into the image by its lure.[22] By the same token, the picture becomes part of nature, a novel display of the role of representation in animal behavior.

The curtain, on the other hand, coalesces at the juncture of the real and the symbolic, since it tricks the human subject into the interpretive act of pulling the veil away in order to dis-cover a hidden meaning behind it. Like the grapes, the curtain "looks real," but now by producing a fictional contrast between an actual curtain and a painting secreted behind it; the curtain functions not as an instinctual stimulus, but as a temporary obstacle to full understanding. In Lacan's vocabulary, the curtain acts as a "cause of desire," an impeding object that sets desire and interpretation into motion by introducing a fundamental discontinuity into an experience retroactively consolidated around it.[23] In seeking a painting *behind* the curtain, Zeuxis finds to his surprise that the curtain *is* the painting; the "realness" of the curtain resides precisely in the gap between seeking and finding, between hermeneutic desire and the element of enigma and surprise that both causes and frustrates that desire. Parrhasius creates *ex nihilo* in the sense that his painting generates a gap; it is not so much that Parrhasius has depicted a curtain (as one might portray any number of other objects of perception), but rather that he has painted occlusion-by-a-curtain, that is, the structural cause of interpretive desire and representation.[24]

Pliny's story is a drama in two acts: in the painting by Zeuxis, an image of *grapes* deceives a *flock of birds*, and in the painting by Parrhasius, the depiction of a *curtain* deceives *another artist*. Vasari's tale of Giotto and Cimabue condenses the two episodes from Pliny into a single anecdote, in which the student's painting of a fly on the master's painting of a face deceives the older artist. In the process, Vasari's novella combines the two modalities of visual deception distinguished by Lacan. Cimabue's swatting of the fly recalls the instinctual reaction that the painted grapes set off in the birds of Zeuxis; in Vasari as in Pliny, a bodily gesture rather than a cognitive judgment marks the uncanny effect of the real within the imaginary. Like the birds of Zeuxis, Cimabue is as much seen by the painting as he is a beholder of it; in this, Giotto's fly resembles the fetish object in Freud's famous example of the *"Glanz auf der Nase,"* the fascinating shine/glance on the nose that, far from situating the viewer in either an intersubjective exchange or a position of visual mastery, gazes at the subject as an opaque, shimmering, illegible object.[25] Insofar as Giotto's fly alights on top of a painted face, the structure repeats that of the curtain of Parrhasius, which deceives the eye by creating the illusion of surface and depth, of a painted plane masked by an actual obstruction. Just as Pliny's Zeuxis wants to draw the painted curtain, so too, Vasari's Cimabue wants to brush away the fly in order to clarify the face beneath it. Giotto's virtuosity, like Parrhasius's, lies not in his mimesis of a particular object but in the generation of the deceptive gap between two registers, the "actual insect"—an irritating mark or smudge—and the "painted figure"—the authorized object of classical viewing.

It is a creation *ex nihilo* that reveals a lack in the current order of representation (the imperfections of Cimabue relative to Giotto) and embodies that lack in the punctual speck that is the fly. The effect of Giotto's trick is to denaturalize the current regime of images by making their conventionality quite literally surface, insofar as the fly de-faces the face beneath, making it sur-face as deflated illusion. Giotto's mythic *trompe-l'œil* flies in the face of the master's techniques by showing the epochal limits of his work—with the result that Giotto becomes the new master, the artist whose art establishes the new conventions for representing nature for the next generation. Thus the life of Giotto begins with the following claim: "painters owe to Giotto, the Florentine painter, exactly the same debt they owe to nature, which constantly serves them as a model [*per essempio*] and whose finest and most beautiful aspects they are always striving to imitate and reproduce [*di contrafarla et imitarla s'ingegnano sempre*]" (Bull I: 57; Ragghianti I: 357). Both the paintings of Giotto and the works of nature can serve as the *essempio* of future artists, since Giotto's paintings help establish what counts as nature, as discursive reality, by revealing anew the exemplary formedness and imitability of nature.

Like the flock of birds drawn to Zeuxis's grapes (and the "flock of starlings" drawn to the Moses of Michelangelo), Giotto's fly is a piece of natural history that has not been naturalized by the signifying framework of its host, a fragment from a different representational order that marks a lack in the initial painting and the system of conventions it instantiates. In the anecdote, Giotto's maneuver serves to install his art as the new model of imitation, reestablishing the homology between art and nature. Yet in the process, the logic of innovation has disclosed another *natura*, not "reality" as the symbolic consistency of lived experience, but rather the "Real," the interval or *nihil* generated by Giotto's *trompe l'œil* on Cimabue's painting. Similarly, the major function of Vasari's allusion to Pliny is to strengthen the *Lives'* narrative of artistic progress by modeling Giotto's career on a classical example of mimetic virtuosity; the episode demonstrates Vasari's selective citation of humanist motifs from Pliny's corpus. Yet, modeled on the *Naturalis Historia*, the episode stages a discourse *on* the thing that has the status *of* a thing in Vasari's text: added to the 1568 edition as one of a series of novellalike anecdotes, this fable after Pliny is detachable from the main *vita*, a textual fly stuck to the central narrative of Giotto's life. The act of citation, like the story it narrates, opens up a breach between discursive registers, a distance, that is, between Vasari's mythically unified art history and the encyclopedic episodism of Pliny.

Just as *disegno* can be read in terms of both the traumatic slash of a single line and the integral image composed by it, so *natura* points to both the formal coherence of the created world (nature as "reality") and the chance encounter with something foreign to representation generated by the very manipulation and crossing of mimetic conventions (nature as the Real). The word *natura* derives from the future participle of the Latin deponent verb *nascor*, "to be born," and thus implies a process of emergence, of an incipient coming-into-existence.[26] In the leaps of innovation that drive the mimetic tradition of art, *natura* momentarily regains its future-participial force, an "about-to-be-born-ness," when representation is both disrupted and immediately reconsolidated around a new point of persistent lack. This *natura* names what is always only nascent, *in statu nascendi*, in the *rinascita* of Vasari, since it emerges in and as the incommensurability between the methodological systems represented by natural history and art history. This incommensurability in turn parallels the embedding of iconoclastic negation in innovative design as both a necessary moment in and a traumatic rejection of the typological retranscription of the *rinascita* as an historical epoch.

For the birth of this emergent *natura* is always a stillbirth, in two senses. First, it always dies into the renovated regime of images that closes over the void that recenters them; the only "realness" carried by *natura* accretes within the field of representation, as a spacing of its registers produced by the obfuscation of a mark or stain. And second, the things of natural history fall into the narrative scene of art history out of the genre of still life, of *nature morte*, as collected, dessicated, or decaying effluvia, their incipient promise of a future only expressable in the past tense of the specimen, the fossil, or the relic, the concentrated temporalities of natural history's taxonomic discourse.[27] Both the grapes and the fly are specimens from natural history, tiny bits of collectible flora and fauna that form the object of both scientific analysis and still-life painting. Even the curtain, a study in the vertical hanging of cloth across a flat plane, is distinct from the draperies that volumetrically articulate the human body in classical sculpture and narrative painting.[28] The anecdote of Giotto's fly superimposes two genres of painting by sliding a miniature still life imported from the discourse of natural history onto the surface of a narrative painting executed in the nascent Italian tradition. It is not that the artist (or the art historian) suddenly looks at nature without the mediation of conventions, but rather that the fungal accretion of one discourse on nature within another unexpectedly distorts or unfixes the dominant terms of representation, forcing them to be rethought around a fragment of the Real.

It is no accident that the other famous example of *trompe-l'œil* in the *Lives* also involves the memorabilia of natural history. In the life of Leonardo, Vasari relates how the artist's father asked him to paint a buckler for a peasant on his farm:

Leonardo started to think what he could paint on it so as to terrify anyone who saw it and produce the same effect as the head of Medusa. To do what he wanted Leonardo carried into a room of his own, which no one ever entered except himself, a number of green and other kinds of lizards, crickets, serpents, butterflies, locusts, bats, and various strange creatures of this nature; from all these he took and assembled different parts to create a fearsome and horrible monster which emitted a poisonous breath and turned the air to fire. . . . Leonardo took so long over the work that the stench of the dead animals in his room became unbearable, although he himself failed to notice because of his great love of painting. . . . So one morning Piero [Leonardo's father] went along to the room in order to get the buckler, knocked at the door, and was told by Leonardo to wait for a moment. Leonardo went back into the room, put the buckler on an easel in the light, and shaded the window; then he asked Piero to come in and see it. When his eyes fell on it Piero was completely taken by surprise and gave a sudden start, not realizing that he was looking at the buckler and that the form he saw was, in fact, painted on it. As he backed away, Leonardo checked him and said:

"This work certainly serves its purpose. It has produced the right reaction, so now you can take it away." (Bull I: 259; Ragghianti II: 603)

Here, too, Vasari emphasizes the shock of representation when it appears not as part of the familiar fabric of reality, but rather on the hallucinatory stage of the Real. Thus the sudden start of Leonardo's father, like the swarming of the birds and the swatting of the fly in the earlier scenes, inscribes the father as a punctual effect of the picture rather than an independent, conscious viewer of it; Piero encounters the painting as something that views *him* rather than as the object of his own perception and judgment. And this is the only purpose, indeed the only being, of the work for Leonardo, a technician of transient impressions and weird novelties more than a designer of permanent works. For Leonardo, the work is a kind of performance piece, a temporary installation whose product is not the painted buckler as such but rather its effect on the viewer, its alienating reduction of the human subject to a pure instinctual response.

These portrayed fragments of *natura* are doubly subject to mortification, since the painting distills them into still life while their collected flesh putrefies in Leonardo's studio. Painted on the curved surface of a buckler rather than the blank ground of a canvas, this painting of disjointed things is itself a thing, a naturalist's curio rather than a history painting. Like the natural historian who trades in marvels with princely collectors, Piero salvages and then sells the buckler to the Duke of Milan as a kind of souvenir, a material memento capable of recalling and repeating the strange temporality of *natura*'s birth-into-decay.[29]

Leonardo's assemblage of weird specimens once again precipitates a *natura* situated between the discourses of natural history and art history as their excluded middle term, the thingly product that marks their negative intersection. The buckler most obviously projects a counter-image to the historical ideal of the art collection and the biographical anthology imagined by the dominant line of the

Lives. Vasari's text approximates the organizational model of Raphael's *School of Athens*, in which the great philosophers of past centuries meet in the secular conversation of a continuous tradition.[30] In the anthology constituted by Leonardo's buckler, fragments of strange animals do not congregate so much as aggregate in a monstrous disunity; the buckler represents the distorted reflection of Vasari's text, in Harry Berger, Jr.'s, analysis, "a parody of those ideals" that gird the program of the *Lives* ("Collecting Bodies" 37).

Yet the painting also diverges from the ideal of the natural history collection. Although the buckler does assemble the items traditionally gathered by the natural historian—"lizards, crickets, serpents, butterflies, locusts, bats"—the principles of dissection and montage that fasten them together into an inorganic organism run counter to the macrocosmic taxonomies and orderly catalogues of the naturalist. Unlike the botanical illustrations of an herbalist, the maps of a geographer, or Leonardo's own anatomical studies, the buckler does not present materials for rational examination and technological instrumentalization, but rather for oneiric recombination. It is as if the grids and shelving that separate and align the objects of the natural history collection had suddenly disintegrated, leaving the items locked inside to meld and reconfigure. The buckler presents the phantasmatic effects produced by Vasari's strategic citation of Pliny's anecdotes outside their natural history context. Rather than projecting natural history as a more inclusive or materialist framework opposed to the aestheticizations of Vasari, the buckler episode represents the weird focalization of that framework in Vasari's discourse. So too, taking the shape of a dragon issuing like Leonardo's famous Madonna "from the dark cleft of a rock," the dissected forms resettle into a burlesque of a history painting, the nonsynthetic symptom of Vasari's project.[31]

Whereas in the life of Giotto, Vasari detaches the episode of Zeuxis and Parrhasius from the comparative framework of natural history, in the *vita* of Leonardo, Vasari develops natural history as a countermodel to art history in order to establish the dramatic agon between Leonardo, the artist as natural historian, and Michelangelo, the consummate painter and sculptor of sacred and human history. For Leonardo's scientific experiments and consequent distraction from the discipline of design finally subordinate his contribution to Michelangelo's in the providential drama of Italian art staged by Vasari. Yet, in the structuring opposition that Vasari draws in these *vite* between the two discourses, the buckler gathers, preserves, and phantasmatically transmogrifies the *realia* of natural history that remain when their epistemological framework is dissolved. Like the spacing of representational registers created by Giotto's fly, this imploded encyclopedia of dead creatures collects that *natura* left over from the dialectical confrontation between the two discourses. It is in that breach or *nihil* that a third rendering of *natura*, produced by its exclusion from both discourses on the artefact, symptomatically arises in Vasari's work.

My point, then, is precisely *not* to criticize Vasari's project from the vantage point of natural history. Instead of rejecting Vasari in favor of an (apparently) more materialist, comprehensive, or interdisciplinary program, I have tried to delimit within Vasari's text both the interaction and the remainder of these two modes. The fly needs a painted nose on which to alight in order to disturb both the picture frame of high formalism and the historicist framework of low contextualism. It is the still-life painting that surfaces within history painting—the fly that alights on the nose of a human figure—rather than still life taken alone that demarcates the site for a future natural history of art. Such a project would reclaim a creation *ex nihilo* misremembered in the annals of genius through the interventions of a *natura* that is continually stillborn into the equalizing coordinates of representation. In Vasari's history of art, the *vecchio* falls out from the movement of Christian secularization as the epochal attribute of all that is rejected in the Renaissance dialectic of the classical and the modern, as this dialectic is mapped onto the exegetical conversion of the Hebrew Bible into the Old Testament. In the process, the *vecchio* reactivates the iconoclastic cut of creation *ex nihilo* carried by Vasari's initial mapping of *disegno* onto the hexameral *logos*. Thus the *vecchio*, apparently opposed to all that is classically modern, ends up emerging, like a dragon from a dark cleft, as a symptomatic novelty, an anecdotal accretion, at the nonmediating center of the scene of *rinascita*.

By placing the so-called fine arts in a continuum with other cultural practices, natural history anticipates the current initiatives of cultural studies, whose interdisciplinary, materialist, and critical imperatives as well as its instrumentalist views of art (art as ideology) are aimed at correcting the idealist monumentalism of the *Lives of the Artists* and the discipline of museological monographs Vasari's example has spawned.[32] Yet it is worth reasserting that Vasari's historiography, like the period term "Renaissance" that he helped found, does not simply impose its values on works that exist independently of it. Instead, Vasari's philosophy and history of *disegno* is immanent in the pictorial and generic concerns of much ambitious painting of the period—hence the interpretive astuteness and foundational effectiveness of Vasari's text in organizing these works and artists in relation to each other. "Canonization," I would insist, is not simply an arbitrary selection of works made by a particular institution in relation to a potentially infinite body of objects; rather, it formalizes and codifies the acts of allusion, imitation, and competitive displacement that constitute the iconographic and stylistic force-fields of the works themselves, and which link them together in a family or "genre" of objects. If the natural history collection seems to predict modern critiques of Vasari's legacy, we should remind ourselves that the interdisciplinary assimilation of the fine arts to the comparativist framework of cultural history effects its own idealist economization of artefacts into vessels of meaning that reflect and constitute a world-picture. The incongruities between the things of the naturalist's collection, the props of a still life, or the unlike artefacts of an interdisciplinary analysis are always regulated by a symbolic network of economic, taxonomic, and ideological exchange values. Such contextualizing *frameworks*, resolving heterogeneous things into exchangeable objects representative of particular periods, classes, institutions, or ideas, can be as idealizing as the much-criticized picture *frame*, which separates the fine arts out from other cultural practices in order to resituate them in an exemplary temporal series of homologous works. Thus I have attempted here

both a critical excavation of the Christian humanism that drives Vasari's historiography and a creative activation of alternative possibilities for thinking the art object carried by Vasari's text. By superimposing natural history and art history at the points where the picture frame excludes the contextual framework and vice versa, we
can momentarily bring into focus a discourse on the artefact that
emerges as the symptom—not the methodological synthesis but the
objectal side-effect—of the current opposition between cultural
studies and the traditional disciplines. This symptomatic object, fran-
gible but not fungible, subsists within the Christian/secular dialectic as both the iconoclastic cause and the typological remnant of its
structuring oppositions. As we shall see in the next chapter, the tension between iconoclasm and typology structures the Renaissance
myth of a work that alludes to Vasari's text, Shakespeare's *The Winter's Tale.*

CHAPTER 7

'The Winter's Tale' and the Gods

ICONOGRAPHIES OF IDOLATRY

In "The Poetics of Incomprehensibility" Stephen Orgel argues that the editorial cruxes of *The Winter's Tale* may never resolve into paraphrasable meanings and satisfying emendations, since the text may have offered similar points of difficulty to a Renaissance audience perfectly happy with obscure passages and esoteric images. In this regard, Orgel points to the "discontinuity between image and text in Renaissance iconographic structures," and then finds precedent for his thesis in Aby Warburg's largely ignored work on Renaissance intermezzi:

> As editors, we all subscribe, however uncomfortably, to some version of Burckhardt's Renaissance, an integrated culture that still spoke a universal language. For theater historians this view of the period was, or at least should have been, seriously compromised when Aby Warburg analyzed two of the learned spectators' accounts of the famous Medici intermezzi of 1589, probably the best documented of the great Renaissance festivals, and observed that the meaning of the performance, and indeed the very identity of the symbolic figures, was opaque to even the most erudite members of the audience. Since Warburg's essay was published in 1895, it is time Renaissance studies began to take it into account: it bears on our general sense of the nature of Renaissance public discourse as a whole. The spectator of *The Winter's Tale* in 1611, we implicitly assume, would have understood it

all. . . . I want to argue on the contrary that Shakespeare's audience
was more like the audience constructed by Warburg than like the audience constructed by Burckhardt. (436–37)

In the name of Aby Warburg and under the sign of iconography,
Orgel recommends that we take the hermeticism of allegorical image-complexes rather than the symbolic resolution of form and
meaning as our model of Renaissance signification. Iconography,
Hellenistic rather than Hellenic, mythographic rather than mythological, treats classical motifs not as living paradigms connecting the
past and the present, but rather as a body of scandalous material that
is either too dead or too alive—mortified beyond recognition or
threatening beyond belief—and thus requiring rationalist, naturalist,
moralizing, or mystical elaboration and retranscription. As Orgel's
comments indicate, the modern study of such exegetical and repre-
sentional strategies is indebted to the work of Aby Warburg, who
studied both the dessication and the reanimation of classical myths in
what he called their *Nachleben* or "afterlife"; as I suggested in Chapter 1, Warburg was drawn to the "iconography of idolatry," the star-
crossed images of a demonized, allegorical antiquity, a paganism visible from the sublime shadows of the Mosaic prohibition against
graven images rather than the beautiful light of the Christian resurrection. To call as Orgel does for a Renaissance studies that displaces Burckhardt by Warburg is also, I would argue, to incite a conception of the Renaissance that both follows out and disturbs the
word's foundations in the historical dialectics and incarnational aesthetics of biblical typology.

The Winter's Tale offers promising ground for the testing of conceptions of the Renaissance as period and canon, since the play, as a
drama of magical resurrection through the power of art coupled
with faith, stages a mythos of aesthetic, seasonal, and spiritual rebirth that rivals Burckhardt's in the sheer force and elegance of its
interlocking metaphors of renewal. *The Winter's Tale* is an exemplary "Renaissance" drama not least because it passes key myths of
classical regeneration (Pygmalion, Proserpina, Flora) through the
typological motifs of Leontes' law corrected by Pauline grace and

faith. We have seen similar programs for a rebirth of antiquity sanctioned by the narratives of biblical typology in the Renaissance world-picture of Burckhardt and in the founding story of *rinascita* offered by Vasari's *Lives of the Artists*, a text to which *The Winter's Tale* not accidentally alludes.

In performing its virtuoso rendition of the Renaissance theme, *The Winter's Tale* enunciates four intersecting discourses on idolatry—Jewish, Greco-Roman, Catholic, and Protestant. Taken as stations in a historical dialectic, the movement of the play as a whole works to transform the stony world of Acts I–III into Act V's symphony of reconciliation by way of Act IV's pagan pastoral. This world-historical *translatio* operates through a set of generic transformations: the modern romance of Act V redeems the ancient tragedy of Acts I–III, a historical and generic sublation facilitated by the minor Alexandrian pastoral staged in Act IV's intermezzo. Yet the Christian-classical synthesis supposedly achieved in the final act remains tainted by signs of Catholicism, sounded in Shakespeare's references to "sects" and "proselytes" (5.1.108–9), to Hermione's "sainted spirit" (5.1.57), and to the "chapel" that houses the statue (5.3.87), an image graven by an artist with "Rome" in his name. As such, the statue scene manifests and comments on a specific moment in the afterlife of the saints: the reduction of the saint to the dead image of idolatry performed by the Protestant assault on visual representation. The play's mythic redemption of the pre-Christian—both Old Testament and Hellenistic—world of Sicily only takes place by precipitating saintly icons out of broken commandments. The detour through pagan Bohemia not only allows the play to cite its mythological precedents in the stories of Flora and Proserpina, but also picks out the paganism residual in Catholicism and the Catholicism residual in reformed England, iconographies that, in their very bankrupting by the Protestant historical vision, together underwrite the hagiographic scheme informing the play.

The play performs, that is, an *iconography of idolatry*, a visual and critical analysis of the religious image in a secular world. Such an analysis is itself always implicated in the objects that it anatomizes; in the phrase "iconography of idolatry," idolatry does not simply present one topic for iconographic research among others, but rather is structurally implicated in iconography as its defining object of analysis, a demonic object, moreover, that threatens to activate the antitypological possibilities of iconography as a mode of historical and aesthetic interpretation. My point is not that *The Winter's Tale* is at heart either a Christian or a pagan play; I wish rather to map the remainders produced by the play's own quintessentially Renaissance coupling of classical and Christian myths of cultural rebirth, in order to show how *The Winter's Tale* constitutes "secular drama" as the reanimation of the fragments left over by the repeated breaking of idols in the history of the West.

Counting (On) the Ten Commandments

The prohibition against graven images, the major proof-text for Jewish and Christian debates about visual representation, follows as the logical consequence of the momentous declaration made by God himself of the principle of monotheism at the beginning of the Decalogue: "I am the Lord thy God, who brought thee out of the land of Egypt, out of the house of bondage" (Ex. 20:2). This opening line of the Decalogue, constituting the first commandment according to the Jewish count, leads immediately into the injunction against idolatry:

> Thou shalt have no other gods before Me. Thou shalt not make unto thee a graven image, nor any manner of likeness, of any thing that is in heaven above, or that is in the earth beneath, or that is in the water under the earth; thou shallt not bow down unto them, nor serve them; for I the LORD thy God am a jealous God, visiting the iniquity of the fathers upon the children unto the third and fourth generation of them that hate Me; and showing mercy unto the thousandth generation of them that love Me and keep My commandments. (Ex. 20:3–6).

The Decalogue unfolds from the central event, at once drama and trauma, of monotheism, the one God crystallized in the definitive statement of Jewish belief, *Sh'ma Israel: Adonai Eloheinu, Adonai echad*: "Hear, Israel: the Lord our God, the Lord is one" (Deut. 6:4)—"one" in the sense of both single and singular, beyond all incarnation in representation or the natural world. In Exodus and Deuteronomy, the sublime singularity and radical alterity of God is set against the plurality and tangibility of the local cults, later displaced by the Greco-Roman pantheon. Accordingly, the prohibition against images appears as a subset and logical extension of the injunction against polytheism, the all-important command to "have no other gods before Me," an injunction that in turn derives from the first commandment, "I am the Lord thy God."[1]

Recall Calum Carmichael's argument that the narrative subtext for the receiving of the Decalogue is the construction of the Golden Calf by the Israelites themselves (316–26). This narrative scene presents idolatry not as an external contamination, but as an ever-resurfacing tendency among the Israelites themselves. In both the creation narrated in Genesis and the revelation given in Exodus, the institution of monotheism serves as a single cut or stroke that brings the background of ancient polytheism into focus as such; the "other gods" (*elohim aherim*) prohibited in the injunction against idolatry are the counterparts both negated and brought into signification by the one/other God (*Eloheinu echod*) of Jewish monotheism.[2]

In the Reformation, Protestant faiths constituted themselves as the repetition of this sublime injunction by projecting the Church's reliance on images and ceremony as an insidious resurgence of paganism. Stephen Batman's 1577 *The Golden Booke of the Leaden Goddes wherein is described the vayne imaginations of Heath Pagans and counterfaict Christians* attributes to Catholicism the idolatrous practices of the Romans. He calls the Catholics "counterfaict Christians" because they are *counterfeiters*, image-makers whose products not only illicitly represent God but also compete with God's own creativity. From the Protestant perspective, Catholicism, especially in the rural practices reflected in Shakespeare's play, disastrously dilutes the monotheistic imperative of the Decalogue by reintroducing the teeming splendor and tactility of polytheism within the confines of the Ten Commandments.

Figure 4, loosely based on Greimas's "semiotic square," maps the dialectical relationship between these four positions. In this scheme, the Decalogue establishes an initial opposition that is both doubled and transformed in its Reformation repetition. Catholicism represents what Greimas calls the "positive complex term" that *combines* the first two contraries, whereas Protestantism offers the "negative complex term" that *rejects* both inaugural positions (Schleifer 25). Protestantism, in projecting Catholicism as both Jewish and pagan, instates itself as neither Jewish nor pagan. Although Protestant theology continues to rely on the Decalogue and indeed reemphasizes it (on the diagram, this vertical axis is "complementary" rather than "contrary"), it nonetheless institutes itself as the cancellation of all ceremony and imagery in order to implicate Catholicism as the vestigial afterlife of both classical paganism and Jewish legalism.

Put otherwise, Protestantism both "counts on" the Decalogue and *re*-counts it, retroactively reorganizing its import by renumbering its ten moments. Whereas both the Jewish and the Catholic tabulations of the Ten Commandments subordinate the prohibition against image-worship to the governing prohibition against polytheism ("Thou shalt have no other gods before Me"), the Protestant assault on Catholicism centered more on images than on multiple gods ("Thou shalt not make unto thee a graven image").[3] As Margaret Aston has meticulously documented, this shifting emphasis eventually led to a renumbering of the Decalogue itself, by granting the prohibition against images autonomy as its own commandment; what had been the first commandment for Catholics was divided into the first and second commandments for Calvinists, one directed against other gods and the other against graven images.[4] The accompanying material, which in the Jewish and Catholic tabulations applies to polytheism, would henceforth be attached exclusively to image worship. Thus in the proscription that "thou shalt not bow down unto *them*, nor serve *them*" (emphasis mine), the pronoun in the Reformed version now refers to "graven images" rather than

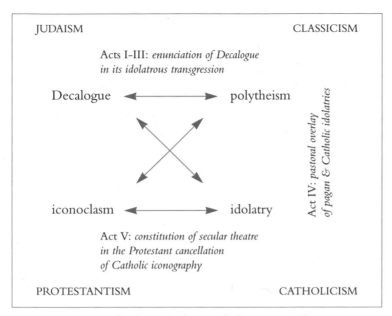

Figure 4. Historico-theological scheme of *The Winter's Tale*.

to "other gods before Me."[5] As one commentator on the commandment against idolatry wrote in 1549, "every man in England
knoweth praying to saints and kneeling before images is idolatry."[6]
Such a statement, seemingly self-evident, presumes that "kneeling"
applies to "images" and not to "other gods."

In my graph, then, the initial opposition concretizes idolatry
as polytheism, whereas the axis that doubles it reconceives of idolatry as the worship of graven images. A crucial switch point between
polytheism and image-worship is the gallery of Catholic saints. On
the one hand, according to the Protestant critique, the vertiginous
multiplicity of saints replicated within the Christian dispensation
the theogony of ancient paganism. Stephen Batman's *The Golden
Booke of the Leaden Goddes*, its title allusively reducing *The Golden
Legend* of Catholic hagiography to the Golden Calf of ancient idolatry, refuses to list all the saints due to their vast number: "Such a

number of preposterous Godds are to bee found: so Saincted &
made by the mayster Demon, that to write them al, woulde con-
tayne an huge volume" (Batman 29). Moreover, the worship of
relics imputed a dangerous divinity to the body and person of the
saint that too much resembled ancient cults of famous people. The
diatribes of Tertullian and Augustine against the Gentile gods could
easily be transferred to the calendar of Catholic saints, dialectically
turning the conflict between monotheism and polytheism into a
schism faulting Christianity itself.[7]

On the other hand, saints were intimately associated with *images*
of saints—the most common means of their medieval worship—
and by extension with visual representation per se. Nicholas Wyse
wrote in 1538 against "pilgrimages unto dead saints and images."[8] In
this telling phrase, "dead" modifies both "saints" and "images," indicating at once the rigor mortis of the relic and the immobile
muteness of manmade representations, the latter much emphasized
in the railings of the prophets against idolatry. The phrase effectively
assimilates the mediating role of the saint in Catholicism into a more
general theory of idolatrous representation. Whereas the first feature entails the saint as *representative* in a scenario of divine intercession, the second aspect emphasizes the saint as *representation* in the
cult of images. From the latter perspective, the danger of the saints
lies not so much in their supplementary relation to divine grace as in
their uncontrolled propagation through imagery, and thus their
insidious dissemination *of* imagery.[9] Sculpture rather than painting
posed the initial threat to the integrity of monotheism, since the
three-dimensional form, invested with a weightier physical presence
as well as transportable in processions and religious dramas, facilitated the belief that a human artefact could concretize divinity (Aston 391–401). The extension of the fear of "popish puppetry"—a
phrase that links Christ's vicar to the icons of the Catholic church—
to two-dimensional images entailed separating out the element of
visual representation per se from the act of localizing and embodying the divine in plastic form.

The fascination of both the saint and the statue, we could say,
stems from their dual status as *idol* and as *icon*. Although both words

are derived from Greek words for image or likeness, the word *ei-dolon* in Jewish and early Christian polemics tended to emphasize the representation of false gods (*OED* I.1), whereas *eikon* was used to refer to representations of all kinds, including but not limited to images of the true God. In order to facilitate the extension of the image prohibition to all religious visualizations, the hermeneutics of Protestant translation increasingly asserted the identity of "idol" and "icon" (Aston 398–99). The Protestant rendering of *eikon* as "idol" was not a mistranslation; it exacerbated a fundamental duplicity inherent in *eidolon*—divided between the signal and the sign, the index and the icon, elements that, mirroring each other, break down the opposition they establish. By polemically translating *eikon* as "idol," the Protestant writers multiplied the cases of possible idolatry while overshadowing the representative materiality of the idol with the representational ideality of the icon. So writes the author of the "Homily against perill of Idolatry," periodically read in every Elizabethan church:

> Although in common speech we use to call the likenesse or similitudes of men or other things images and not idols: yet the Scriptures use the sayd two words (idols and images) indifferently for one thing alway. They be words of divers tongues and sounds, but one in sense and signification in the Scriptures. (12)

Whereas the Decalogue's emphasis on the idol focuses on the danger of concretizing and localizing the divine in physical receptacles that would "represent" God in a political or hieratic sense, the Protestant inflection of the idol as icon generalizes and escalates the danger of mimetically visualizing God. In Exodus, the offensiveness of the artefact as idol lies more in its characteristics as a physical thing purporting to precipitate a piece of the transcendent Real in empirical reality; for the reformers, the hazard of the artefact as icon lay more in its status as a visualization of the divine.

Indeed, this distinction and rapprochement between "icon" and "idol" underwrites and complicates the relationship between the two terms of this chapter's subtitle, "Iconographies of Idolatry." In its current use, the word "iconography" covers the keying of images to a system of meanings as well as the encyclopedic or analytic study of the image-complexes so produced—the project of art and cultural history established by the Warburg school. An iconography of idolatry, then, would categorize and interpret the different verbal and visual images (the Golden Calf, for example) through which conceptions of idolatry have been formalized and transmitted. In the plural, the phrase "iconographies of idolatry" implies that those images fall into distinct clusters or discourses, in this case, the Jewish, Greco-Roman, Catholic, and Protestant ideologies of the religious image. The problem posed by an "iconography of idolatry," however, is the historical and conceptual derivation of the first term (iconography) from the object (idolatry) it purports to study. First, "iconography" describes not simply an approach *to* the Renaissance, but a crucial mode in which Renaissance scholars, artists, and poets understood their own modes of signification. The term "iconology," moreover (the Renaissance predecessor of "iconography"), emerges in this period precisely out of the humanistic study of the Gentile gods—in this sense, iconography as a discipline began as the iconography of idolatry. Vasari's introduction to *The Lives of the Arists* historically (though not conceptually) derives human art from idolatry (26); more expansive histories of ancient paganism introduce such mythographic works as Cartari's 1556 *Le Imagini degli dei de gli antichi* and Natalis Comes's *Mythologiae*. And, in the context of a reformed England, Stephen Batman's 1577 *The Golden Booke of the Leaden Goddes*, called by its modern editor Stephen Orgel "the first English iconography," is an exposé of imagery both Catholic and classical; it is an "iconography of idolatry" with the expressed goal of demonstrating that iconography is itself idolatrous.

The phrase "iconography of idolatry" effects the translation of idol into icon, transforming the material representative into a principle of mimetic representation by exploiting an ambiguity constitutive of the *eidolon* itself. The convergence of the terms "icon" and "idol" within Protestant hermeneutics implicates the very possibility of an iconography in the dubious resources of an idolatry that it also fundamentally mistranslates. It is this paradoxical relation between iconography and idolatry that informs *The Winter's Tale*'s relation to "the gods." On the one hand, *The Winter's Tale* mobilizes competing discourses (or "iconographies") of the image that are articulated across two clearly defined and dialectically produced axes: the Decalogue is to polytheism as Calvinist iconoclasm is to Catholic idolatry. Both Catholic and classical iconographies can only emerge in Shakespeare's text as conditioned and undercut by the Jewish and Protestant discourses that construe them as idolatrous; in the modern West, "the gods" only signify as the opposite of "one God" (*Adonai echad*). At the same time, insofar as "iconography" in the West is pagan iconography (and, secondarily, Catholic iconography, especially the iconography of the saints), the phrase "iconographies of idolatry" names the vertiginous implication of the discursive means of analysis in a material object that always exceeds the representational impulses that it mobilizes. In this sense, an iconography of idolatry could never be performed—or its "performance" should be understood in a dramatic sense, as the mise-en-scène of the ambiguity of the image as representative representation, rather than a successful anatomy of it.

'The Winter's Tale,' Acts I–III: Idolatry and Adultery

Acts I–III are dominated by the tragic fixation of Leontes as he rapidly succumbs, unaided by any Iago, to a jealous fantasy of his own concoction. The turning point in his destiny takes place during his notoriously difficult speech on affection, in which the meaning of the word shifts with fatal indeterminancy between the supposed licentiousness of Hermione (affection as lust) and the imputations of adultery taking shape as we listen to Leontes speak (affection as the jealous imagination). These lines constitute the first installment of what amounts to one long, interrupted soliloquy divided between the topic of jealousy (1.2.138–46) and the specter of the adulterous neighbor (1.2.192–98). As so often in Shakespeare, Leontes' extended speech takes place in a careful mise-en-scène of characters and positions, a staging that locates him in a social and familial scenario without, however, compromising the radical solitude of thought. The first segment, on affection, is supported by Leontes' address to his son as a mirror, simultaneously a confirming reflection of himself and ironic proof of his wife's fidelity and his own delusion, as Leontes observes, like Satan in Milton's garden, the maddening tableau of the hostess and her guest joined in intimate conversation. This apostrophe to affection breaks off at the arrival of Polixenes and Hermione, whose departure after a brief interchange leads to the next movement of Leontes' monologue, his reflections on the over-nighness of the neighbor.

Between the two segments of this double soliloquy, Leontes produces his jealous fantasy by crossing the Decalogue's injunctions against idolatry, adultery, and covetousness. By generating Leontes' jealousy out of the matrix of transgressions drafted by the Ten Commandments, Shakespeare typologically locates the ethos of Acts I–III in a stony world of law unredeemed by grace in order to establish the romance movement of the drama, which constitutes itself as the historical and generic renovation of the tragedy staged in the first half of the play. At the same time, the biblically endorsed coupling of idolatry and adultery sets up Hebrew monotheism, its iconoclastic tenets repeated by radical Protestantism, as an enduring contradiction to the typological dream of incarnational reconciliation that dominates the historial, spiritual, and artistic vision of the play.

Leontes' apostrophe to affection demonstrates the mechanisms of identification, projection, and reversal that determine the tragic mood and structure of Acts I–III. Distracted by the sight of Hermione and Polixenes nearby, Leontes interrupts his loving yet troubled chatter to his son Mamilius with a violent apostrophe:

> Affection! Thy intention stabs the centre:
> Thou dost make possible things not so held,
> Communicat'st with dreams;—how can this be?—
> With what's unreal thou coactive art,
> And fellow'st nothing: then 'tis very credent
> Thou may'st conjoin with something; and thou dost,
> (And that beyond commission) and I find it,
> (And that to the infection of my brains
> And hardening of my brows.) (1.2.138–46)

Speaking to his son while looking at Hermione and Polixenes, Leontes' conversation with Mamilius about their resemblance ("we are almost as like as eggs" 1.1.129–30) shifts into the soliloquy of a pained yet triumphant self-consciousness divided and created by the strength of its delusion. The speech enacts a symbolizing process whereby a difference inherent in mirroring likeness, already reflected against the image of a neighboring dyad, becomes internalized as the cut or fold of self-difference.[10] As critics have pointed out, the difficulty and the irony of the passage lie in the double valence of the word "affection"; the passage begins as a meditation on the errant desire of Hermione (affection = adulterous love), but it seems to end as both a realization of and a retroactive commentary on Leontes' own jealousy. In the first reading, desire finds an object to body forth its lustful fantasies; in the second gloss, jealousy confirms its obscene misgivings in the glances and gestures of social intercourse. This ambiguity has posed several difficulties to readers: the anatomy of affection seems to describe jealousy better than adultery, yet such a reading makes less sense in terms of the dramatic and psychological situation, in which Leontes is convincing himself of his wife's infidelity. If Leontes understands the deceptive operations of his own imagination, why does he so readily lend credence to his fears? On the other hand, if the passage indeed describes adulterous desire, why is the topic pursued in such contortedly ontological terms ("unreal," "something," "nothing") rather than ethical ones? I contend that the Hebrew Decalogue offers a legal armature, a grammar of motives, for understanding the reflexive transformation of adulterous affection into jealous infection, a mutation effected by a devious imagination conceived through the Decalogue as both idolatrous and covetous.

A reading of Leontes' jealousy as a species of idolatry has already been suggested by James Siemon's account of The Winter's Tale in Shakespearean Iconoclasm (289–92); Charles Frey's visual reading of the play's tragic movement isolates "four pulsations of madness," a quadrature of "statue scenes" in which Leontes "points an accusatory finger at a woman, centrally observed, and charges her with artifice and deceit" (95, 97–98). Finally, Lowell Gallagher has brilliantly demonstrated the dialectic between doubling idols and iconic images in the representational economy of *The Winter's Tale*. These astute readings serve as invitations to explore more intensively the scenario's specific verbal and logical manipulations of the Decalogue as the legal proof-text of idolatrous transgression. Leontes' analysis of affection as that which "fellowst nothing" and "communicat'st with dreams" resembles Protestant accounts of "inner idolatry" as the fount of all future errors of visualization; in the concise expression of William Perkins, "A thing feigned in the mind by imagination, is an idol" (cited Aston 453). Just as the idolator, prone to visualize the godhead, comes to materialize divinity in the things around him, "affection" in this passage grants reality to its erotic fantasies by con-firming and real-izing them in the world.

In the Decalogue, the injunctions against idolatry and adultery are metaphorically and conceptually linked. In the prophetic and rabbinic traditions that conceive the relationship between God and Israel as one of marriage, the Decalogue institutes a *ketuba* or marriage contract, in which the injunction against idolatry legislates that marriage as a monogamous one. It is within this marital framework that the God who punishes idolaters appears as "a jealous God"; as the great medieval commentator Moses Maimonides argued, "A Jew who worships another god is like a spouse willfully engaging in adultery; the betrayed partner—God—is justified in His anger" (paraphrased Feuer 33). The motif of Israel's marriage to God underwrites the alignment of the second commandment of the first tablet (against idolatry) with the second commandment of the second tablet ("Thou shalt not commit adultery") (Goldman 80). Just as the idolator takes on a second and illegitimate god, the adulterer takes on a second and illegitmate lover. Thus Ezekiel figures the idolatrous Israel as an "adulterous wife, / Who under her husband takes strangers" (16:32), and the Book of Hosea takes the prophet's God-commanded marriage to a prostitute as a metaphor for God's relation to idolatrous Israel: "Go, take to yourself a wife of harlotry and have children of harlotry, for the land commits great harlotry by forsaking the Lord" (Hos. 1:2). Calvin, writing in the tradition of the reforming prophets centuries later, referred to "that vilest species of adultery, the worship of images" (cited Aston 468).

In *The Winter's Tale*, the initial reading of "affection" as lust echoes the biblical logic that links idolatry and adultery—hence the tortuously ontological terms of Leontes' analysis. In this first gloss, Hermione's desire, "coactive" "with what's unreal," comes to "co-join with something" insofar as an illicit fantasy ("what's unreal") is obscenely consummated in action ("co-joins with something"). The distinct verbal parallel between "coactive" and "co-join" at once alludes to and contaminates the ideal of marital union, insofar as the "co-joining" names an adulterous liaison at the same moment that it evokes the sacramental "joining" of husband and wife in St. Paul (Eph. 5:31).[11] Moreover, the movement of the passage as a whole works to "co-join" or adulterate the apparent contrast between the "unreal" and the "something," since the "something" pursued by illicit desire presents the consummation rather than the opposite of the "unreal" of fantasy. Whereas God creates something out of nothing (the doctrine of creation *ex nihilo*), the false images of the idolator and the false love of the adulterer create nothing out of something by rendering reality itself into a vain fiction, a web of deceptions and betrayals.[12]

If the apostrophe to affection displays adultery as a form of idolatry, the internalization of af-fection as in-fection ("the infection of my brains / And hardening of my brow") reveals the jealous imputation of adultery as itself a form of idolatry. The ambivalence of the passage concerning the referent of "affection" implies an identificatory reflexivity between adultery and jealousy, a reflexivity that informs, for example, Leontes' first accusation of Hermione in her closet:

> *Hermione*: You, my lord,
> Do but mistake.
> *Leontes*: You have mistook, my lady,
> Polixenes for Leontes. (2.1.80–82)

Hermione generously excuses Leontes' accusation as an interpretive error, a visual "mistake"—as an idolator might mistake an image for the thing it represents. Leontes turns his jealousy into her adultery by taking "mistaking" not as a hermeneutic error of *representation* but as a problem of false *representatives*, a mis-taking or substituting of one person for another. The idolatrous "mistakes" of both adultery and jealousy are constructed here as inversions of each other, projecting the adulterer as a polygamous polytheist and the jealous spouse as a promiscuous worshipper of false images.

What coordinates and metastases are mapped by this reconfiguration of adultery into jealousy, both in the affection passage and in the tragic movement of Acts I–III? According to Freud, male delusional jealousy is produced by a precise grammatical operation on an initial expression of homosexual desire, "I (a man) *love him* (a man)," a sentence revised under repression into "It is not *I* who love the man—*she* loves him" (*SE* XII: 64). Such a formulation is clearly relevant to the homosocial economy of *The Winter's Tale*, in which Leontes' self-mirroring love of Polixenes (they were like two "twinn'd lambs," 1.2.67) is shatteringly reorganized into hate through its displacement onto Hermione. The disastrous difference represented by the wife, however, already inhabits the union of two figured in Camillo's early lyrical description of the two kings:

> Sicilia cannot show himself over-kind to Bohemia. They were trained together in their childhoods, and there rooted betwixt them then such an affection which cannot help but branch now. (I.1.21–23)

The pastoral image of the tree vigorously branching upwards and outwards from its strong roots already carries the threat of rivalrous division—of branching *apart*—within its promise of brotherly love (I.1.22–23).[13] Here, the play's first utterance of the word "affection" describes a homoerotic liking of likes which will later be violently rearticulated as the woman's adultery on the one hand and the husband's jealousy on the other. To follow the Freudian logic, the action of the play takes an initial statement, "I, Leontes, like and am like Polixenes," in order to dramatically redistribute and affectively reverse it in the secondary fantasy, "It is Hermione, not I, who loves Polixenes—therefore I hate them both."

Through its particular calculation of the Decalogue, *The Winter's Tale* provides an analogous syntactic diagnosis of pathological jealousy. Crucial here is the figure of the adulterer as *bad neighbor*, as the one who, in the language of the tenth commandment, covets his neighbor's house and wife. The commandment against covetousness is unique in the Decalogue for forbidding an internal state rather than an action; as such, this final, consummate commandment separates out desire or, in Leontes' term, "affection," as the origin of the other transgressions (Goldman 187–88). And, like the injunction against idolatry, the commandment attempts to reticulate the intersubjective dimension (neighbor to neighbor, husband to wife) with the order of material things (the idols manifested by the neighbor's house and goods).

The "next-to-ness" of metonymy is crucial to the delimiting of desire in the tenth commandment; just as the neighbor is defined as the one who lives "next to" or "near" the ethical subject, the metonymic criterion of contiguity helps generate the potentially infinite list of household goods and chattel whose coveting is prohibited. In the architecture of affection drafted by the Decalogue as a whole, the plural *metonymies of desire* encountered in the tenth commandment are opposed to the singular *metaphor of love* instituted by the first commandment's declaration of the one God, "I am the Lord thy God."[14] So too, in the Decalogue conceived as a marriage contract, the singularity of God as a primal metaphor opposes the metonymic pluralities of both idolatry (the second commandment) and the objects of coveting (the tenth commandment).

In the resumption of his musings after the interchange with Hermione and Polixenes, Leontes pointedly echoes the language of the Decalogue in his evocation of adultery as a crime of and against the neighbor:

> And many a man there is (even at this present,
> Now, while I speak this) holds his wife by th'arm,
> That little thinks she has been sluic'd in 's absence
> And his pond fish'd by his *next neighbour*, by
> Sir Smile, his *neighbour*, nay, there's comfort in't,
> Whiles other men have gates, and those gates open'd,
> As mine, against their wills. (1.2.192–98, emphasis mine)

The repetition of the word "neighbour" implicates the imagining of adultery within the proscription of covetousness. The "next-to-ness" of the other ("his next neighbour" in Leontes' expression) implicates the rival in the metonymization of desire that the tenth commandment attempts to regulate. Thus later in the play, we are told that the Shepherd's estate has grown "beyond the imagination of his neighbours" (4.2.40–41), a phrase that tellingly binds the key words of "imagination" and the "neighbour" through the mediating image of coveted goods. In Leontes' evocation of the bad neighbor, jealousy is constituted as a *coveting in reverse*, an imputation of desire to the rivalrous other. In both the Decalogue of *The Winter's Tale* and Freud's analysis of delusion, the coordinates of the fantasy of jealousy are ternary, involving not simply a reversal of terms (from love to hate; from coveting of to coveted by) but also a projection that redistributes them. Thus Leontes' fantasy of jealousy converts the coveting *of* the neighbor's wife into the coveting of one's wife *by* the neighbor. The emphasis, that is, shifts from the neighbor's wife as the object of forbidden desire to the figure of the neighbor himself as desiring.

Furthermore, through the syntactic transformations of fantasy, not only does jealousy emerge as the projection of the neighbor's illicit desire, but in the new scenario, through the crossing of adultery and covetousness the adulterous wife surfaces as the bearer of an overwhelming enjoyment; if covetousness is the crime of and against the neighbor, 'adultery is traditionally the crime of the wife against the husband.[15] In the structure of jealousy, the specter of the wife's dangerously proximate enjoyment precipitates out of the metonymic chain of coveted objects as an immobile, invasive quantity, an infecting affect. Leontes ragefully cries out to Hermione, "O thou thing" (2.1.82), an expression whose very inarticulateness serves to index the scandalous character of the adulteress's obscene enjoyment, an enjoyment that congeals not as an object of desire and exchange but as a nonsignified thing of feminine *jouissance* swelling up at the branching divide of narcissistic rivalry.[16] Leontes' infantile invective registers the materialization of the idol at the intersection of covetousness and adultery.

In the infamously difficult passage on affection, I would argue that this reverse identification with the covetous neighbor underwrites the reflexive relation between adultery and jealousy. If we return to the ontological contortions of Leontes' speech, moreover, we can reconceive the "something" with which affection co-joins not simply as that empirical reality wherein both adulterous desire and jealous delusion find false confirmation, but as the thingly element within idolatrous representation that gives fantasy its particular charge and persistence. This something neither opposes nor consummates fantasy but inhabits it, constellating what Freud calls a psychic reality whose coordinates repetitively dictate the behavior of the subject. As Leontes says to Hermione, "Your actions are my dreams" (3.2.83), an acknowledgment of the effects of fantasy within the texture of the everyday.

The first installment of Leontes' soliloquy presents the two faces of "affection" as aspects of idolatry, linking the prohibition against adultery on the second tablet to its counterpart on the first tablet. When Leontes resumes his reflections, the vector of adultery now points to the figure of the neighbor, the obligations to whom are spelled out on the second tablet. One result of Leontes' jealousy so configured is to demote Polixenes from the position of the Friend, imagined in a narcissistic economy of Edenic similitude, to that of the Neighbor, taken now as the merely proximate fellow man, neither kin nor kind, whose needs and interests, irritatingly present, come forward precisely insofar as they fail to mirror or advance one's own. Polixenes describes the face of Leontes as he had seen it just after the affection speech:

> The king hath on him such a countenance
> As he had lost some province, and a region
> Lov'd as he loves himself. (1.2.368–70)

Polixenes' echo here of the biblical injunction to love thy neighbor as thyself registers his own fall in the eyes of Leontes from Friend to Neighbor, the figure of sheer contiguity who mobilizes the vicious cycle of covetousness. The lines measure loss ("As he had *lost* some province") in terms not of the disappearance of a specific object, but rather of the dissolution of a certain relationship; what is lost or *perdita* in the play is the mirroring on which both friendship and good-neighborliness is founded, namely, the possibility of loving the other as oneself. The Bad Neighbor emerges here as the friend-turned-stranger, the splintered, piercing remnant of a shattered specularity.

If the tragic *mythos* of Acts I–III structurally depends on the breaking of biblical commandments, how do we account for the pagan setting of the play's Sicily, especially the episode of the oracle, the play's most vocal message from—and therefore about—*elohim aherim*? G. Wilson Knight writes of Act III's Apollo that he "is as mysterious and awful as Wordsworth's gigantic mountain-presences; he is both the Greek Apollo and the Hebraic Jehovah" (23). Knight alludes here to the sublime unintelligibility of God's voice at Sinai: "And all the people perceived the thunderings, and the lightnings, and the voice of the horn, and the mountain smoking; and when the people saw it, they trembled, and stood afar off" (Ex. 20:18). Cleomenes may echo this passage in his description of the oracle's overpowering effect: "But of all, the burst / And the ear-deaf'ning voice o' th'Oracle, / Kin to Jove's thunder, so surpris'd my sense, / That I was nothing" (3.1.8–11). There remains, however, a felt disparity between the sound of the oracle and its pedestrian content: "Hermione is chaste; Polixenes blameless; Camillo a true subject; Leontes a jealous tyrant; his innocent babe truly begotten. . . . " (3.2.132–34). The oracle of *The Winter's Tale* reads like a cliché of the pagan, the profoundly riddling prophesies of Sophocles reduced to a plain-speaking moral ledger. At the same time, we might say that in the dialectic of the Western tradition, the conventions of pagan culture are *rendered as cliché* precisely by the trauma of monotheism. Thus, while I agree with Knight's discernment of a "Hebraic" mood and structure determining the pagan fiction of Acts I–III, I would insist that the relation of "Jove" and "Jehovah," the pagan and the Jewish, is not one of proto-Romantic complementarity resolvable in the synthesis of a symbol. In the dialectic of the West, polytheism conceived as a distinct theology or worldview is doubly an aftereffect rather than a ground of monotheism. First, in the Hebrew Bible, idolatry, the contaminatingly contiguous sin of the neighbor and the brother (recall that Aaron, Moses' brother, instigates the building of the Golden Calf) is most scandalous when practiced within the gates of the Jewish household and community, its procedures made visible as idolatrous precisely by the institution of monotheism that outlaws it; idolatry is in this sense an effect of the law that forbids it. And second, the plurality of paganism, which empirically pre-exists monotheism, is nonetheless signified as "pagan" by the single stroke of monotheism that emerges against a ground both articulated and forever discounted by its mark. In *The Winter's Tale*, the sublime *sound* of the oracle is to its mundane *message* as the giving of the law at Sinai is to making of the Golden Calf that violates the new injunction. That is, the multiple significations of polytheism appear as the retroactive products of the unpronounceable name of monotheism.

In Acts I–III, the Decalogue functions as a "constitution," in the physiological and legal senses—as, that is, a disposition or biology laying out certain ethical and narrative trajectories, and a set of terse injunctions subject to decomposition and recomposition during crisis.[17] Leontes, as both the critic and the performer of idolatry—as both idolator and idolatry's iconographer—may derive some of his stature and pathos from the great Jewish kings. Like Jonathan's love for David, the love of Polixenes "to [him] was wonderful, passing the love of women" (*Oxford Bible* II Sam. 1:26). And, like David, Bathsheba, and Uriah, Leontes finds himself in a compromising love triangle that threatens to break all the laws (in the case of Leontes, idolatrous jealousy leads to attempted murder, false witness, and blasphemy). Acts I–III achieve a Hebraicizing of classical tragedy—the grafting of an Old Testament ethos onto a Hellenistic setting and form. Perhaps Shakespeare eschews any Iago in his depiction of Leontes' jealousy in order to remove all traces of the Christian morality play, without, however, returning to a classical conception of fate. In *The Winter's Tale*, jealousy is neither the work of a Fury nor the unholy offering of a tempter, but rather takes shape between an absolutely unpersonified Law and its fatally free transgression, in the dreadful solitude of a soliloquy voiced at the heart of a social and domestic scene.

Act IV: The Scattered Flowers of Country Paganism

Casting Perdita as Flora, her young lover Florizel grandly describes the sheep-shearing festival as "a meeting of the petty gods" (4.4.4), and goes on to read the *Metamorphoses* as a tale of pastoral masking: "The gods themselves, / Humbling their deities to love, have taken / The shapes of beasts upon them" (4.4.25–27). Florizel's pastoral readings of mythology emphasize not the natural settings and seasonal etiologies of the *Metamorphoses*, but rather the Ovidian delight in deception and masking; in the argument of Florizel's allusion, the metamorphosed gods are to the seduced mortals as the courtier in shepherd's clothing is to the courted peasant girl. In Florizel's handling, the gods represent not a higher providential plane of truth in a mystic allegory of nature, but a "petty" principle of fiction and theatricality carried out in the *sermo humilis* of pastoral. We characterized the paganism of Acts I–III as bordering on cliché, the classical gods and rites reduced to "mere" literary convention through the defining contrast with the monotheistic revolution. Here we again meet the literary conventionality of paganism, not, however, in the form of a depleted and painfully misunderstood plot device, but as a vehicle for poetic allusion and theatrical masquerade. It is no accident that the highly conventional discourse of pastoral, with its fondness for disguise and witty references, remained one of the most hospitable literary asylums for the exiled gods through the end of the Renaissance. The shift from the high classical form of tragedy to the lower, later, form of pastoral casts the sheep-shearing festival as a generic and historical intermezzo, a festive interlude of iconographic pageantry that separates and mediates between the Old Testament Sicily of Acts I–III and its romance renovation in Act V. If, as Roy Battenhouse has suggested, *The Winter's Tale* forms a "diptych" modeled on the Bible, "with its two-phased story of the logic of grace within history and time"

("Theme and Structure" 137), Act IV forms the gilded frame dividing the two halves and thus supporting the set of correspondences that link them.[18]

Taking a hermeneutic cue from Florizel's treatment of the gods as erotic fictions should serve as an antidote against any bluntly archetypal or hermetic reading of seasonal mythology in *The Winter's Tale*. It is not enough, however, to emphasize the "literariness" of the pagan references over their folkloric efficacy, nor even to derive that literariness from the monotheistic encounter, as I did in the last section. Instead, we need to trace both the cancellation and the survival of paganism in the Christian discourses that historically mark the Renaissance understanding of idolatry. If Acts I–III dramatize the signification of polytheism as an aftereffect of monotheism, activating the upper level of our initial diagram, the pastoral world of Act IV takes paganism as its initial starting point, insofar as the play's first elaborate allusions and enactments of Ovidian myth are here played out. At the same time, the Bohemian scene is also distinguished by a rustic English paganism, the country remnants of Catholic syncretism, which overlay and modernize the ancient setting, preserving the ritual dimensions of classical paganism left over from their sublimation into the language of literature as a secular scripture. Finally, the play's topical references to Puritanism abruptly bring this rustic, "garden-variety" Catholicism up against its modern abrogation in the crisis of the Reformation.

Throughout Act IV, the pastoral language of flowers provides the shared discourse in which these different iconographies of idolatry are gathered up and set against each other. Perdita's famous allusion to Proserpina initiates a sequence of pagan, Catholic, and Protestant associations that sample the ambivalent strata of Bohemia's relationship to the gods:

> Perdita: Now, my fair'st friend, [*to Florizel*]
> I would I had some flowers o' th' spring, that might
> Become your time of day; and yours, and yours,
> [*To Mopsa and the other girls*]
> That wear upon your virgin branches yet
> Your maidenheads growing; O Proserpina,

> For the flowers now that, frighted, thou let'st fall
> From Dis's waggon! daffodils,
> That come before the swallow dares, and take
> The winds of March with beauty; violets, dim,
> But sweeter than the lids of Juno's eyes
> Or Cytherea's breath; pale primroses,
> That die unmarried, ere they can behold
> Bright Phoebus in his strength (a malady
> Most incident to maids); bold oxlips and
> The crown imperial; lilies of all kinds,
> The flower-de-luce being one. O these I lack,
> To make you garlands of; and my sweet friend,
> To strew him o'er and o'er!
> *Florizel*: What, like a corpse?
> *Perdita*: No, like a bank, for love to lie and play on;
> Not like a corpse; or, if—not to be buried,
> But quick, and in mine arms. Come, take your flowers:
> Methinks I play as I have seen them do
> In Whitsun pastorals; sure this robe of mine
> Does change my disposition. (4.4.112–34)

As Northrop Frye and others have amply demonstrated, the reference to Proserpina renders explicit the play's structuring reliance on this ancient winter's tale of a mother's stony mourning for a daughter first lost then found (Frye 138).[19] The pagan world of gods and goddesses is, however, in Frye's term, "displaced" through the limited narrative rationalizations of romance. The use of the Demeter-Proserpina myth here borders on the Aristotelian sense of "mythos" as plot, a model or primal scene whose formal properties rather than hermetic import are exploited by the action of the play.

Note, however, that Perdita's allusion to the Proserpina myth elicits negative as well as positive parallels between Shakespeare's play and the ancient tale. The dominant theme of the myth brought forward in Perdita's reference is the mourning for the loss of virginity, a de-floration emblematized by the scattered flowers of Proserpina's tossed bouquet. Perdita, however, contrasts her own condition with Proserpina's by using the story to mourn not defloration, but *defloration's lack*: "O these I lack," she laments, a virgin still, "to make you garlands of." The deflection of the myth calls attention to the fact that the contrast between Sicily and Bohemia is not that of winter to spring but, "the year growing ancient" (4.4.79), of winter to "middle summer" (4.4.107). If the chronology of the play has "slid o'er sixteen years," the seasonal calendar of *The Winter's Tale* has managed to skip spring entirely, moving into the period of sheepshearing, and of rosemary and rue, the season, that is, of remembering, including the remembering of pagan myth.

Through its negation, the original myth's mourning for lost virginity is intensified and redirected into a nostalgia for the classical, the pagan springtime of the West. Borrowing and extending Frye's reference to displacement, I would suggest that through such transformations, Shakespeare "displaces" or metamorphoses *mythology* into *mythopoetics*, that is, into a specifically literary "learned" discourse whose primary function is to establish Shakespeare's text within the literary tradition of the classical poets. Such a displacement of myth into mythopoetics does not render Shakespeare's references to classical myth any less serious or any less structuring; instead, it determines that the stakes of allusion are carried out within the poetic dynamics of the literary tradition—indeed, that the stakes of such allusions are precisely to constitute that tradition *as literary*. (Not accidentally, this passage counts as one of the play's most cited poetic set pieces.) It is not, then, that the archetypal theme of seasonal revival has been undercut, debunked, or ironized, but rather that its energy has been displaced onto the cycles of literary transmission itself, in order to help formalize and maintain them.[20] The tale of Proserpina, like that of Pygmalion, is quintessentially a story of renaissance. Through such allusions to Proserpina, paganism flourishes again as the gathered flowers of literature, conceived as the secular negation and sublation of Christian writing that allows the *translatio* of ancient myth into modern poetry.

Yet the classical reference and attendant self-canonizing gesture does not exhaust the passage. Perdita's floral catalogue, though sprinkled with further classical allusions (Juno, Cytherea) is not, as we might expect, an especially Ovidian bouquet; although the motif of the catalogue is likely derived from the account of Proserpina in Ovid's *Fasti*, in the bouquet itself we find "daffodil" where we might have heard "Narcissus," and the Anglo-Saxon oxlip rather than the hyacinth or the anemone, while both the crown imperial and the flower-de-luce suggest an international but no more classical context. Indeed, the provenance of Perdita's imagined bouquet is closer to Spenser and to the Renaissance herbals than to Virgil or Ovid, sources that suggest the native Englishness of this literary landscape.[21] Furthermore, this contemporary countryside is a residually Catholic one, harboring its own version of paganism.[22] As John Guillory has argued, Perdita's classicizing reference to Proserpina's bouquet swirls into a barely masked figuration of Florizel as a garlanded maypole, that rustic fertility symbol erected under the purview of a benign Catholicism: "O these I lack, / *To make you garlands of*; and my sweet friend, / *To strew him o'er and o'er*."[23] This surging image of the maypole is exposed and confirmed in the reference to "Whitsun pastorals" that closes Perdita's speech; as the Arden note points out, the festivities surrounding the springtime feast of Pentecost included "May-games" as well as Robin Hood plays (97n). In her desire to gather and weave the scattered flowers of Proserpina into the entwining garlands of May Day, Perdita's speech retraces the brilliant synthesis of monotheism and paganism forged by the popular customs of the Church. So too, the braiding of literary and extraliterary discourses, of classical flowers and country weeds, distinguishes the Shakespearean contribution more than mythopoesis alone in the poetic transactions and retroactions of the canon. In Act IV Shakespeare uses the constitutive dialogue within pastoral between "hard" and "soft" modes of representation in order to counterpoint an idealized, hyperliterary classical paganism against "realistic" moments of Catholic anachronism in a singing contest held between two different iconographies of idolatry.[24] These two strands represent the double senses of "pagan," which indicates not only the classical world of gods and goddesses but also the rustic religion of the *pagani*, villagers or countrymen—both the learned *Fasti* of Ovid and the popular feasts of the rural hamlets.

For the maypole, we could say, is the Golden Calf of an indigenous agricultural idolatry, its phallic staff insistently raised in response to Protestant enforcements of Sabbath rest. Christopher Hill reports the response of the Earl of Nottingham when a maypole bearing King James I's coat of arms was pulled down: "If it had the picture of any saint . . . I should mislike it as much as any; but the arms of his majesty, or any other arms of noblemen or gentlemen, I do not see but that it is lowable" (Hill 185). The word "saint" stands in here for Catholic idolatries in general; the sight of a maypole topped by a saint bore home to this Protestant the lasting affinities between Catholic visual practices and an unregenerate local heathenism. And, indeed, this Protestant response is itself registered in Perdita's withdrawal in the name of Whitsuntide from the verbal splendor and erotic energy of her own glorious conceit. When she says, "Come, take your flowers: / Methinks I play as I have seen them do / In Whitsun pastorals," the anachronism serves to distance Perdita from the rituals and religious dramas traditionally performed around Pentecost even as it draws together Catholic and pagan rites.[25] In rejecting these Catholic pastorals, Perdita is playing the iconoclast, virtuously retiring from the idolatrous implications of her iconographic virtuosity. In this, she directs the message of her critique of grafting, also a rejection of art, against those festive practices that had bound for centuries the ancient rites of agriculture to the holy days of the Catholic year. In the world-historical calendar drafted by the shifting mood and setting of the play, winter is the season of transgressed commandments, while spring is the imaginary moment of a double pagan plenitude remembered from the late summer of their passing into Protestantism. Rather than equating "Perdita" with "Spring" in a symbolic renewal of the classical archetype, the play mourns the fact that Spring itself is *perdita*, insofar as the pagan world of mythic correspondences, what we could call the "springtime of the West," is lost as such to the current regime of representation, which substitutes the allegorical distancing of mythography for the seductive resonances of mythology.

The Ovidian references wound into the pagan costume of Perdita situate her in the iconographic tradition of the pagan *nympha*

that Aby Warburg elaborated throughout his career, beginning with
his early studies of Botticelli's mythological paintings and ending
with "Mnemosyne," his massive, unfinished archive of imagery devoted to representations of the female figure in motion. In his 1893
work on Botticelli, Warburg first analyzed the depiction of women
in graceful movement, the dance of their bodies captured in still
images by the motif of "accessories in motion" (*ausserlich bewegten
Beiwerks*): the sway of hair, garments, ribbons, or garlands in response to the turns and steps of the body and the flow of an often
personified breeze (*Gesammelte Schriften* I: 5). Warburg's essay on
Botticelli, which definitively identified the cluster of figures at the
right-hand side of the *Primavera* as the story of Flora, traces the
theme of pastoral rape in Ovidian and neo-Ovidian poetry, and
then goes on to link the figure of the *nympha* in flight to the frantic
dance of maddened Maenads (33–37). Between these two sets of
associations, the *nympha* came to embody for Warburg the potential
violence of paganism, in which women figure alternately as the object of rape in myths of seasonal transformation (Daphne, Flora,
Persephone), and as Dionysian head-hunters who end male virility
or poetic expression with the cut of decapitation (the Orphic Maenads, the Bacchae). In one fragment, Warburg makes an associative
list of such *nymphae*:

> On headhunting: Judith, Salome, maenad, via the Nymph as a
> bringer of fruit, Fortuna, the Hora of Autumn, to the server of water
> at the well, Rachel at the well, the fire-fighter at the Borgo fire. (cited
> Gombrich, *Aby Warburg* 287)

The switch-point between the themes of decapitation and defloration—the loss of heads and maidenheads—is the basket of fruit,
whether carried by seasonal allegories, falling from the laps of maid-
ens pursued by gods, or filled with the decapitated spoils of sexual
conquest by the Judiths and Salomes of a classicized repertoire of
biblical iconography. Such nascent bits of still life deposit the objects of natural history within the narrative *istoria*, sedimenting the
reified attributes of an iconographic *Nachleben* within the symbolic
unfolding of the Renaissance *mythoi* of seasonal or spiritual rebirth.[26]

Shakespeare's Perdita clearly activates the cluster of icons derived from stories of pastoral rape; explicitly affiliated with Flora
and Proserpina, Perdita is emblematized by the collection of real
and imagined flowers that she presents with such iconographic,
mythographic, and herbalogical finesse to the guests at the sheep-
shearing festival. Moreover, the dialogue that follows her floral presentation addresses the paradox of stillness-in-movement, the representational problem at once classically solved and baroquely exacerbated by Warburg's "accessories in motion." Perdita, prettily
presenting her mythopoetic speech as a pastoral gift to her lover,
becomes herself a fixed and transfixing icon in the rapt gaze of
Florizel:

> What you do,
> Still betters what is done. When you speak, sweet,
> I'd have you do it for ever: when you sing,
> I'd have you buy and sell so, so give alms,
> Pray so, and, for the ord'ring your affairs,
> To sing them too: when you do dance, I wish you
> A wave o' th' sea, that you might ever do
> Nothing but that, move still, still so,
> And own no other function. Each your doing,
> So singular in each particular,
> Crowns what you are doing, in the present deeds,
> That all your acts are queens. (4.4.135–46)

James Siemon detects a "possible tyrannical aspect to the act of shaping that paradoxical stillness" (293); put otherwise, Florizel "idol-
izes" Perdita, distilling from her pagan discourse the very fact of
imaging. In the process, a speech about *idols* (Perdita on the flowers
of myth) comes to be voiced by a living *icon*, a spectacle of feminine grace who, "moving still, still so," anticipates the living statue of
the play's final scene. This moment consummates Florizel's initial
reading of paganism as a form of masquerade, insofar as the icon of
Perdita embodies pure theatricality, projecting drama as an art of
the moving image. Here theater and idolatry coincide not through
the allusive reenactment of the Proserpina plot or mythos (their
symbolic signification), but rather through their shared visual

medium as *opsis*, their imaginary effect and real presence in a baroquely Renaissance dance.

The image of Perdita as a wave of the sea further transmutes
into a figure of Perdita as reflective surface in the Shepherd's lyric
description of Florizel's love: "for never gaz'd the moon / Upon
the water as he'll stand and read / As 'twere my daughter's eyes"
(4.4.174–76). In this image of nature's imaging, the moon above the
water looks at the reflection of its own reflected light. Between the
two passages, the dancing of Perdita becomes the glancing of light
upon water; in the process, the captivating shimmer of pure *reflectivity* dazzlingly radiates from the horizon line of self-conscious *reflexivity* inscribed by the figure of the moon gazing at itself. One
rabbinic gloss reads the injunction against representing anything
"that is in the water" to include reflected images (Goldman 140);
following a similar logic, the pair of watery comparisons twice re-
fracts the pagan content of Perdita's language (a speech about the
gentile gods), yielding up idolatry as iconicity. Perdita is first projected as an emblem of the theatrical image—the dance of the
wave—and then sublimated into an abyssal figure whose endless
mirroring exhausts its own mimetic production: the reflected image
of borrowed light in brightened water.

The scene's transformation of Perdita from a poet of paganism
into a spec(tac)ular icon is brought short by the rage of Polixenes,
who angrily rejects her as a "fresh piece / Of excellent witchcraft"
(4.4.422–23). The discourse of witchcraft employed intermittently
throughout the play points to the diabolical flip side and pagan
background of Florizel's act of erotic idolization. Before the Calvinists divided and renumbered the commandment against idolatry,
pastors took the injunction primarily as a prohibition against superstition and witchcraft (Aston 409–10). Whereas within Catholicism the saint and the witch present opposed emblems of good and
evil, from the perspective of the reformers, their tricks and miracles belong to the same basic iconography of idolatry (see Shakespeare's own Joan of Arc). The winter's tale told by Mamilius relies
on the conventions of "sprites and goblins" (2.1.26), the Halloween
harbingers of All Saints' Day; Shakespeare's identification of his play

with Mamilius's tale implicates the drama in the popular discourse of a demonized Catholicism.

Polixenes' phrase violently shatters the icon of beauty into an idol of superstition, a "piece," fetish, or thing of uncanny power. Cast as a picture that "moves still, still so" and as a "piece of excellent witchcraft," Perdita, like the Catholic saints debunked by the Reformation, is both icon and idol, both pure image and material relic, a "most peerless piece of earth" (5.1.94). Even Perdita's name registers her Cordelia-like status as a mute *infans* cast off by the paternal order: "Perdita" means, in Antigonus's etymological gloss, "poor thing, condemn'd to loss" (2.3.191).[27] Indeed, the very name "Antigonus," his fate tied to the infant he exposes, must remind a modern reader of "Antigone," Cordelia's Greek sister and Perdita's distant cousin. In the lost-and-found economy of *The Winter's Tale*, Paulina will not restore the calumnied and mortified Hermione until Perdita, "that which is lost" (3.2.135), is recovered. Yet the finding of Perdita is first only a refinding, and second a refinding of the object as lost. That is, the loss of Perdita is not the initiating trauma in a tragic chain of events, but rather one episode in a series of losses (lost childhood, lost trust, lost time). Consequently, the finding of Perdita cannot redeem the entire sequence; "Perdita" remains "Perdita" at the play's end. The shared "thingness" of Perdita and Hermione, marking a leaden immobility, a fascinating fixation within the displacements of exchange, relentlessly records the tragic losses sustained by the play's comic economy. Just as the Shepherd forgets about his lost sheep ("Let my sheep go," he tells his son, 3.3.124), so *The Winter's Tale* lets Mamilius and Antigonus go as poor things condemned to loss, the persistent remainders of the comic resolution. The figure of the lost sheep pinpoints a hollowed space of nonrecuperable loss within pastoral— the object of melancholia rather than mourning—which Shakespeare's play activates, weaving its text *ex nihilo*, around an inherited nothing.[28]

The allusive rhythm of Perdita's Proserpina speech and its associative ripples play out the dialectic of idolatry set into motion by the transgressions of Acts I–III. In the suggestive waves of the passage each moment is already conditioned by the next. The rustic contemporaneity infusing the scene's classical pastoralism already presses the evocation of paganism into a nostalgia for it, dissolving idol into idyll through the reflected light of the theatrical icon. So too, the festive mood of an ageless English countryside is insistently shadowed and historicized by its Protestant abrogation, its definitive sheep-shearing. Even the pastoralizing conflation of Catholicism with paganism implies the historical position of reform; this is *not* the vision of Catholic worship we would meet in an Italian or French work of the period. The shifting emphases within Perdita's speech and their vicissitudes in the props and imagery of the scene surrounding her, however, are as nothing compared to the governing opposition between the two settings of the play. The pagan iconographies of Act IV constitute a pastoral counter-world to the Sicily of Acts I–III, the site of those sublime transgressions that bring into signification this romantic landscape.

Act V: Versions of Pygmalion

The statue scene that ends *The Winter's Tale* and epitomizes its special power is also the site of the play's most protracted and involved meditation on idolatry. Crucial here is Shakespeare's deployment of the Pygmalion myth, which unfolds in two distinct hermeneutic traditions: on the one hand, it tells a story of artistic rebirth, of cultural renaissance, and on the other, it recounts a parable of idolatry that critiques the resurrectional and incarnational metaphors informing "the Renaissance" as a historical fiction. *The Winter's Tale* crosses these two versions of Pygmalion. The dominant trajectory of the play celebrates the softening of stone into life; in the overlapping typological registers of the play, the law makes way for grace, tragedy is supplanted by romance, and classical myth lives again in Renaissance art. Yet the play's coding of Paulina's chapel-gallery as the reliquary of both pagan and Catholic traces of idolatry mobilizes the second reading of Pygmalion, a trajectory that does not subordinate Judaism to Christianity in the classic typological sequence, but rather opposes iconoclasm—both Jewish and Protestant—to idolatry—both Catholic and pagan. Although, as G. Wilson Knight has argued, the final scene brilliantly overlays Christian and pagan myths, I would insist that its language and visual staging at once marks and distances the "Christianity" of the scene as Catholic. The idolatrous ambience of the Church serves to heighten the sense of mystery and magic; when this supernaturalism is finally naturalized, however, the play does not dissipate its energy so much as surreptitiously transport it onto the dramatic image itself. So too, the final act not only corrects Act I–III's world of broken laws with the grace of the resurrected Hermione, it also plays the iconoclasm shared by Judaism and radical Protestantism against the incarnational aesthetics of a natural art, establishing the Hebraic world of Acts I–III as the contradiction as well as the foundation of the Christian-classical synthesis. The play's dream of an art "as lawful as eating" points to a naturalistic aesthetic along the lines of Polixenes' speech on grafting, and to a conception of art as the bearer of iconographic and allegorical significations not reducible to the seamless digestion of meaning in form.

In his reading of The Winter's Tale, Leonard Barkan takes the story of Pygmalion as a model for the rebirth of paganism in the Renaissance. He weaves the theme of the animated statue into the metaphorics of the Renaissance as a period: "the motif of the statue coming to life was alive and well in Shakespeare's time. . . . Following [its] history offers us. . . . an insight into the growth of several ideas that flower in the Renaissance" ("'Living Sculptures'" 639–40; emphasis mine). In his Ovidian reading of the play, Barkan pairs the oracle of Act III with the gallery of Act V, identifying both as pagan spaces in a drama that constitutes "Shakespeare's last hommage to the world in which metamorphosis was born" (Gods Transformed 287). By reading the play as a reanimation of antiquity that structurally enacts as well as thematically retells the story of Pygmalion, Barkan's forthrightly pagan analysis dovetails with its apparent opposite: the Christian-typological interpretation of the play. Thus Roy Battenhouse had also paired the oracle and the chapel, reading the one as the "surpassing antitype" of the other, a typological interpretation that presents modern Christian art as the rebirth of classical hu-

manism through the redemption of Leontes' rocky heart ("Theme
and Structure" 138). Both Battenhouse and Barkan emphasize the
role of "faith" in bringing a world of stone to new life, the one
from an Ovidian, the other from a Pauline perspective; for both,
the reanimation of the statue represents a cultural rebirth, classical
for Barkan and Christian for Battenhouse. The unexpected structural affinities between the pagan and the Christian readings of the
play demonstrate once more the derivation of the Renaissance conceit from exegetical patterns of periodization hidden beneath their
apparent opposition.

There is, however, another Pygmalion, the counter-Pygmalion
who suffers from an idolatrous love intensified rather than redeemed
by the animation of the statue. In his 1598 "Metamorphosis of Pygmalion's Image," John Marston compares the love-struck artist during the period before Galatea's transformation to a Catholic worshipper kneeling before a silent icon:

> Look how the peevish Papists crouch and kneele,
> To some dum Idoll with their offering,
> As if a senceles carved stone could feele
> The ardor of his bootles chattering,
> So fond he [Pygmalion] was, and earnest in his sute
> To his remorsles Image, dum and mute.[29]

If Barkan takes Pygmalion as a figure of the Renaissance rebuild-
ing of the ruins of the classical past, J. Hillis Miller gives voice to
the Reformation reading of the myth as expressed in Marston's simile, which, in the manner of the Hebrew prophets, emphasizes the
dumb muteness of senseless stone and the fallacy of projecting life
onto it. Miller, who cites "Thou shalt not make unto thee any
graven image" as the epigram to his book *Versions of Pygmalion*, emphasizes not the redemptive trajectory of the myth as a story of renaissance, but rather its staging of idolatry, the fashioning of a dead
image which is then (mis)taken for reality (8). Miller's reading of
Pgymalion combines the Old Testament prohibition against images
with the Protestant critique of Catholicism insofar as that critique
diverges from the humanist ideals of the Renaissance. We need to

distinguish, that is, between the Protestant historiography of the nineteenth century (Hegel, Burckhardt), which sees itself as the synthesis of classical and Christian culture at the expense of Judaism, and the Lutheran rejection of all transubstantial unities, a rejection that reinstates the sublimity of Hebrew iconoclasm at the expense of pagan, Catholic, and secular syncretisms (Luther, Kierkegaard, Löwith). In Miller's reading of Pygmalion, Jewish and Protestant iconoclasm separates out from the Christian-secular schemes it makes possible. Miller links the story of Pygmalion to his broader insistence on the figurative condition of human signification and the error implicit in any belief that language incarnates the world, or that form manifests meaning. Following Walter Benjamin's anti-typological historiography, we could say that Miller's Pygmalion figures a Baroque rather than a Renaissance aesthetic, becoming an emblem for the epistemological and ethical errors carried by myths of renovation and the consequent stationing of mythographic and iconographic representation in the place of mythological and symbolic forms, with their dreams of incarnation.

These two versions of Pygmalion emblematize the way in which the tokens of idolatry fall out of the dominant typological movement of the final scene of *The Winter's Tale*. The renewed Sicily to which we return at the end of the play is produced through the redemptive transcription of key words and images from the fallen Sicily of Acts I–III. In Act III, Leontes, acknowledging his wrong, describes himself as "transported by my jealousies" (3.2.158), whereas Leontes in front of the statue is "so far transported that / He'll think anon it lives" (5.368).[30] "Transport" names the dangerous power of the visual image to carry the viewer out of himself; from one end of *The Winter's Tale* to the other, the transports of the imagination are themselves transported from Leontes' diseased opinion to Paulina's healing art. One of Leontes' early accusations against Polixenes as "he that wears [Hermione] like her medal, hanging / About his neck" (1.2.308–9) is repeated and corrected in the closing image of the restored Hermione embracing her husband: "She hangs about his neck!" (5.3.113). Both lines conflate Hermione with her medallion—the first, however, within the paranoid circuit of idolatrous jealousy, and the second within the Pauline emblematics of married love. This miniature recuperation of the portrait miniature recapitulates the general movement by which the statue scene typologically repeats and redeems the spectacle of Hermione's trial, effectively Christianizing the Sicily of broken laws and deadly idolatry into the Sicily of a redeeming faith and a resurrected art.[31] In this way, the play's doubling of key images uses the reflective resources of the icon in order to renew its vision of the image.

The generalized "Christianity" produced by this doubling is at the same time iconographically coded as Catholic. The return to Sicily converts the Old Testament profile of the play's sublimely rageful Leontes into a living emblem of saintly penance. Leontes has, Cleomenes reassures him, "performed a saint-like sorrow" (5.1.2), assumedly by having carried out his pledge to visit "once a day . . . the chapel where they lie," the "tears shed there" his only "recreation" (3.2.238–40). Later in Act V, the supposed death of Hermione is "bravely confessed and lamented by the king" (5.2.84–85), who, assuming his guilt as his shield, comes to personify the saint as repentant sinner. The "sainted spirit" of the dead Hermione, on the other hand, epitomizes the tradition of the virtuous martyr, in this case one who, like St. Dorothea, has managed to convert the very tyrant who had mocked her. Together the increasingly typical, iconic figures of the king and queen choreographically crystallize and counterpoint the two fundamental careers of the saint, "the one through tears and penance and the other through martyrdom" (Voragine, *Golden Legend* 224), the careers opposed and reworked in the characters of Angelo and Isabella in *Measure for Measure*.

This proliferation of hagiographic imagery had already begun in the tragic aftermath of Act III. Paulina, come to announce Hermione's death, casts Leontes as the pagan tyrant of martyrology:

> What studied torments, tyrant, hast thou for me?
> What wheels? racks? fires? what flaying? boiling?
> In leads or oils? What old or newer torture
> Must I receive, whose very word deserves
> To taste of thy worst? (3.2.175–79)

Paulina's list of tortures is a shorthand catalogue of hagiographic *re-alia*: the wheel of St. Catherine, the rack of a St. Vitus or a St. Margaret, the flaying of St. Bartholomew, and the boiling of St. Juliana (in lead) and St. John (in oil). Paulina goes on to predict the impossibility of the tyrant's redemption:

> But, O thou tyrant!
> Do not repent these things, for they are heavier
> Than all thy woes can stir: therefore betake thee
> To nothing but despair. A thousand knees
> Ten thousand years together, naked, fasting,
> Upon a barren mountain, and still winter
> In storm perpetual, could not move the gods
> To look that way thou wert. (3.2.207–14)

Paulina's infinite calculus ("a thousand knees ten thousand years together") sets up the repetitive machinery of remorse that will have stamped Leontes into a pattern of penance during the great hiatus of the play; the passage shows a particular representation (the icon of regret) emerging from the sheer repetition of a key gesture (kneeling). At the same time, Paulina's sentence, insisting on the hopelessness of Leontes' redemption, implicitly undercuts the Catholic capitalization of works that the tableau imagines; in the Pauline gift economy of grace, only one of the parties can accumulate debt. Roy Battenhouse describes Paulina's "spiritual progress from an initially moralistic rigidity to a more gracious shepherding, analogous perhaps to the growth of the biblical Saul of Taurus into a St. Paul" ("Theme and Structure" 137). The connection between Paulina and Paul does indeed describe the generic and historical progression of the play from Old Testament tragedy to Christian comedy; what Battenhouse's reading misses, however, is the way in which the character and name of Paulina not only symbolizes the typological movement of the play but also materializes the remainders of that movement by brandishing the reified fragments of an annulled hagiographic discourse.

Those remainders are collected in Paulina's gallery, a setting loaded with the signs of both Italian secular art and Catholic forms of worship. As Leonard Barkan and Stephen Orgel have suggested independently, the reference in *The Winter's Tale* to "that rare Italian master, Julio Romano" may demonstrate Shakespeare's familiarity with the life of the artist recounted by Vasari. Vasari, who names Pygmalion as a classical artist in his Preface, praises Giulio for depicting the stones of Rome in his Mannerist paintings.[32] In representing the life of Constantine, Romano studied "the ancient columns of Trajan and Antoninus that are in Rome" as well as "the very bath made by Constantine himself" (213). In his painting of the life of Constantine, at once the first Christian emperor and the emblem of classical Rome's decline and fall, Giulio Romano's archaeological references and Vasari's reconstructions of them stage the imperfect incorporation of the decadent style of the late empire into the awkward icons of Christianity's earliest state art—the nontypological appropriation of a post-classical aesthetic.[33] As a Roman artist, moreover, Giulio was subject to the vagaries of papal patronage; the Florentine Vasari writes that, with the return of a Medici, Clement VII, to the papacy, "all the arts of design, along with all the other virtuous skills, were *restored to life*" (211). In this line, Shakespeare may have encountered the Renaissance metaphor, but in the contaminating context of the papal politics abhorred by the reformers. As emblematized by his name, Vasari's Giulio Romano is a pointedly *Roman* artist, a painter of antiquities and an iconographer and servant of the Roman Church, the Catholic patron of classical rebirth.

Critics have worried the fact that Romano, skilled in the other arts, was not a sculptor; rather than a slip on Shakespeare's part, I would suggest that Vasari's emphasis on Giulio's skills as a painter and architect made him a strangely fitting candidate for his role as the maker of a fictive statue. Vasari describes Romano's design of a Medici villa in Rome:

> He made the facade to the front of the palace in the form of a semicircle, like a theatre, with a range of niches and windows of the Ionic order. . . . And Giulio executed many pictures in the living rooms and elsewhere, and particularly beyond the first vestibule in a very

fine loggia, adorned all round with niches large and small, [with] a great quantity of ancient statues, including one of Jove. (Bull II: 210)

Giulio has constructed a space that is both a theater and a gallery, a semicircular building of niches that hold Roman statuary. Not himself a sculptor, Giulio appears instead as the fashioner of *theatrical spaces for sculpture*, a designer of galleries and, like Paulina, himself a collector of antiquities (228). Recall here the *trompe-l'œil* veil painted by Pliny's Parrhasius, which, in Stephen Bann's formulation, created "the illusion of a space in which figuration was bound to appear" (*True Vine* 35). Just as Parrhasius's veil produces the illusion that a representation lies behind it, in Shakespeare's play the name of "Julio Romano," associated with statues, ruins, and idols both ancient and modern, creates the niche, the conceptual and theatrical space, in which we can believe that the actor is "really" a statue. By mapping in advance the inner stage as a niche, as space-for-a-sculpture, the evocation of "Julio Romano" prepares us to take the actor's living body as the stony replica of Hermione.

In the next scene, when we finally confront the statue, the niche of a Roman gallery now appears as a "chapel" (5.3.87) where viewers can kneel to the image of Hermione. Early in the scene, Perdita responds to the presentation of her mother's statue by supplicating the image:

> And give me leave,
> And do not say 'tis superstition, that
> I kneel, and then implore her blessing. Lady,
> Dear queen, that ended when I but began,
> Give me that hand of yours to kiss. (5.3.42–46)

Perdita's words resemble a prayer to the Virgin, that other "Lady, dear queen," and mother whose iconography was outlawed under Protestantism. Paulina's response, "Patience!"—though quickly turning into an admonition not to touch the artwork ("The statue is but newly fix'd, the colour's / Not dry," 5.3.47–48)—provides a momentary gloss of the emblematic tableau. The caption of "Patience" brings into play the Griselda motif that informs the Hermione-

Leontes couple; note the basic configuration of the tyrannous husband, the patient wife, and a daughter who, separated from her mother at birth, returns as a bride.[34] Iconographically, Paulina's gloss evokes other Shakespearean statues of Patience, in which the stoniness of statuary and the perseverance of the virtue reinforce each other. Thus Viola "sate like Patience on a monument, / Smiling at grief" (*Twelfth Night* 2.4.114–15), an image that recurrs in *Pericles*, where Marina "dost look / Like Patience gazing on kings' graves, and smiling / Extremity out of act" (*Pericles* 5.1.137–39). In the related imagery of *Measure for Measure*, Mariana beseeches the novice Isabella to join with her in kneeling for Angelo's acquittal: "As this is true / Let me in safety raise me from my knees, / Or else for ever be confixed here, / A marble monument" (5.1.229–32).[35] The conversion of the hardened heart of Leontes through the grace of Hermione mirrors Hermione's mollification from a statue of marital patience into a warm and loving wife.

In the whispered echo of such hagiographic imagery in *The Winter's Tale*, Perdita becomes herself a statue transfixed before and by the statue, kneeling like a donor in an Italian painting of the Virgin. As a replay of the Pygmalion story, the figure of Hermione is now closer to the altar of Venus worshipped by the artist than to the Galatea he has fashioned; Hermione as statue has become a kind of Venus–Isis–Madonna figure who bestows her gifts on those who pray in her Roman chapel. The mortifying tableau vivant formed by the mother and child, evoking the pagan background of Marian iconography, activates the second strand of Pygmalion exegesis, culminating in Perdita's voiced defensiveness about the "superstition" of her act. It is as if, kneeling before the figure of her mother, Perdita recollects the commandment stressed by the reformers, "thou shalt not bow down unto them." Following the iterative logic of the play, Perdita will both repeat and remedy her first supplication before the supposed statue by kneeling again before her living mother: Paulina requests of Perdita, "Please you to interpose, fair madam, kneel / And pray your mother's blessing" (5.3.118–19). The filial piety of the second bowing corrects and covers over the superstition of the first while continuing to borrow its iconographic charge.

During Leontes' initial viewing of the statue, he asks, "does not the stone rebuke me / For being more stone than it?" (V.iii.37–38), words which, as the play's editor J. H. P. Pafford points out, echo the prophet Habakkuk: "Thou hast consulted shame to thine owne house, by destroying many people, and hast sinned against thine owne soule. For *the stone shall crie out of the wall.*"[36] The allusion distinguishes Leontes' stoniness from Hermione's frozen grace by citing an Old Testament text, raising the moral difference between husband and wife into a typological distinction between two kinds of covenant. Yet, when the voice of Habakkuk emerges a second time, it enunciates a different historical logic. Paulina's incantation, "Music, awake her; strike! / 'Tis time; descend; be stone no more," uncannily recalls the idolatrous tableau pictured by the prophet a few lines later: "Woe to him who says to a wooden thing, Awake; / to a dumb stone, Arise!" (Hab. 2:19). By infusing the scene of Christological resurrection with the austerity of Hebrew monotheism, the second allusion to Habakkuk introduces the counter-rhythm of iconoclasm—both Jewish and radical Protestant—into the dominant typological patterning of the play, distorting the ideological clarity of the play's thematic, historical, and spiritual resolution of stone into life.

Throughout the scene, characters express concern over the "lawfulness" of a transaction whose purpose seems to be the idolatrous attribution of a dead image with life. Paulina says, "those that think it is unlawful business / I am about, let them depart," and Leontes cries out, "If this be magic, let it be an art / Lawful as eating" (5.3.110–11). Leontes' enigmatic response is most commonly taken as the play's naturalist manifesto, expressing Shakespeare's "concrete, physical delight" (Neely 86) in "warm human actuality" (Knight 42). In such readings, which assimilate Leontes' line to the logic of the grafting metaphor by taking "lawful" as a synonym of "natural," the art of the statue scene is defended as a part of nature rather than an idolatrous affront to it. Yet "lawful" is not simply reducible to "natural," since law and nature are opposites as much as synonyms; in a nature bereft of grace, laws intervene in and reorganize animal drives. From this perspective, human eating is "lawful" in the sense of *regulated by law*, a valence that reinstates the world of prohibitions and their tragic transgression from the earlier Sicily. Leontes' reference to the lawfulness of eating "transports" the violated Jewish laws of Acts I–III into the Christian frame(s) of faith and grace that redeem Act V, reasserting both the tragic foundation of the romance redemption and the stone tablets of law on which the play's dream of a natural art is written. By proposing that the magic of the animated statue—and by extension, the magic of the play—be as lawful as eating, Leontes suggests not that it be as natural, as spontaneous, and as vital as the appetites that man shares with beasts, but rather that this magic be as subject to signification and ritualization as food itself, entering into the calendars and tables of divine laws for human activity.

In the suspenseful moments before the statue's magic dissolves into art, the scene evokes Christological and sacramental resonances; in the seventeenth century, *The Winter's Tale* was scheduled at least once for performance on Easter Tuesday, exploiting this eucharistic theme (Laroque 27). We soon learn, however, that the apparent resurrection of the statue is symbolic rather than actual; as G. Wilson Knight notes, "Hermione's restoration not only has nothing to do with black magic; it is not even transcendental" (42). Put in Protestant terms, the only "lawful eating" of the Eucharist is one conceived as a symbolic commemoration rather than a real transubstantiation, the latter doctrine coming to epitomize Catholic idolatry in Reformation polemics. The play's rationalizing deflation of its carefully staged mystery definitively undercuts the Catholic iconography the scene so powerfully evokes, enacting the movement from the Church to its Reform. It is not a statue after all, but Hermione herself, whose "actions shall be [as] holy" as Paulina's "spell is lawful" (5.3.104–5). No heretical transubstantiation or pagan magic, we are assured, has in fact taken place.

The statue scene, then, stages the visual conditions of Catholic image worship, but only as canceled, with equal emphasis on both the act of staging and the fact of cancellation. How successful, however, can this abrogation be, and what effect does it have on the status of theater? In reassuring us that all is legal here, Shakespeare manages to distract us from the power of his own art: the reassurance that the statue is "really" Hermione allows us to forget that Hermione is not really Hermione but an actor. The scene similarly finesses its classical analogue in the story of Pygmalion. In *The Winter's Tale*, Hermione only *seems* to be a statue come to life, reanimating a pagan fiction of reanimation; unlike the Ovidian metamorphosis, Hermione was alive all along, thus dissolving both the pagan mystery of the myth and the Catholic resonances it has gathered. This staging of iconoclasm is itself only apparent, since another metamorphosis is occurring through the verbal and optical media of theater—namely, that we take the actor "for" Hermione, as both a representative and a representation, a proxy and a mimesis. Shakespeare, like Pygmalion, conceals his art with art (*ars adeo latet arte sue, Metamorphoses* X.252). The point is not that we are fooled into thinking that the actor playing Hermione is not really an actor; instead, a particular kind of fictionality emerges as the double negation of both the ritual truth of a sacramental or magical theater (the metamorphosis of the Pygmalion story) and the nominalist truth of iconoclastic discourse (Pygmalion exposed as idolator). In both staging idolatry and iconoclastically breaking the illusion, but only within the borders of the narrative, *The Winter's Tale* smashes the Catholic idols in order to extract their fascinating power, or, to change the metaphor, in order to draw new wine from their old skins. The presentation of Hermione-as-statue privileges the mimetic illusion of the icon over the material presence of the idol; when the statue reveals itself as human, the representational icon is reduced once more to the presentational idol, but within the scene of dramatic fiction, whose staging of human bodies recycles the mimetic iconicity and the epiphanic idolatry of pagan and Catholic rites. The power of secular theater is constituted by *The Winter's Tale* as both the quotient of paganism retained within the modern framework that cancels it and the critique of representation carried over from Judaism into the typological mythos that iconoclasm must finally repudiate.

I submit that *The Winter's Tale* is a Christian play in this sense, and in this sense only. It is not Christian if by this we mean a faithful transmission of a homogeneous tradition's redemptive message, nor is it Christian in the sense of deciding "for" or "against" either the Protestant or the Catholic dispensation. Instead, *The Winter's Tale* registers Christianity as a discourse repeatedly turned against both itself and its pagan and Jewish others by the cycles of typological renovation and iconoclastic destruction. Moreover, it is out of these tropic conversions and syntactic repunctuations that new lives of the image are born for an art and drama that establishes itself as the afterlife of the saints. Each movement of the play inflects a different moment and modality in that ongoing process. Acts I–III dramatize the transgression of the Decalogue as its commandments take shape against the field of a polytheism always uncannily native to it. The pagan pastoralism of Act IV emphasizes the confluence of classical and Catholic idolatry, already autumnally shadowed by the crisis of the Reformation. The return to Sicily in the final act construes the secular theater as the ghost of paganism—the reanimation of Pygmalion but in the figure of the idolator—which emerges between the Christian resurrection of classical art (the story of Renaissance) and the iconoclastic interruption of typology (the Baroque critique of incarnational aesthetics). *The Winter's Tale* neither melancholically glorifies the icons of the Church nor manically participates in their smashing; rather, it takes up the fragments of the idols *as* fragments, stones of Rome whose vestigial thaumaturgy and iconographic redeployments animate Shakespearean drama.

Reference Matter

Notes

Introduction

1. Howard Hibbard points out the borrowing (*Caravaggio* 159).
2. On biblical typology as a literary and historical logic, see especially Erich Auerbach, "Figura," in *Scenes from the Drama of European Literature* 11–76. See also the second half of Northrop Frye's *The Great Code*. Karl Löwith's *Meaning in History* demonstrates the often invisible contributions of Christian typology to the German philosophy of history; see especially chapters 8 and 11 as well as the Conclusion and Epilogue. For an example of typology applied to pagan-Christian relations, see Augustine, *On Christian Doctrine* XL.60. (This passage is examined in more detail in Chapter 1.)
3. See Jacob Neusner, *Introduction to Rabbinic Literature*, on the origins and genres of rabbinic literature.
4. Much recent work in classics, taking anthropology as its main method, has struggled to revise the view of the ancient world inherited from nineteenth-century idealism (Vernant and Vidal-Naquet; Paige du Bois). As such, it develops initiatives already present in Nietzsche's *Birth of Tragedy* as well as the work of Aby Warburg.
5. See, for example, John Guillory's *Cultural Capital*, one of the most discerning and balanced contributions to the progressive side of the debate, which nonetheless subordinates the intertextual dynamics of literary change to the external function of institutional ideologies and technologies (e.g., the syllabus): "The canon achieves its imaginary totality, then, . . . by retroactively constructing its individual texts as a *tradition*, to which

works may be added or subtracted without altering the impression of totality or cultural homogeneity. A tradition is 'real,' of course, but only in the sense that the imaginary is real. A tradition always retroactively unifies disparate cultural productions . . . while such historical fictions are perhaps impossible to dispense with, one should always bear in mind that the concept of a given tradition is much more revealing about the immediate context in which that tradition is defined than it is about the works retroactively so organized" (*Cultural Capital* 33–34). Retroactive determinations of meaning appear in Guillory's analysis not as a fundamental principle of literary signification, but as an illusion or deception brought off by the teacher of literature interpellated in the official library of his or her school. Guillory implies that these unnatural meanings can be at least partially or provisionally removed through recourse to "historical contextualization," the main technique left to such a perspective (43). To the contrary, I would insist that the retroactivity of signification is performed not only by the syllabus on otherwise rooted, context-bound works, but by one literary text on another as the very means and process of writing itself, which is intrinsically disruptive and deracinating.

6. On the narrativity of history, see Hayden White, *Metahistory*. On the sedimentation of literary forms, see Fredric Jameson, "Magical Narratives," in *The Political Unconscious*. Natural history is a key term in the works of Walter Benjamin and Theodor Adorno. Adorno writes of Benjamin's letters: "Benjamin brought to them an uninhibited talent for antiquities; he celebrated the wedding of a vanishing institution to its utopian restoration. What enticed him to write letters was thus connected with his habitual mode of experience; for he regarded historical forms—and the letter is one such form—as nature that required deciphering, that issued a binding commandment. His posture as a letter-writer inclines to that of the allegorist: letters were for Benjamin natural-history illustrations of what survives the ruin of time" (Benjamin, *Correspondence* xix).

Chapter 1

1. The works of Deborah Shuger have done much to revise the old sense of the Renaissance as a proto-secular revolution. For the supplementation of "Renaissance" by "early modern," see Margaret Ferguson et al., eds., *Rewriting the Renaissance*, who write that "The new name, which poses its own set of problems for theories of periodization, generally does not replace the old one but supplements it" (xvii). Leah S. Marcus writes that "early modern approaches" allow us to "set aside the implicitly hierarchical agenda of 'Renaissance' in its traditional sense for a more prosaic,

level mode of analysis that strives for a greater cultural inclusiveness" (43).

2. On Burckhardt and the establishment of the Renaissance mythos, see Wallace Ferguson, *The Renaissance in Historical Thought*, Wolfgang Hardtwig, *Geschichtsschreibung*, and Hannelore and Heinze Schlaffer, *Studium zum ästhetischen Historismus.*

3. In *Weltgeschichtliche Betrachtungen* Burckhardt mocks Hegel's philosophy of history and distances himself from "alles Systematische," especially "'weltgeschichtliche Ideen'" (1–2). E. H. Gombrich, however, has demonstrated the Hegelian provenance of many of Burckhardt's historical leitmotifs, as well as noting what he calls the "Trinitarian speculations" that inform Hegel's dialectic (*In Search of Cultural History* 10–11, 8).

4. This distinction is already at work in Panofsky's "Iconography and Iconology," where the two methodological terms counterposed in the essay's title also correspond to the medieval and Renaissance modes of signification, the first ruled by allegory, and the second by a high-mimetic realism identifiable with the aesthetics of the symbol. See also Panofsky's *Renaissance and Renascences*, whose title words instate a similar opposition.

5. Thus Gadamer, one of the last great commentators on and participants in the German aesthetic tradition, writes, "the Greek fathers used this kind of neoplatonist thinking in overcoming the old testament's hatred of images when it came to christology. In this overcoming of the ban on images we can see the event through which the development of the plastic arts became possible in the christian West" (*Truth and Method* 125). For a brief reading of the anti-Semitism implicit in Hegel's dialectic of religion, see Zizek, *Sublime Object* 201–7.

6. Hegel writes of the Jewish deity, "God, as Lord of the world that serves him, [is] not incarnate in the external world but withdrawn out of mundane existence into a solitary unity. What in symbolism proper was still bound into one, thus falls apart here into two sides—the abstract independence of God and the concrete existence of the world" (Hegel, *Aesthetics* I: 373). For a related reading of Hegel's appropriation of typology, see John Smith, *Spirit and Its Letter*, 132–37.

7. Luther to Eoban Hess, March 29, 1953. Cited Ferguson, *Renaissance in Historical Thought* 54.

8. In the Northern European historical imagination, Italy may be the home of the *Renaissance*, but the North is the home of Enlightenment, that is, of cultural *Mundigkeit* or maturity, as Kant puts it in "What is Enlightenment?" Emmanuel Lévinas's implicit rejoinder to Kant, in his essay on Judaism entitled "A Religion for Adults," challenges the Protestant claim to cultural maturity.

9. Panofsky argues that "the reintegration of classical themes with classical motifs which seems to be characteristic of the Italian Renaissance as opposed to the numerous sporadic revivals of classical tendencies during the Middle Ages . . . is a most important element of what Burckhardt and Michelet called 'the discovery of both the world and of man'" (*Meaning* 54; compare Burckhardt, *Culture* II: 279).

10. Gombrich notes that Warburg "was to quote this saying of Burckhardt's throughout his life" (*Aby Warburg* 63).

11. As Warburg notes in these remarks on Burckhardt, the older historian did not treat art works per se in *Die Kultur der Renaissance in Italien*, nor were his art-historical writings especially cultural or contextual.

12. For biographical background on these figures, see Gombrich on Warburg, Joist Grolle on Saxl, Michael Ann Holly on Panofsky, and Hugh Lloyd-Jones on Edgar Wind.

13. Warburg did, however, have many connections with the University of Hamburg, which was founded during the heyday of the Warburg library in the 1920's.

14. The story probably originally served to allegorize the relationship between the Israelites and their enemies the Edomites (named after Jacob/Israel and Esau respectively) (*Eerdman's Bible Dictionary* 346). Later midrashim later associated Esau with Rome (A. Cohen, ed., *Soncino Bible* 155n).

15. On the anthropological vision of Warburg, see Peter Burke, "Aby Warburg as Historical Anthropologist." On the Warburg school as the repository of German humanism, see Fritz Saxl, librarian of the Warburg Institute for many years, who defines the goal of the library in 1933 as "the idea of creating a centre of learning outside Germany where the old tradition of German humanism should be preserved" ("The History of Warburg's Library" 336).

16. Gombrich cites Warburg's notes to his lecture on Amerindian serpent ritual, where Warburg recalls a serious illness of his mother during a stay at an Austrian resort; the depressing nature of the events was mitigated by the proximity of a lending library and a nonkosher delicatessen (*Aby Warburg* 20).

17. On Warburg's place in the internally divergent German tradition of reading antiquity, see Gombrich, *Aby Warburg* 12, and Ferretti, *Cassirer, Panofsky, and Warburg* 12.

18. See Hibbard, *Michelangelo* 108. Hibbard in turn cites Warburg scholar Edgar Wind on the typological scheme of the Sistine Chapel ("Michelangelo's Prophets and Sibyls.")

19. On the historical situation of the writing of *Mimesis*, see Richard

Regosin, "Critical Discussions" 1357. In his recent work on St. Paul, Daniel Boyarin has argued against distinguishing between allegory and typology in the epistles that crystallize typology for Christian exegetics (*Radical Jew* 34, 86).

20. Auerbach quotes Hegel's assessment that the *Divine Comedy* "plunges the living world of human action and suffering and, more particularly, the deeds and fates of individuals" into the "changeless existent" of God's plan. *Aesthetics* II: 1103; see Auerbach, *Mimesis* 191, 194. Throughout the *Aesthetics*, Hegel protects Dante from being judged "merely" allegorical, not unlike Panofsky and Gombrich's sheltering of Warburg from the label of iconographer; Hegel writes of Beatrice that she "hovers (and this constitutes its beauty) between allegory proper and a transfiguration of his youthful beloved" (*Aesthetics* I: 402). Edgar Schell, in his typological reading of medieval drama, reasserts Auerbach's Hegelian point: "Preserving the historical integrity of biblical types is essential to a carefully worked out typological scheme, for, as St. Augustine has pointed out, unless we imagine the type realistically, unless we understand that what is said to have happened really did happen just as it is narrated, we 'seek to build as it were in the air'" (149).

21. Warburg, *Gesammelte Werke* II: 473. See Warburg's analysis of the different strata of mythological and astronomical representation in the fresco cycles at the Palazzo Schifanoja in Ferrara (461–81). Gombrich comments on Warburg's attention to artistic resistance as a disproof of *Zeitgeist*: "What he wanted to bring out in Rembrandt, after all, was, if anything, the artist's resistance to that spirit [of the age]. . . . Himself the victim of conflicts, he responded not to the superficial unity but to the conflicts of past ages" (*Aby Warburg* 314).

22. See, for example, Peter Burke, "Aby Warburg as Historical Anthropologist," or Margaret Iversen's "Retrieving Warburg's Tradition," a feminist rereading of Warburg.

23. Indeed, the word "Romanticism" seems to activate its full Hegelian scope, to encompass the rise of Christian culture as such.

24. In many Nativity scenes and some Annunciations as well the Holy Family appears in a ruined building, symbolizing the Synagogue abrogated by the Christ child. Erwin Panofsky explores the typological iconography of the ruin in *Early Netherlandish Art* I: 133–40. Panofsky describes the typological program of Pucelle's calendar in the *Hours of Jean d'Evreux*: "The *bas-de-pages* . . . illustrate the concordance between the Old Testament and the New by showing how the Twelve Apostles convert the sayings of the Prophets into the Articles of the Faith . . . by the Prophet's tearing a stone out of the fabric of the Synagogue and passing it on to the Apostle so that

it might serve as building material for the Church, a process which naturally results in the gradual ruination of the Synagogue. A handsome edifice in January and February, it begins to show traces of wear and tear by the middle of the year and is completely reduced to rubble in November and December" (33).

25. Löwith summarizes his thesis: "There are in history not only 'flowers of evil' but also evils which are the fruit of too much good will and of a mistaken Christianity that confounds the fundamental distinction between redemptive events and profane happenings, between *Heilsgeschehen* and *Weltgeschichte*" (discourses, I would add, that Löwith has shown earlier to be wholly interdependent) (203).

26. Take, for example, the Pilgrim's protest in the *Inferno*, "Io non Enëa, io non Paulo sono [I am not Aeneas, I am not Paul]" (*Inferno* II.32). Dante's coupling of Aeneas and Paul compares the Roman *translatio* of Troy to the Christian conversion of the old law, and it uses this typological equation to tap a quotient of Judaism's theme of national redemption for application to the Christian world order. By pairing the City of Men with the City of God (and thus diluting Augustine's intransigent opposition) Dante crosses the historicity of the one realm with the eternity of the other, charging both the pagan temporality of Rome and the profane history of the Church with a remainder of the national self-consciousness carried over by Paul's New Covenant from Judaism.

27. Here I cite Rainer Nägele again, a critic whose reading of Benjamin's Judaism as a structuring feature of his thought rather than a sociological accident is exemplary for me: "Hegel's secularized Christian theology is confronted with the Jewish theology of the Messiah who has not yet come and a world that is still waiting for redemption. These historical and theological models are not a matter of personal opinion or faith. They structure the political unconscious that Benjamin's thought attempts to outline" ("Reading Benjamin" 13).

28. On Schmitt and Benjamin, see Samuel Weber, "Taking Exception to Decision: Walter Benjamin and Carl Schmitt," and Gillian Rose, *Judaism and Modernity* 179n. On Löwith and Schmitt as theorists of secularization and its discontents, see Chantal Mouffe, *The Return of the Political* 123.

29. "The exception in jurisprudence," writes Schmitt, "is analogous to the miracle in theology" (36).

30. The editor of a recent anthology of essays on cultural studies offers the following provisional definition: "Cultural studies is, of course, the study of culture, or, more particularly, the study of *contemporary* culture" (During, *The Cultural Studies Reader* 1). It is telling that the growing focus

on context, undertaken in the name of historicization, is so often accompanied by a radical reduction in chronological scope. This was certainly not the case for Raymond Williams, frequently cited as the founder of cultural studies, but it has increasingly characterized the evolving discipline, as witnessed in During's opening statement. With the rise of multiculturalism (a word with "culture" in its middle), geographical diversity has begun to supplant historical diversity as the goal of humanistic inquiry.

Chapter 2

1. The literature on the symptom is vast, and I am restricting myself here to the Lacanian articulation of the symptom. In addition to Lacan's seminar on the *sinthome*, see Slavoj Zizek's *Sublime Object of Ideology*, especially the chapter "From Symptom to *sinthome*" (55–84), and *Enjoy Your Symptom!* See also Jacques-Alain Miller, "Reflections on the Formal Envelope of the Symptom," and his unpublished seminar, "Du Symptôme au fantasme et retour."

2. I use Graesse's Latin edition and the Ryan and Ripperberger translation; the texts diverge in many ways. For a reception history of the *Golden Legend*, see Sherry Reames, *The Legenda Aurea: A Reexamination of Its Paradoxical History.*

3. See Alison Goddard on this division: "*Passiones*, accounts of martyrs, differ substantially from *vitae*, tales of confessor saints such as the desert hermits. Both tell stories about heroes, but the type of hero and the specific mode his heroic action takes are not identical. While in all cases the ultimate goal is the same, the attainment of the kingdom of heaven, the road taken is a different one" (11).

4. A core group of the *Acta* has been edited and translated by Herbert Musurillo, *The Acts of the Christian Martyrs.*

5. My own typology, restricted to the denouement of martyrdom, begins with the sequence covered by Boreau's middle term and ends with the postmortem treatment of the body.

6. Thus Lacan explains later in the seminar that consistency "means that which holds together, and it is for that very reason that it is in this case symbolized by the surface. The only idea of consistency that we have, unfortunately for us, is that which makes a sack or dust-cloth. Even the body we feel as a skin holding in its sack a pile of organs" (*Le séminaire, livre XXIII*, Jan. 13, 1976).

7. Lacan's counter-intuitive identification of beauty here with that which suspends rather than leads on desire anticipates Lacan's later account in *Seminar XI* of that element in painting which "invites the person to

whom this picture is presented to lay down his gaze there as one lays down one's weapons" (*Seminar XI*, 101).

8. Thus St. Julitta was "flayed alive, plunged into boiling pitch, and at last beheaded" (316). In the romance of St. George the saint is dragged through the city and then his head is cut off (237). St. Margaret survives racking, scourging, burning, and boiling, until finally "the prefect, fearing still other conversions, ordered her beheaded as quickly as possible" (354). St. Cyriacus submits to boiling pitch poured on his head, then to the rack, and is "finally beheaded with his companions" (437).

9. Thus Lacan comments on the biological fable of the praying mantis who eats the head of her lover that "it is less the part which is preferred to the whole than—in the most horrible way, and in a way which almost allows us to short-circuit the function of metonymy—the whole that is preferred to the part. Let us not omit in effect that, even in an animal structure as far removed from us in appearance as that of the insect, the value of concentration, reflection, and totality of the cephalic extremity" (*Seminar VIII*, in a typescript translation by Bruce Fink, 254).

10. Boreau characterizes hagiographic decollation as "the summary and sign of a martyr" (123).

11. In Lacan's formulation, "A signifier is that which represents the subject to another signifier. This signifier will therefore be the signifier for which all other signifiers represent the subject" (*Écrits* 316).

12. As Alain Boreau characterizes the role of the relics in Jacobus de Voragine's collection, "Intercession is not anchored in any particular place or activity because it expresses a relation that can vary over the course of Christian history" (160).

13. Another class of postmortem miracles involves the cult of the saint apart from the place of burial, often entailing the invocation of the name of the saint. The Miracles of the Virgin exemplify this paradigm (see *Golden Legend* 207–8; 455–65). Examples of this type in secular literature include Chaucer's Prioress's Tale and, in a more comic vein, the story of the devotee of St. Julian the Hospitaler, *Decameron* 2.2.

14. In the following passages from *Le séminaire, livre XXIII*, Lacan associates the symptom with creation *ex nihilo*: "In what way can artifice expressly aim at that which first presents itself as symptom? How can art, or the artisan, elude that which is imposed by virtue of the symptom?" (Nov. 18, 1975). "How can art aim, in a manner expressly divinatory, to substantialize in its consistency, and also in its ex-istence, the fourth term essential to the knot, how can it aim to render it as such, to get at it as closely as possible?" (Dec. 9, 1975). "One imputes to God that which is the concern of the artist. The first model of God, as everyone knows, is the potter,

of whom one says that he has molded . . . this thing [*truc*] called, and not by accident, the universe—which means but one thing, that there is something of One [il y a de l'Un]" (Jan. 13, 1976).

15. The language of the sacrament, moreover, is deictic rather than metaphoric, as Louis Marin has argued in his analysis of the Port Royal grammarians (*Food for Thought* 13–17). On the sentence, "This is my body," Marin writes, "For 'this'—which means 'the thing that is present'—is subject to two successive determinations: at the beginning of the proposition, it is clearly determined as 'bread' and, at the end, as 'my body.' The contradiction to which the Protestant ministers point and which they seek to resolve through metaphor and heresy, turns out not to be a contradiction at all" (16).

Chapter 3

1. On Chaucer's *Legend of Good Women*, see especially Lisa J. Kiser, *Telling Classical Tales*, and Robert Worth Frank, Jr., *Chaucer and the Legend of Good Women*. All citations from Chaucer are from the *Riverside Chaucer*, ed. Larry D. Benson.

2. The Levitical law of gleaning probably represents an ethical reorientation of "ancient harvest regulations," originally designed as an offering for the spirits of the soil, but "reinterpreted as a charitable gift for *the poor and the alien*" (Porter 153).

3. Rabbinic commentaries on Ruth are attuned to the figuration of the widow as a kind of remnant; thus the *Midrash Rabbah* glosses the fate of Naomi, left alone by her sons as well as her husbands, as "the remnants of the remnants [of the meal offering]" (cited Cohen, ed., *Five Megilloth* 140).

4. "Dixitque Ruth moabitis ad socrum suam: Si iubes, vadam in agrum et *colligam* spicas, quae fugerint manus metentium, ubicumque clementis in me patrisfamilias repperero gratiam" (Ruth 2:2; emphasis mine).

5. As Lisa Kiser has argued, Chaucer's poem shows the limits of the "inadequate fruit/chaff model, which implies that fictional aspects of a work are wholly expendable" (81).

6. Chapter 19 of Leviticus, a compilation of laws concerning God and neighbor written for the instruction of priests but prescribing the obligations of all Israelites, has been called "the priestly Decalogue" because of its echoes of Exodus 20 within a Levitical (priestly) context (Porter 151–52). Gordan J. Wenham has divided the 37 commandments of Leviticus 19 into three segments: religious duties, good neighborliness, and miscellaneous duties; in this division, the law about gleaning closes the first segment, and the injunction to love thy neighbor as thyself closes the second (263–64).

7. Which is not to say that the Christian account of charity is purely narcissistic, since love for the neighbor is always triangulated by love for God, and pride remains one of the ethical threats haunting acts of charity. It is fair to say, however, that in the Christian scheme, the self and the neighbor are taken as interchangeable, reflective units, whereas in Lévinas's reading of Jewish ethics, the neighbor is finally as radically different in kind from the subject as God is; indeed, we intuit God's difference precisely from the shock of our encounter with our neighbors.

8. *Eerdman's Bible Dictionary* glosses Boaz's generosity to Ruth as assistance "beyond the letter of the law" (420). Such an interpretation, implicitly opposed to the "legalism" of Judaism, serves to present Boaz as a proto-Christian figure. Boaz, however, *fulfills* the law in the sense of following it *fully*, with a sense of joy—the essence rather than the opposite of so-called Jewish legalism.

Chapter 4

1. So too, for Joy Potter, Stories I.1 and X.10 form an internal frame to the *Decameron*'s tales (148). Patricia Phillippy has argued for the function of the Griselda tale as a palinode or formal retraction ("Love's Remedies"). All citations from the *Decameron* are from G. H. McWilliam's English translation and Vittore Branca's Italian edition, marked "E" (for English) and "I" (for Italian) respectively.

2. De' Negri takes the story as an exercise in Bollandist criticism of the saints' legends executed *avant la lettre* and with other tools: "To religious legend, [Boccaccio] opposed not so much the arguments of criticism, but a similar manner of constructing tales by means of examples and legends" (179).

3. Petrarch writes of his Latin translation, "My object in thus re-writing your tale was not to induce the women of our time to imitate the patience of this wife, which seems to me almost beyond imitation, but to lead my readers to emulate the example of feminine constancy, and to submit themselves to God with the same courage as did this woman to her husband" (Musa and Bondanella 186). Marga Cottino-Jones' reading of Griselda is in the same tradition, though less generically sensitive than de' Negri's.

4. On the reception of Job in medieval liturgy and literature, see Besserman.

5. Branca notes the allusion, 1243n.

6. Thus Boccaccio's example is the burning bush on Mount Sinai rather

than, say, the parable of the sowers: "the Holy Spirit wanted to proclaim through the very green bush in which Moses beheld God almost like a burning flame the virginity of that woman who was purer than any creature, who was destined to become the dwelling place and haven of all nature" (38).

7. As John Guillory has pointed out, once literature becomes the new scripture, the Bible in turn can become that modern hybrid, "the-Bible-as-literature": "The 'line' of poetry descending from Spenser and Milton is aggressively scriptural, and it is a great irony of its success that the Bible has now been annexed in university curricula 'as literature.' It is no longer audacious to make this substitution since the originative reversal—'literature as scripture'—has for very long been the ground of poetic authority" (*Poetic Authority* viii).

8. The translator discusses the connections between the *Trattatello* and hagiography, xxvii–ix.

9. See Mazzotta on Gualtieri as the condensation of Satan and God (*World at Play* 125).

10. On "clerkly discourse" and on the structure of palinode in the Griselda tales of Boccaccio, Petrarch, and Chaucer, see Phillippy, 148–58. For the French and Latin texts of Chaucer's Petrarchan source, see Severs.

11. Dioneo comments, "Who else but Griselda could have endured so cheerfully the cruel and unheard of trials that Gualtieri imposed upon her without shedding a tear?" (E 824). Petrarch writes, "My object in thus rewriting your tale was not to induce the women of our time to imitate the patience of this wife, which seems to me almost beyond imitation . . . " (Musa 186).

12. To these stories we could also append IV.6, in which Gabriotto dreams that a black greyhound is ripping out his heart; this story, however, belongs more prominently to a second sequence of tales in Day IV. IV.10 also includes a minor motif of dismemberment in the planned amputation of a man's leg; I have chosen, however, not to address this comic tale here.

13. In IV.8, a story that does not fit into this sequence, the mother is the obstacle to love, filling out Boccaccio's list of hindrances in the preface.

14. The lovers of IV.7 and IV.8 are also buried together. On the translation and double burial of Lawrence and Stephen, see Voragine on the Feast of the Invention of St. Stephen, *Golden Legend* 408–12.

15. For tragedies with sources in the novella and sharing its ambiance, see, for example, Shakespeare's *Romeo and Juliet* and *Othello*; for a tragicomedy, see *Much Ado*.

16. IV.10, told by Dioneo with his usual license to break the rules of the

day, is a comic story, and, though linked in some ways to the themes of
Day IV, falls along with IV.2 outside of the tragic collection.

17. Christine de Pizan, for example, retells IV.1 and IV.5 in succession
in *The Book of the City of Ladies*, clearly seeing these as paired tales
(193–202).

18. A similar structure appears in Dante's Bertran de Born, who mo-
notonously swings his severed head like a lantern well below his trunk (*Inferno* XXVIII), or in *Othello's* image of the *anthropophagi*, "men whose heads
/ [Do grow] beneath their shoulders" (I.iii.144). Joel Fineman has read the
passage from *Othello* in terms of the "headless subject" elaborated in Lacan's
theory of castration as absolute alienation in language (Fineman 149–50).

19. On the distinction between introjection and incorporation, see the
work of Nicolas Abraham and Maria Torok as well as Laplanche and Pontalis's glosses of the terms in *The Language of Psychoanalysis*.

20. In Exodus, the plague of frogs is followed several plagues later by
"boils breaking out in sores on man and beast" (Ex. 9:9).

21. The trials of the unkind widow in VIII.7 superimpose the fates of
the saints Lawrence and Bartholomew. Because a young woman inflicted a
dangerous night in the cold on the scholar who courted her, the scholar re-
taliates by stranding her naked on the roof of a tower in the hot sun. Boccaccio emphasizes the effects of the heat on her tender flesh: "not only did
it scorch every part of her flesh that was exposed to its rays, but it caused
her skin to split into countless tiny cracks and fissures [*che non solamente le
cosse le carni tanto quanto ne vedea ma quelle minuto minuto tutte l'asperse*]" (E
639; I 968). Her recovery is equally painful: "The physicians promptly set
to work upon the lady, but since she shed the whole of her skin several
times over because it kept sticking to the bedclothes, she suffered untold
agony" (E 644).

22. In Lacanian terms, dismemberment symbolizes the real through the
incisions of *capitonnage*; interment realizes the symbolic by outlining the
voids which decomplete the order of signification; and swelling yokes the
imaginary and the real in the primary processes of oneiric metastases.

23. Branca notes that "*punsa e trafissi*" is the "single reproach" made by
Griselda (1247n).

24. *Pillicione* is a variation of *pellicione*, meaning "little fur" and a euphemism for the female pudenda; its root is *pelle*, skin. The idiom *scuotere il
pillicione* occurs elsewhere in the *Decameron*, including VIII.7, the story of
the radical sunburn (I 966), and the tenth tale of Day IV, the day of the
plague (I 581).

Chapter 5

1. G. Wilson Knight writes that "Isabella stands for sainted purity" (74), although she "behaves to Claudio . . . like a fiend" (92). M. C. Bradbrook (1941), Roy Battenhouse (1946), and Nevill Coghill (1968) treat Isabella as a saintly exemplar of Mercy. Earlier praises of Isabella's piety or sanctity include Drake (1817), Jameson (1832), and Ruskin (1882), who wrote, "She is Shakespeare's only 'Saint'" (excerpts in *Measure for Measure: A New Variorum*, ed. Mark Eccles). Marc Shell's *End of Kinship* discusses the hagiographic analogues and background of *Measure for Measure* in ways that I have found especially helpful.

2. On Foxe and hagiography in Reformation England, see Helen C. White, *Tudor Books of Saints and Martyrs*.

3. Darryl Gless has also pointed out the allusion, which he reads as an Anglican parody of Mariolatry (103).

4. Thus Nereus and Achilleus are two eunuchs who persuade the niece of the Emperor to embrace virginity through an extended homily against the estate of marriage: "'They told her that the wife was subject to her husband, that often she was exposed to blows and kicks, and often brought forth misshapen offspring" (Voragine, *Golden Legend* 282).

5. Like vocation, the Annunciation entails an explicitly verbal calling from the divine to the human; hence Mary is often depicted reading a book—generally Isaiah—when the Angel appears in her chamber or *cubiculum*. The homology between vocation and Annunciation as scenes of religious calling is evident in representations of the evangelists that borrow their disposition of figures from the iconography of Mary. Irving Lavin has pointed out that Caravaggio's *Second St. Matthew* follows the type of the "back-handed Annunciation," in which the Angel surprises Mary from behind (Lavin 79). And, since the story of the Annunciation to Mary occurs only in the Gospel of Luke, that saint, the patron of painters, has a privileged relation to Mary, who sometimes appears in a vision before the evangelist who paints her. Panofsky describes Roger van der Weyden's portrayal of Luke and the Virgin: "'[St. Luke] maintains a graceful and reverent attitude which can best be described as genuflexion, and thereby the static and secular group of painter and model is transformed into something closely resembling an Annunciation scene, St. Luke taking the place of the Angel Gabriel" (*Early Netherlandish Painting* 254). Whereas the St. Matthew paintings emphasize the saint as the elected receiver of a divine message—placing the Evangelist, like Cecilia, in the place of Mary—Roger van der Weyden's St. Luke is the privileged witness to a holy scene, like Valerian before his beloved Cecilia.

6. See Eric Nicholson, "The *Decameron*'s Magic Theatre"; Nicholson first pointed out to me the possible allusion to "St. Luke" in the name "Lucio."

7. Gless makes a similar analysis of the disguised-ruler motif: "The motif belongs to folklore, more immediately to the broad genre of romance. . . . Our preliminary generic conception therefore begins to specify a range of possibilities about the category of language to which *Measure for Measure* belongs" (15–16). Gless's account differs from mine in stressing anticlerical satire rather than hagiography and hagiographic parody as the genre informing Isabella's character. In method, Gless uses genre to fix textual meaning in relation to an ideal Jacobean audience, rather than, as in my approach, taking genre as a flexible, dynamic set of practices with an unpredictable "effective history" informing present criticism as well as past audiences.

8. As critics have pointed out, the bed trick takes place in a "garden circummur'd with brick" that evokes the Marian *hortus conclusus* (Shell 144). Cf. Battenhouse 1035 and Kirsch 100.

9. St. Catherine of Alexandria was one of the most popular female saints; English versions include an Anglo-Norman verse legend by the nun Clemence of Barking (d'Ardenne xxvii).

10. St. Catherine, as famed for her "mystical marriage" to Christ as for her learning, is said to have been greeted by Christ at her martyrdom, "Come unto me, my fair love and my spouse" (Caxton VII: 25). In John Foxe's Protestant *Actes and Monuments*, the 20-year-old Joan Lashford "being brought unto the stake, there washed her clothes in the blood of the lamb . . . to whom most lovingly she espoused herself" (VII: 750).

11. For the political valences of tyranny, see Isabella's maxim, "O, it is excellent / To have a giant's strength, but it is tyrannous / To use it like a giant" (II.ii.108–10). (These lines in turn echo the complex hagiographic language of Sonnet 94.) Humanist political discourse reappears in reduced, comic form in the figure of the pimping "Pompey."

12. On the nostalgia for martyrdom among fourteenth-century saints, see Kieckhefer 66–68.

13. Thus Raymond of Capua, in his efforts toward the canonization of Catherine of Siena, represents her painful death after a long illness as proving her worthy of the martyr's crown.

14. Shell has explored these equivalences most intensively.

15. For an historical view of the desert fathers, see especially the work of Peter Brown. On the literary implications of the theological symbol of the desert, see Mazzotta, *Dante: Poet of the Desert*.

16. Thus the loaves delivered to Paul and Anthony in the desert echo the manna that fed the Jews during their exodus from Egypt.

17. It is no accident that the life of St. Anthony forms the first link in the chain of imitative conversions that lead up to the climax of Augustine's own conversion in Book IX of the *Confessions*.

18. In the terms of Alain Boreau, the "crucial" merits of the martyr are replaced by the "chronic" merits of the hermit (136).

19. "For asceticism," writes Geoffrey Galt Harpham, "the desert was both an antiworld, a nonplace from which the world could be condemned, and a metaphor for the world itself" (*Ascetic Imperative* 21).

20. Rajna cites Boccaccio's story as a possible source for Ariosto's narrative.

21. On Isabella as "hysterical," see Lever, lix, lxxx, 75; Gless, 178; Kirsch, 96, 97. These attacks replicate the accusation in Act V by the Duke and Angelo that Isabella suffers "th'infirmity of sense" (V.i.50). In a provocative footnote, Shell redirects the term "hysteria" from a moralizing label to a principle of exclusion and marginalization (227).

22. The allegorical reading is exemplified by M. C. Bradbrook, "Authority, Truth, and Justice in *Measure for Measure*."

23. Isabella's status as saintly novice begging for intercession on behalf of another aligns her with the New Dispensation over against the Law that it fulfills; at the same time, as Gless has argued, the Protestants of Shakespeare's England would have read the strange habits of the Catholic orders as the Law requiring re-formation.

24. Gless argues that the Sermon on the Mount is "the primary ethical standard *intrinsic* to *Measure for Measure*"; I am building on his analysis (43ff.)

25. According to Jacqueline Rose, these lines have helped provoke the critical scapegoating of Isabella as a figure of female excess and deficiency ("Sexuality" 108–9). Marc Shell, in his brilliantly single-minded monograph on incest in *Measure for Measure*, takes these lines as the drama's most explicit commentary on its own incestuous economy.

26. The siblings' double marriage to death is proof of their paternity and thus of their kinship. This is "a kind of incest," yet one founded on the saintly substitution of sex with death, in which the martyr embraces darkness as a bride. When soon after Claudio replaces death with sex in his plea for Isabella's charity, she wards against the physical incest it implies by revoking the morbid kinship in paternity affirmed earlier.

27. See also Pompey's intentionally absurd proposal for legal reform, "Does your worship mean to geld and splay all the youth of the city?" (II.i.227–28).

28. See *Totem and Taboo*: "The dead father became stronger than the living one had been" (*SE* XIII: 143).

29. Freud rightly associates the conversion of external law into conscience not with Christian mercy, but with Mosaic morality and the repeated reforms of the prophets. See *Moses and Monotheism* (*SE* XXIII: 51, 64, and *passim*), and *Future of an Illusion* (*SE* XXI).

30. Compare IV.ii.59–60.

31. See *Totem and Taboo* on Christianity: "A son-religion replaced the father-religion" (*SE* XIII: 154).

32. I have not addressed Isabella's rejection of incest, since Marc Shell has devoted an entire book to it. Important here would be the argument (in Freud and Lévi-Strauss) that incest is the originary object of prohibition, and that the reform of sexual licentiousness in Angelo's Vienna has as one of its goals the prevention of unwitting incest. See Shell 31–46.

33. In the Duke's "Measure still for Measure" speech, he says to Angelo, "We do condemn thee to the very block / Where Claudio stoop'd to death" (V.i.412–13); the scene is thus marked by different versions, whether staged or described, of kneeling.

34. Compare her initial plea for mercy: "I have a brother is condemn'd to die; / I do beseech you, let it be his fault / And not my brother" (II.ii.34–36).

35. On allegory as the figure of disjunction in signification, see Paul de Man, "The Rhetoric of Temporality"; his ideas are in turn indebted to Walter Benjamin, *The Origin of the German Tragic Drama*.

36. The possible connection between Barnadine / Barabbas and Bartleby was pointed out to me by Matthew Potolsky in a graduate seminar.

Chapter 6

1. On the life and work of Vasari from the perspective of art history, see T. S. R. Boase, *Giorgio Vasari: The Man and the Book*. In a 1960 essay, Svetlana Alpers analyzes Vasari's *ekphrastic* practices. Harry Berger, Jr., has excavated with his usual interpretive brilliance the classical myths of mimetic idealism that inform both the conscious program and the literary unconscious of Vasari's *Lives* ("Collecting Body Parts"). By far the most extended literary readings of Vasari that I have seen appear in Paul Barolsky's trilogy on the *Lives* (*Why Mona Lisa Smiles*, *Michelangelo's Nose*, and *Giotto's Father*); I am indebted throughout these pages to Barolsky's careful and creative tracking of literary and scriptural allusions in the *Lives*. On the con-

solidation of artistic career models through biography in the early modern period, see Rudolph and Margot Wittkower, *Born Under Saturn*; on Enlightenment developments, see Lawrence Lipking, *The Ordering of the Arts*, and works by Robert Folkenflik. On the idea of "Renaissance" in Vasari's writings, see Ferguson, *The Renaissance in Historical Thought* 59–67; he notes that the metaphor of rebirth was familiar "in the field of religious thought."

2. The *Lives of the Artists* was published by Vasari in 1550 and then extensively revised and expanded by the author in the second edition of 1568. The selected translation by George Bull follows the second edition, as does Licia and Carlo Ragghianti's complete Italian text of 1971. The more recent Luciano Bellosi and Aldo Rossi edition (1986) reproduces the 1550 edition. In general, I cite passages from Vasari's second edition, but follow the more architectonic scheme of the first edition, which ends with the life of Michelangelo. The theoretical introduction to the lives is available in English in *Vasari On Technique*, identified here as *Technique*; otherwise, editions are identified by editor and volume number.

3. Ti'amat is the salt-water goddess, and Apsu is the sweet-water god; in a series of intergenerational wars, Ti'amat is ultimately inflated and then dismembered by the conquering god Marduk in the creation of the world (Heidel 3–8). E. A. Speiser notes the verbal and thematic parallels in his commentary on Genesis in the *Anchor Bible*; see also John H. Walton, *Ancient Israelite Literature in Its Cultural Context* 19–44.

4. On *Grund* and *Abgrund*, see Rainer Nägele, *Benjamin's Ground* 19, 33–34.

5. Vasari plays on his foundational analogy between God's creation and the artist's when he describes the Sistine ceiling in the life of Michelangelo, a work that demonstrates "the perfection of art and the greatness of God" (Bull I: 355).

6. In Vasari's hexameral fable, God sculpts first, then paints, a privileging of sculpture that serves ultimately to establish the shaping function of *disegno* within painting, insofar as line gives "pose and contour" (*attitudini e contorni*) to the "softness," "light," and "shadow" (*morbidezza, lumi, ombre*) that characterize the coloristic resources of painting. As my student Draza Fratto pointed out in a seminar paper, the hierarchical couple of *disegno-colore* is implicitly modeled or designed after the couple of Adam and Eve in the scene of creation. The academic tradition that would grow out of Vasari and his circle affirmed this alignment of *disegno* with the masculine and *colore* with the feminine; thus the French academician Charles Blanc wrote in 1876, "The union of drawing and color is necessary to engender painting, as is the union of man and woman to engender humanity; but draw-

ing must predominate over color. If it is otherwise, painting courts its ruin; it would be lost through color as humanity was lost through Eve" (22). I thank James Herbert for this reference.

7. Vasari sets forth this point with special explictness in the opening remarks to the life of Masaccio (Bull I: 124).

8. The frame-tale of the *Heptameron*, first published in 1558, begins with a disastrous flood that serves to bring the noble company together; the flood is Marguerite's patently scriptural substitution for Boccaccio's plague. The *Heptameron*'s use of biblical typology is, of course, an analogue rather than a source for Vasari's double appropriation of the novella and the saint's legend. Barolsky comments on the Flood reference (*Giotto's Father* 4).

9. This is the role of the commentator prescribed by Leon Baptista Alberti, whose early humanist tract *Della Pittura* (1435–36) sets forth the requirements of the *istoria*, the composition of the history painting: "In an *istoria*, I like to see someone who admonishes and points out to us what is happening there; or beckons with his hand to see; or menaces with an angry face and with flashing eyes, so that no one should come near; or shows some danger or marvellous thing there; or invites us to weep or to laugh together with them" (78). In Leonardo's famous half-length portrait of St. John, the demonstrative function of pointing, separated from a central vision, has become an open invitation to the viewer to think ahead.

10. Thus Paul Barolsky emphasizes the figuration of Cimabue as John the Baptist to Giotto's Christ; although I have staged Cimabue as Abraham and Giotto as the Baptist, the power of typology lies in its retroactive transferrablity from one pair of artists to another.

11. Vasari's more obvious borrowings from the novella insert humorous anecdotes into individual lives in the style of Boccaccio's brief tales of witty repartee; in these episodes, Vasari's novella-derived tendencies are distinct from his hagiographic ones. Boase comments on this kind of use of the novella form (51). Examples include the episode of Giotto's "O," the nose of Michelangelo's David, the smile of Mona Lisa, and so on; on these scenes, see Paul Barolsky's excellent analyses in *Michelangelo's Nose* and *Why Mona Lisa Smiles*.

12. Vasari attributes at least four paintings of the subject to Lippi, and describes one in some detail: "For the church of Santa Maria Primerana, on the piazza of Fiesole, Fra Filippo did a panel picture of the Annunciation of Our Lady, finished with wonderful care, in which the figure of the angel is so beautiful that one can hardly doubt it comes from heaven" (Bull I: 216). On the historical details of the Lucrezia incident, see Wittkower and Wittkower 156.

13. Barolsky writes, "Through the power of the statue, they turned away from their laws, from the commandments brought to them by Moses himself, and turned toward Christ" (*Michelangelo's Nose* 43).

14. Compare Vasari's "*a schiera . . . come gli storni*" to Dante's simile of the carnal sinners, "*come li stornei ne portan l'ali / nel freddo tempo, a schiera larga e piena*" (*Inferno* V.40–41).

15. Thus Vasari distinguishes the ancient from the merely old: "I want to give a simple definition of what I call old [*vecchio*] and what I call ancient [*antico*]. Ancient works of sculpture are those which were produced in Corinth, Athens, Rome, and other famous cities, before the time of Constantine. . . . Old works of art are those which were produced from the time of St. Silvester by a few surviving Greek artists, who were dyers rather than painters" (Bull I: 45–46; Ragghianti I: 256).

16. Rainer Nägele, citing work by Beryl Schlossman, discusses the resurgence of the same coalition in Baudelaire and Kafka's "curious Catholic-Jewish subversion of Protestant secularization" (*Theater, Theory, Speculation* 184). And, in the same context, Nägele discusses Walter Benjamin's isolation of those elements of ancient tragedy that are not assimilated into the central dialectic of Western philosophy and culture: "Its discontinuity [with classical Greece] would shatter constitutive elements of a discourse of modernity embedded in the tradition of the *querelle des anciens et des modernes*" (183). Following Nägele's example, I am tracing the overlap between a nonclassical antiquity, an unconverted Judaism, and a pre-Tridentine Catholicism that fall out of Vasari's historical dialectic.

17. In this regard, Freud cites Jacob Burckhardt's description of the statue: "Moses seems to be shown at that moment at which he catches sight of the worship of the Golden Calf, and is springing to his feet. His form is animated by the inception of a mighty movement and the physical strength with which he is endowed causes us to await it with fear and trembling" (*SE* XIII: 216).

18. Freud cites the phrase from Max Sauerlandt (*SE* XIII: 213).

19. Alberti's *Della pittura* relies extensively on Pliny, as does Castiglione's brief commentary on painting and sculpture in *The Book of the Courtier*. Cristoforo Landino was both a friend of Alberti and a translator of Pliny's *Historia Naturalis* who gave a brief history of Florentine painting in his commentary on the *Divine Comedy* (Baxandall, *Painting and Experience* 114–38).

On Pliny's theory of art, see Jacob Isager, *Pliny on Art and Society*. For an art historiography modeled on natural history, see Svetlana Alpers, *The Art of Describing*. On natural history and *typography* (not typology), see J. Abbot Miller, ed., *Printed Letters: The Natural History of Typography*.

20. Pliny states the project of these two books on what we call art: "We have now practically indicated the nature of metals, in which wealth consists, and of the substances related to them, connecting the facts [*ita connexis rebus*] in such a way as to indicate at the same time the enormous topic of medicine [*immensa medicinae silva*] and the mysteries of the manufactories and the fastidious subtlety of the processes of carving and modelling and dyeing" (XXXV.1.1). The series constituted by carving, modelling and dyeing, linked to both medicine and coinage under the subject of metals, conceptualizes what will have come to be the fine arts as simply one set of natural manipulations among others within an immense taxonomy of technologies.

21. See, for example, Vasari's programmatic statement in the technical introduction to the *Lives* that "design cannot have a good origin if it has not come from continual practice in copying natural objects [*cosè naturali*], and from the study of pictures by excellent masters [*pitture d'eccellenti maestri*] and of ancient statues in relief" (*Technique* 211; Ragghianti I: 181). Here, there is both a distinction and a tacit equation between *cose naturali* and the *pitture d'eccellenti maestri*.

22. Thus Lacan, channeling the natural history of Roger Caillois into the discourse of psychoanalysis, comments on the function of mimicry in animal life: "To imitate is no doubt to reproduce an image. But at bottom, it is, for the subject, to be inserted in a function whose exercise grasps it" (*Seminar XI* 100).

23. Lacan describes the function of cause as "impediment, failure, split. . . . There, something other demands to be realized—which appears as intentional, but of a strange temporality. What occurs, what is *produced*, in this gap, is presented as *the discovery*" (*Seminar XI* 25).

24. Compare Stephen Bann's analysis of Pliny's anecdotes: "Parrhasius had managed to create *the illusion of a space in which figuration was destined to appear*" (*The True Vine* 35). Cf. Bryson, *Looking at the Overlooked* 30–32, 79–80.

25. See Freud, "On Fetishism," *SE* XXI: 152, and Lacan's account of the gaze as a disembodied thing that looks at the subject; Lacan's example is the gleam of an abandoned sardine can encountered on a boating trip with men of another social class (*Seminar XI* 95).

26. Auerbach notes the apparent syntactic similarity between *natura* and *figura*, saying of the latter that "this peculiar formation expresses something living and dynamic, incomplete and playful . . . the notion of the new manifestation, the changing aspect, of the permanent runs through the whole history of the word" (*Scenes from the Drama of European Literature* 11–12).

27. In this sense, even a "live specimen"—as in a zoo—is dead.

28. Many Dutch paintings in the tradition traced by Svetlana Alpers have *trompe-l'œil* curtains at the threshold of the pictured space, or mounds of meticulously described fabric with no body underneath; for a painting that combines both phenomena, see Vermeer's *Woman Reading a Letter* in the Staatliche Kunstsammlung, Dresden.

29. The life of Leonardo is riddled with naturalist anecdotes: the buckler comes alive in Leonardo's tamed lizard with fabricated wings; his balloons in the form of animals are curiosities; his allegory of genius (a balloon that fills an entire room and then deflates) is another performance piece.

30. Indeed, the cover of the Bellosi and Rossi edition frames off the detail of Raphael's self-portrait from the *School of Athens*, a choice of illustration that casts Vasari's project as a School of Artists. On Raphael's painting as a paradigm for the Christian-humanist historiographical project, see Leonard Barkan, *Consuming Passions* 10–19.

31. Leonardo's piece both imitates and dissolves the encylopedic function of another famous buckler: the shield of Achilles, which catalogues and calendars the daily life of Homeric Greece in an extended ekphrasis.

32. For a critique of Vasari that is both feminist and transalpine, see Svetlana Alpers, "Art History and Its Exclusions." For a Foucauldian critique of art history after Vasari, see Donald Preziosi, *Rethinking Art History: Meditations on a Coy Science.*

Chapter 7

1. The First Commandment is recast as a prologue in Christian traditions. On the links between the *sh'ma* and the Decalogue, see Feuer 63.

2. The medieval commentator Rashi was concerned enough by the apparent similarity between "other gods" and the otherness of the one God that he glossed *elohim aherim* as "gods of others" or, alternately, as "gods that are unable to answer when their devotees call to them and so appear as strangers" (paraphrased Goldman 135; see Feuer 28). I have in mind here as well the Lacanian distinction between S_1 (the singular, unary signifier; the signifier without signification specifically compared by Lacan to the tetragrammaton) and S_2 (the set of all other signifiers, the signifying chain).

3. In this, the Church fathers are closer to the Jewish and Catholic configuration of the commandment; thus Tertullian is concerned less with representing the Deity than with paying tribute through any kind of "form" or "formula"—his translation of *eidolon* (85).

4. In order to keep the number at ten, the reformers, following Jewish precedent, reunited the final two commandments in the Catholic count,

those against covetousness. In the Jewish count, the so-called prologue ("I am the Lord thy God") counts as the first commandment. For a full "accounting," see Goldman 30 and Aston 371–75.

5. So too, the threats and promises of the jealous God are attached to idolatry rather than polytheism in the revised Decalogue.

6. John Hooper, *Declaration of the ten holy commandments,* 1549. Cited Aston 435.

7. See, for example, the second part of the "Homilie against perill of Idolatry," on the authority of the Church fathers (21–26).

8. Nicholas Wyse, *A consolation for christian people to repair again to the lord's temple, with certain places of scripture truly applied to satisfy their minds for the expelling of idolatry,* 1538. Cited Aston 429.

9. This formulation intentionally recalls what Lacan, following Freud, called the "representative of representation," the *Vorstellungsrapräsentanz.* Moses Maimonides' gloss on this commandment discusses idols conceived as "ministers" of God—as "representatives" more than "representations" of God (Feuer 30).

10. See William Morse's careful exposition of the passage as "Leontes' self-representation, his own impulse to rational subjectivity" (292).

11. "For this reason a man shall leave his father and mother and be joined to his wife, and the two shall become one." Paul's proof-text is Gen. 2:24.

12. The idolator's inversion of creation *ex nihilo* culminates in Leontes' speech on "nothing" ("Is whispering nothing? / Is leaning cheek to cheek? . . . is this nothing? / Why then the world, and all that's in't, is nothing, / The covering sky is nothing, Bohemia nothing, / My wife is nothing, nor nothing have these nothings, / If this be nothing" 1.2.284–96). This is the nihilism of the idolator, who in insisting on the truth of his image uncreates God's creation by rendering it a lie.

13. See René Girard's related reading of the play in terms of mimetic desire, and Leslie Fiedler's analysis of homosocial desire (151–52).

14. The proof-text here is once more the definitive Deuteronomic statement of Jewish belief, the *sh'ma* prayer, whose statement of God's absolute singularity (*Adonai echad*) is followed immediately by the injunction to *love* that single God: "Thou shalt love the Lord thy God with all thy heart, and with all thy soul, and with all thy might" (Deut. 6:5).

15. "Technically, adultery is sexual intercourse of a married woman with any other man than her husband (Lev. 20:10, *et al.*)." (Goldman 182–83) See also Biale, *Women and Jewish Law* 183–89.

16. Lacan associates the incursive closeness of the neighbor with the intimate alterity of *das Ding*: "The *Ding* is the element that is initially iso-

lated by the subject in his experience of the *Nebenmensch* [neighbor] as being by its very nature alien, *Fremde*" (52). See Lacan's further discussions of the neighbor (39, 76, 151–52) and the Decalogue (79–83) in the same seminar. On the Thing in Shakespeare, see Lupton and Reinhard.

17. For the physiological sense, I am taken by the title of Wolfgang Wickler's book *The Biology of the Ten Commandments*, although he means something very different by it (an ethological naturalization of the last seven commandments).

18. This account of the generic and historical progress of the play from Judaism to Christianity via classicism, and from tragedy to romance via pastoral, is indebted to Harry Berger, Jr.'s account of Spenserian poetics as "evolutionary" and "retrospective" (*Revisionary Play* 243). It is no accident that *The Winter's Tale* is Shakespeare's most Spenserian work.

19. See also Neely 81.

20. Such allusive promises are seeds rather than blossoms, their fertility confirmed only by their effectivity in future poets; there may be, for example, a hint of Shakespeare in Milton's rather different negative citation of Proserpina in his description of Eden as "*Not* that fair field / Of Enna, where Proserpine gathering flow'rs / Herself a fairer flow'r by gloomy Dis / *Was* gathered" (*Paradise Lost* IV.268–71, emphasis mine).

21. Compare the bouquet of Spenser's "Aprill" eclogue to Perdita's flowers, both here and in the famous grafting speech:

> Bring hether the Pincke and purple Cullambine,
>> With *Gelliflowres*:
> Bring *Coronations*, and Sops in wine,
>> worne of Paramours.
> Strowe me the ground with *Daffadowndillies*,
> And *Cowslips*, and Kingcups, and loued *Lillies*:
>> The pretie Pawnce,
>> And the Cheuisaunce,
> Shall match with the fayre *flowre Delice*.

Italics indicate shared or related flowers.

On the other hand, Proserpina's bouquet in the *Fasti* does have several flowers in common with Perdita's: the lily, the violet, and perhaps the rose (compare to Shakespeare's "primrose"; *Fasti* IV.435–44. It may be more accurate to say that Perdita's bouquet combines Ovid's and Spenser's.

22. Noting that "the May Queen is turned into Flora," François Laroque writes that the Proserpina reference institutes "a parallel between the sacred calendar of Greek ritual and the profane calendar of agricultural activity and of seasonal rejoicing" (26).

23. John Guillory pointed out this allusion in his graduate seminar on pastoral at Yale in 1984.

24. I would insist, of course, *pace* the Arden editor, J. H. P. Pafford, that such "realistic" gestures are themselves part of the conventionality of pastoral, a dialectic staged most definitively in Virgil's *Eclogue* I, which counterposes exile and idyl at the inaugural threshold of Latin pastoral. See Patterson, "Vergil's *Eclogues*: Images of Change" and my "Home-Making in Ireland" 120–23.

25. Compare Laroque: "Perdita's anachronic reference to *Whitsun pastorals* (IV.4.134) is one sign among others in the play that the hints at the English church year and at its annual cyle of festivals were almost inseparable from the more obvious pagan allusions" (27).

26. One of Warburg's most obsessively analyzed images is Ghirlandaio's *Birth of John the Baptist*, which features a striding serving girl carrying a basket of fruit on her head (Gombrich, *Aby Warburg* 106ff and *passim*). It is no accident that the story of John the Baptist, forerunner of Christ within the confines of the New Testament, is such a powerful figure for typological readings, or that Warburg would concentrate so exclusively on the figure of the servant girl, both thematically and formally marginal to the central scene.

27. Compare Cordelia's characterization of the mad Lear as "poor *perdu*" (4.7.35).

28. Compare the function of the lost sheep in Virgil's *Eclogue* I, where the loss of the livestock emblematizes the exile of Meliboeus.

29. Stanza 14; cited Siemon 35.

30. Again, the later usage of Milton helps fix the meaning of Shakespeare's words; in Book VIII of *Paradise Lost*, Adam, falling into idolatrous uxoriousness, recalls his first experience before Eve, "transported I behold, / Transported touch" (VIII.529–30). Adam's idolatry is echoed in Satan's momentary hesitation in the face of Eve's pastoral beauty, "with what sweet / Compulsion thus transported to forget / What hither brought us" (IX.473–75).

31. On repetition in *The Winter's Tale*, see especially Frey, "Tragic Structure" and Siemon, "Iteration in *TWT*."

32. Stephen Orgel commented on the epigraphs to the life of Giulio Romano in a lecture on *The Winter's Tale* delivered at the University of California, San Diego, Sept. 1992. Barkan emphasizes Vasari's life of Michelangelo as an analogue for Shakespeare's play, and also discusses the theatricality of Romano's Sala dei Giganti in the Palazzo del Te ("'Living Sculptures'" 655). Of Pygmalion Vasari writes, "It was Pygmalion of whom the story goes that, in answer to his prayers, the girl he had carved from

stone was brought to life"; Vasari's Pygmalion is clearly a prototype of Renaissance (Bull I: 28).

33. The Arch of Trajan and the baptismal font of Constantine are both overdetermined references for Vasari; in his Preface to the *Lives*, Vasari associates the first with the classical heyday of Roman arches, pointedly contrasted to the decadence of Constantine's arch (Bull I: 32), and the font, "ornamented with sculptures made a long time ago" (34), becomes a figure of the Christian pillaging and resignification of classical art.

34. Pafford notes the comparison: Shakespeare, *The Winter's Tale*, lxiii.

35. Compare Barkan's discussion of Michelangelo's "Night" as a subject that reinforces the medium of sculpture ("'Living Sculptures'" 648).

36. Hab. 2:10–11; cited by Pafford in Shakespeare, *The Winter's Tale*, 156.

Bibliography

Abraham, Nicolas, and Maria Torok. *L'écorce et le noyau*. Paris: Flammarion, 1978.

Almansi, Guido. *The Writer as Liar: Narrative Technique in the "Decameron."* London: Routledge and Kegan Paul, 1975.

Alpers, Svetlana. *"Ekphrasis* and Aesthetic Attitudes in Vasari's *Lives." JWCI* 23 (1960).

————. "Art History and Its Exclusions." In Norma Broude and Mary D. Garrard, eds., *Feminism and Art History: Questioning the Litany*. New York: Harper and Row, 1982. 182–99.

————. *The Art of Describing: Dutch Art in the Seventeenth Century*. Chicago: University of Chicago Press, 1983.

Alter, Robert, and Frank Kermode, eds. *The Literary Guide to the Bible*. Cambridge, Mass.: Harvard University Press, 1987.

Altman, Charles. "Two Types of Opposition and the Structure of Latin Saints' Lives." *Medievalia et Humanistica* 6 (1975): 1–11.

Ambrose, Saint. *Hexameron, Paradise, and Cain and Abel*. New York: Fathers of the Church, 1961.

Ariosto, Ludovico. *Orlando Furioso*. Ed. Emilio Bigi. Milan: Rusconi Libri, 1982.

Aristotle. *Poetics*. Trans. W. Hamilton Fyfe. Harvard, Mass.: Loeb Classics, 1927. Rev. 1932. Rpt. 1982.

Aston, Margaret. *England's Iconoclasts. Volume I: Laws against Images*. Oxford: Clarendon Press, 1988.

Athanasius. *The Life of Antony and the Letter to Marcellinus.* Trans. and introduction by Robert C. Gregg. New York: Paulist Press, 1980.

Auerbach, Erich. "Figura." In *Scenes from the Drama of European Literature.* 1959. Minneapolis: University of Minnesota Press, 1984. 11–76.

———. *Mimesis: The Representation of Reality in Western Literature.* Trans. Willard R. Trask. Princeton: Princeton University Press, 1953.

Augustine, Saint. *On Christian Doctrine.* Trans. D. W. Robertson. Indianapolis: Bobbs-Merrill, 1958.

———. *The City of God.* Trans. Henry Bettenson. Harmondsworth, Middlesex: Penguin Books, 1972.

———. *Confessions.* 2 vols. Trans. William Watts. Cambridge, Mass.: Harvard / Loeb Library, 1912.

Bann, Stephen. *The True Vine: Visual Representation and Western Tradition.* Cambridge, Eng.: Cambridge University Press, 1989.

Barkan, Leonard. "'Living Sculptures': Ovid, Michelangelo, and *The Winter's Tale.*" *ELH* 48.4 (Winter 1981): 639–67.

———. *Transuming Passions: Ganymede and the Erotics of Humanism.* Stanford, Calif.: Stanford University Press, 1991.

Barolsky, Paul. *Giotto's Father and the Family of Vasari's "Lives."* University Park: The Pennsylvania State University Press, 1992.

———. *Michelangelo's Nose: A Myth and Its Maker.* University Park: The Pennsylvania State University Press, 1990.

———. *Why Mona Lisa Smiles and Other Tales by Vasari.* University Park: The Pennsylvania State University Press, 1991.

Batman, Stephen. *The Golden Booke of the Leaden Goddes, wherein is described the vayne imaginations of Heathe Pagans, and counterfaict Christians.* 1577. Facsimile ed. Stephen Orgel. New York: Garland Press, 1976.

Battenhouse, Roy. "*Measure for Measure* and Christian Doctrine of Atonement." *PMLA* 61.4 (1946): 1029–59.

———. "Theme and Structure in 'The Winter's Tale.'" *Shakespeare Survey* 33 (1980): 123–38.

Baxandall, Michael. *Giotto and the Orators: Humanist Observers of Painting in Italy and the Discovery of Pictorial Composition, 1350–1450.* Oxford: Clarendon Press, 1971.

Benati, Pino. *Santa Cecilia nella Legenda e nell'Arte.* Milan: Luigi Alfieri.

Benjamin, Walter. *The Correspondence of Walter Benjamin, 1910–1940.* Ed. and ann. Gershom Scholem and Theodor W. Adorno. Trans. Manfred R. Jacobson and Evelyn M. Jacobson. Chicago: University of Chicago Press, 1994.

———. *One Way Street and Other Writings.* Trans. Edmund Jephcott and Kingsely Shorter. London: Verso, 1979.

————. *Ursprung des deutschen Trauerspiels.* Ed. Rolf Tiedemann. Frankfurt: Suhrkamp, 1955. Trans. as *The Origin of German Tragic Drama* by John Osborne. London: New Left Books, 1977.

Bennett, Jennifer. *Lilies of the Hearth: The Historical Relationship between Women and Plants.* Camden, Ont.: Camden House Books, 1991.

Benson, Larry D., ed. *The Riverside Chaucer.* Third ed. Boston: Houghton Mifflin, 1987.

Berg, William J., Michel Grimaud, and George Moskos. *Saint/Oedipus: Psychocritical Approaches to Flaubert's Art.* Ithaca: Cornell University Press, 1982.

Berger, Harry, Jr. "Collecting Body Parts in Leonardo's Cave: Vasari's *Lives of the Artists* and the Erotics of Obscene Connoisseurship." Presented at the Twenty-Fifth Annual Faculty Research Lecture, University of California, Santa Cruz, June 6, 1991.

————. *Revisionary Play: Studies in the Spenserian Dynamics.* Berkeley: University of California Press, 1988.

Besserman, Lawrence. *The Legend of Job in the Middle Ages.* Cambridge, Mass.: Harvard University Press, 1979.

Biale, Rachel. *Women and Jewish Law: An Exploration of Women's Issues in Halakhic Sources.* New York: Schocken Books, 1984.

The Bible. *The Oxford Annotated Bible, Revised Standard Edition.* Ed. Herbert G. May and Bruce M. Metzger. New York: Oxford University Press, 1962.

Biblioroum Sacrorum iuxta Vulgatam Clementium. (The Vulgate.) Ed. Aloisius Gramatica. Rome: Vatican, 1959.

Blanc, Charles. *Grammaire des arts du dessin: architecture, sculpture, peinture.* 1st ed., 1876. Paris: Librairie Renouard, 1876.

Bloom, Harold, ed. *William Shakespeare's "The Winter's Tale": Modern Critical Interpretations.* New York: Chelsea House, 1987.

Boase, T. S. R. *Giorgio Vasari: The Man and the Book.* Washington, D.C.: National Gallery of Art, 1971. Bollingen Series 35, Princeton University Press.

Boccaccio, Giovanni. *The Decameron.* Trans. G. H. McWilliam. Middlesex: Penguin, 1972.

————. *Decameron.* Ed. Vittore Branca. Turin: Giulio Einaudi, 1980.

————. *The Elegy of Lady Fiametta.* Ed. and trans. Mariangela Causa-Steindler and Thomas Mauch. Chicago: University of Chicago Press, 1990.

————. *The Life of Dante (Trattatello in Laude di Dante).* Trans. Vincenzo Zin Bollettino. New York: Garland, 1990.

————. "Trattatello in Laude di Dante." In Vittore Branca, ed., *Tutte le opere di Giovanni Boccaccio.* Vol. 3. Milan: Mondadori, 1974. 423–538.

Boureau, Alain. *La légende dorée: le système narratif de Jacques de Voragine.* Preface by Jacques le Goff. Paris: Les Éditions du Cerf, 1984.

Boyarin, Daniel. *A Radical Jew: Paul and the Politics of Identity.* Berkeley: University of California Press, 1994.

Bradbrook, M. C. "Authority, Truth, and Justice in *Measure for Measure.*" *Review of English Studies* 62.68 (1941): 385–99.

Bramly, Serge. *Leonardo: Discovering the Life of Leonardo da Vinci.* Trans. Siân Reynolds. New York: HarperCollins, 1991.

Bredekamp, Horst, Michael Diers, and Charlotte Schoell-Glass, eds. *Aby Warburg: Akten des internationalen Symposiums Hamburg 1990.* Weinheim: VCH Verlagsgesellschaft, 1991.

Brodersen, Momme. "Wenn Ihnen die Arbeit des Interesses wert erscheint . . . Walter Benjamin und das Warburg-Institut: einige Dokumente." In Bredekamp et al., *Aby Warburg.* 87–94.

Brown, Judith C. *Immodest Acts: The Life of a Lesbian Nun in Renaissance Italy.* New York: Oxford, 1986.

Brown, Peter. *The Cult of the Saints: Its Rise and Function in Late Antiquity.* Chicago: University of Chicago Press, 1981.

———. *Society and the Holy in Late Antiquity.* Berkeley: University of California Press, 1982.

Bryson, Norman. *Looking at the Overlooked: Four Essays on Still Life Painting.* Cambridge, Mass.: Harvard University Press, 1990.

Burckhardt, Jacob. *Die Kultur der Renaissance in Italien: Ein Versuch.* 1860. Ed. Walter Goetz. Stuttgart: Alfred Kröner Verlag, 1976. Trans. S. G. C. Middlemore as *The Culture of the Renaissance in Italy.* 2 vols. New York: Harper and Row, 1958.

———. *Weltgeschichtliche Betrachtungen: Über geschichtliches Studium.* Munich: Deutscher Taschenbuch Verlag, 1978.

Burke, Peter. "Aby Warburg as Historical Anthropologist." In Bredekamp et al., *Aby Warburg.* 39–44.

Bushnell, Rebecca. *Prophesying Tragedy: Sign and Voice in Sophocles' Theban Plays.* Ithaca: Cornell University Press, 1988.

Bynum, Caroline Walker. *Holy Feast and Holy Fast: The Religious Significance of Food to Medieval Women.* Berkeley: University of California Press, 1987.

Carmichael, Calum M. *Law and Narrative in the Bible: The Evidence of the Deuteronomic Laws and the Decalogue.* Ithaca: Cornell University Press, 1985.

———. *The Origins of Biblical Law: The Decalogues and the Book of the Covenant.* Ithaca: Cornell University Press, 1992.

Cartari, Vincenzo. *Le imagini de i dei de gli antichi*. Venice, 1556. Reprinted 1571. Facsimile edition, ed. Stephen Orgel. New York: Garland, 1976.

Caxton, William, trans. *The Golden Legend, or Lives of the Saints*. By Jacobus de Voragine. 7 vols. London: J.M. Dent, 1900.

Certaine Sermons or Homilies Appointed to be Read in Churches in the Time of Queen Elizabeth. Ed. Mary Ellen Rickey and Thomas B. Stroup. Facsimile of 1623 ed. Gainesville, Fla.: Scholars Facsimiles and Reprints, 1968.

Christine de Pizan. *The Book of the City of Ladies*. Trans. Earl Jeffrey Richards. New York: Persea, 1982.

Coghill, Nevill. "Comic Form in *Measure for Measure*." *Shakespeare Survey* 8 (1955): 14–27.

Cohen, A., ed. *The Five Megilloth*. Hebrew text and English translation. London: Soncino Press, 1984.

———. *The Soncino Chumash: The Five Books of Moses with Haphtaroth*. Hebrew text and English translation. 1947. Rprt. Brooklyn, New York: Soncino Press, 1983.

Cole, Bruce. *Sienese Painting From Its Origins to the Fifteenth Century*. New York: Harper and Row, 1980.

Cottino-Jones, Marga. "Fabula vs. Figura: Another Interpretation of the Griselda Story." In Musa and Bondanella, eds., *The Decameron*. 295–305.

Curtius, Ernst Robert. *European Literature and the Latin Middle Ages*. Trans. Willard R. Trask. Princeton: Princeton University Press, 1973.

Dante Alighieri. *The Divine Comedy*. 3 vols. Trans. and commentary by Charles Singleton. Princeton: Princeton University Press, 1970; 1977.

d'Ardenne, S. R. T. O., and E. J. Hobson. *Seinte Katerine*. Oxford University Press and the Early English Text Soceity, 1981.

Delahaye, Hippolyte, S. J. *The Legends of the Saints: An Introduction to Hagiography*. Trans. V. M. Crawford. 1907. Rpt. Indiana: University of Notre Dame Press, 1961.

Deleuze, Gilles, and Félix Guattari. *A Thousand Plateaus: Capitalism and Schizophrenia*. Trans. Brian Massumi. Minneapolis: University of Minnesota Press, 1987.

de Man, Paul. "The Rhetoric of Temporality." In de Man, *Blindness and Insight*, rev. ed. Minneapolis: University of Minnesota Press, 1983. 187–228.

de'Medici, Lorenza. *Florentines: A Tuscan Feast*. Illustrations by Giovanna Garzoni, 1600–1670. New York: Random House, 1992.

de' Negri, Enrico. "The Legendary Style of the *Decameron*." *Romanic Review* 5.43 (1952): 166–89.

Derrida, Jacques. "La Loi du Genre / The Law of Genre." Trans. Avital Ronell. *Glyph* 7: 172–232.

Detienne, Marcel, and Jean-Pierre Vernant. *The Cuisine of Sacrifice Among the Greeks*. 1979. Trans. Paula Wissing. Chicago: University of Chicago Press, 1989.

Dollimore, Jonathan. "Transgression and Surveillance in *Measure for Measure*." In Dollimore and Sinfield, eds., *Political Shakespeare*. 72–87.

————, and Alan Sinfield, eds. *Political Shakespeare: New Essays in Cultural Materialism*. Ithaca: Cornell, 1985.

Dombrowski, Robert S., ed. *Critical Perspectives on the* Decameron. London: Hodder and Stoughton, 1976.

Drakakis, John, ed. *Alternative Shakespeares*. Cambridge, Eng.: Cambridge University Press, 1985.

duBois, Page. *Sowing the Body: Psychoanalysis and Ancient Representations of Woman*. Chicago: University of Chicago, 1988.

During, Simon, ed. *The Cultural Studies Reader*. London: Routledge, 1993.

Eccles, Mark, ed. *Measure for Measure: A New Variorum*. New York: MLA, 1980.

Eerdman's Bible Dictionary. Rev. ed. Allen C. Meyers. Grand Rapids, Mich.: William B. Eerdmans, 1987.

Elton, William. *King Lear and the Gods*. Rev. ed. Lexington: University of Kentucky Press, 1988.

Eusebius Pamphili. *Ecclesiastical History*. 2 vols. Trans. Roy J. Deferrari. New York: Fathers of the Church, 1955.

Felman, Shoshana. "To Open the Question." In Felman, ed., *Literature and Psychoanalysis: The Question of Reading: Otherwise*. Baltimore: The Johns Hopkins University Press, 1982. 5–10.

Ferguson, Margaret, Maureen Quilligan, and Nancy J. Vickers, eds. *Rewriting the Renaissance: The Discourses of Sexual Difference in Early Modern Europe*. Chicago: University of Chicago Press, 1986.

Ferguson, Wallace. *The Renaissance in Historical Thought: Five Centuries of Interpretation*. Boston: Houghton Mifflin, 1948.

Ferretti, Silvia. *Cassirer, Panofsky, and Warburg: Symbol, Art, and History*. Trans. Richard Pierce. New Haven: Yale University Press, 1989.

Feuer, Avrohom Chaim, trans. and commentary. *Aseres Hadibros / The Ten Commandments: A New Translation with Commentary Anthologized from Talmudic, Midrashic, and Rabbinic Sources*. New York: Mesorah, 1981.

Fiedler, Leslie. *The Stranger in Shakespeare*. New York: Stein and Day, 1972.

Fineman, Joel. "Fratricide and Cuckoldry: Shakespeare's Doubles." In Schwartz, *Representing Shakespeare*. 70–109.

―――. *The Subjectivity Effect in Western Literary Tradition: Essays Towards the Release of Shakespeare's Will.* Cambridge, Mass.: MIT Press, 1991.

Flaubert, Gustav. *La tentation de st. Antoine.* Ed. Jacques Suffel. Paris: Garnier Flammarion, 1967.

Folkenflik, Robert. "Patronage and the Poet-Hero." *Huntington Library Quarterly* 48 (1985): 363–79.

―――. *Samuel Johnson, Biographer.* Ithaca: Cornell University Press, 1978.

Foucault, Michel. "Fantasia of the Library." In Foucault, *Language, Counter-Memory, Practice: Selected Essays and Interviews.* Ed. Donald F. Bouchard. Trans. Donald F. Bouchard and Sherry Simon. Ithaca, N.Y.: Cornell University Press, 1977. 87–109.

―――. "The Father's 'No.'" In Foucault, *Language, Counter-Memory, Practice.* 68–86.

Foxe, John. *Acts and Monuments.* 8 vols. New York: AMS Press, 1965.

Frank, Robert Worth, Jr. *Chaucer and the Legend of Good Women.* Cambridge, Mass.: Harvard University Press, 1972.

Freud, Sigmund. *The Standard Edition of the Complete Psychological Works.* 24 vols. Trans. and ed. James Strachey. London: Hogarth Press, 1955, 1958.

Friedlaender, Walter. *Caravaggio Studies.* Princeton: Princeton University Press, 1955.

Frey, Charles. "Tragic Structure in *The Winter's Tale*: The Affective Dimension." In Bloom, ed., *Shakespeare's "The Winter's Tale."* 89–100.

Frye, Northrop. *Anatomy of Criticism: Four Essays.* Princeton: Princeton University Press, 1957.

―――. *The Great Code: The Bible and Literature.* Orlando, Fla.: Harcourt Brace Jovanovich, 1982.

Gadamer, Hans-Georg. *Truth and Method.* Trans. Garrett Barden and John Cumming. New York: Crossroads Publishing, 1975.

Gallagher, Lowell. "Ambivalent Nostalgia in *The Winter's Tale.*" *Exemplaria* 7.2 (Fall 1995): 465–98.

Georgianna, Linda. "The Protestant Chaucer." In C. David Benson and Elizabeth Robertson, eds., *Chaucer's Religious Tales.* Cambridge, Eng.: Boydell and Brewer, 1990. 55–69.

Girard, René. "Jealousy in *The Winter's Tale.*" In Brigitte Cazelles and René Girard, eds., *Alphonse Juilland: D'une passion l'autre.* Palo Alto, Calif.: Stanford French and Italian Studies, 1987. 39–62.

―――. *Violence and the Sacred.* Trans. Patrick Gregory. Baltimore: Johns Hopkins University Press, 1977.

Gless, Darryl J. *Measure for Measure, the Law, and the Convent.* Princeton, N.J.: Princeton University Press, 1979.

Goddard, Alison Elliott. *Roads to Paradise: Reading the Lives of the Early Saints*. Hanover: University Press of New England, 1987.

Goldman, Solomon. *The Ten Commandments*. Chicago: University of Chicago Press, 1956.

Gombrich, Ernst. *Aby Warburg: An Intellectual Biography*. Oxford: Phaidon Press, 1986.

———. *In Search of Cultural History*. Oxford: Clarendon Press, 1969.

Gregory the Great. *Dialogues*. Trans. Odo John Zimmerman, O.S.B. New York: Fathers of the Church, 1959.

Greene, Thomas M. "Forms of Accommodation in the *Decameron*." In Dombrowski, ed., *Critical Perspectives*. 113–28.

Guillory, John. *Cultural Capital: The Problem of Literary Canon Formation*. Chicago: University of Chicago Press, 1993.

———. *Poetic Authority: Spenser, Milton, and Literary History*. New York: Columbia University Press, 1983.

Hardtwig, Wolfgang. *Geschichtsschreibung zwischen Alteuropa und moderner Welt: Jacob Burckhardt in seiner Zeit*. Göttingen: Vandenhoeck and Ruprecht, 1974.

Harpham, Geoffrey Galt. *The Ascetic Imperative in Culture and Criticism*. Chicago: University of Chicago Press, 1987.

Hegel, G. W. F. *Aesthetics: Lectures on Fine Arts*. 2 vols. Trans. T. M. Knox. Oxford: Clarendon Press, 1975.

Heidel, Alexander. *The Babylonian Genesis: The Story of Creation*. Chicago: University of Chicago Press, 1942. Second ed. 1951.

Hibbard, Howard. *Caravaggio*. New York: Harper and Row, 1983.

———. *Michelangelo*. Second ed. New York: Harper and Row, 1974.

Hill, Christopher. *Society and Puritanism in Pre-Revolutionary England*. London: Secker E. Warburg, 1964.

Holderness, Graham, ed. *The Shakespeare Myth*. Manchester: Manchester University Press, 1988.

Holly, Michael Ann. *Panofsky and the Foundations of Art History*. Ithaca: Cornell University Press, 1984.

Hunter, G. K. "Tyrant and Martyr: Religious Heroism in Elizabethan Tragedy." In Maynard Mack and George de F. Lord, eds., *Poetic Traditions in the Renaissance*. New Haven: Yale, 1982.

Isager, Jacob. *Pliny on Art and Society: The Elder Pliny's Chapters on the History of Art*. London: Routledge, 1991.

Isidore of Seville. *Etymologiae*. 17 vols. Ed., trans., and commentary by Jacques André. Paris: Société d'Édition "Les Belles Lettres," 1981.

Iversen, Margaret. "Retrieving Warburg's Tradition." *Art History* 16.4 (Dec. 1993): 541–53.

Jameson, Fredric. *The Political Unconscious: Narrative as a Socially Symbolic Act.* Ithaca: Cornell University Press, 1981.

Jerome, St. "Letter to Eustochium." In *Selected Letters of Saint Jerome.* Trans. F. A. Wright. 1933. Rpt. Cambridge, Mass.: Harvard / Loeb, 1954. 53–159.

———. "Life of St. Paul the Hermit." Trans. Sister Marie Luguori Ewald. In Roy J. Deferrari, ed., *Early Christian Biographies.* Volume 15 of *The Fathers of the Church.* General ed. Roy Joseph Deferrari. Washington, D.C.: Catholic University Press of America, 1964. 217–38.

———. "Vita S. Pauli Primi Eremitae." In J.-P. Migne, ed., *Patrologiae, Series Latina.* Vol. 23. Paris: 1883. 18–30.

Johnson, Phyllis, and Brigitte Cazelles. *Le vain siècle guerpir: A Literary Approach to Sainthood through Old French Hagiography of the Twelfth Century.* Chapel Hill: North Carolina Studies in the Romance Languages and Literatures, No. 205, 1979.

Kant, Immanuel. "Beantwortung der Frage: Was ist Aufklärung?" In Otto F. Best, ed., *Die deutsche Literatur in Text und Darstellung: Aufklärung und Rokoko.* Stuttgart: Reclam, 1980. 42–45.

Kieckhefer, Richard. *Unquiet Souls: Fourteenth-Century Saints and Their Religious Milieu.* Chicago: University of Chicago Press, 1984.

Kierkegaard, Sören. "The Ancient Tragical Motif as Reflected in the Modern." In *Either/Or,* Vol. 1. Ed. and trans. Howard V. Hong and Edna H. Hong. Princeton: Princeton University Press, 1987. 139–64.

Kirsch, Arthur. "The Integrity of *Measure for Measure.*" *Shakespeare Survey* 28 (1975): 89–105.

Kiser, Lisa. *Telling Classical Tales: Chaucer and the* Legend of Good Women. Ithaca: Cornell University Press, 1983.

Knight, G. Wilson. "'Great Creating Nature': An Essay on *The Winter's Tale.*" In Bloom, ed., *Shakespeare's "The Winter's Tale."* 7–45.

———. "*Measure for Measure* and the Gospels." In Knight, *The Wheel of Fire,* rev. ed. New York: Oxford, 1949. 73–96.

Krauss, Rosalind. *The Optical Unconscious.* Cambridge, Mass.: MIT Press, 1993.

Kunstmann, Pierre. *Treize Miracles de Notre Dame.* Ottawa, Canada: Éditions de l'Université d'Ottowa, 1981.

Lacan, Jacques. "Intervention on Transference." Trans. Jacqueline Rose. In Charles Bernheimer and Claire Kahane, eds., *In Dora's Case: Freud—Hysteria—Feminism.* New York: Columbia University Press, 1985. 92–104.

———. *Le séminaire, livre VII: L'éthic de la psychanalyse.* Text established Jacques Alain-Miller. Paris: Editions du Seuil, 1986. Trans. as *Seminar*

VII: The Ethics of Psychoanalysis. Trans. Dennis Porter. New York: Norton, 1992.

——. *Seminar XI: The Four Fundamental Concepts of Psychoanalysis*. Text established Jacques-Alain Miller. Trans. Alan Sheridan. New York: W. W. Norton, 1978.

——. *Le séminaire, livre XXIII, 1975–76: Le Sinthome*. Text established Jacques-Alain Miller. Published in *Ornicar?* 6 (1976): 3–20; 7 (1976): 3–18; 8 (1976): 6–20, 9 (1977): 32–40; 10 (1977): 5–12; 11 (1977): 2–9.

Laplanche, Jean, and J.-B. Pontalis. *The Language of Psychoanalysis*. Trans. Donald Nicholson-Smith. New York: Norton, 1973.

Laroque, François. "Pagan Ritual, Christian Liturgy, and Folk Customs in *The Winter's Tale*." *Cahiers Élisabéthains*. 22 (Oct. 1982): 25–34.

Lavin, Irving. "Divine Inspiration in Caravaggio's Two Saint Matthews." *Art Bulletin* 56 (1974): 59–81.

Leavis, F. R. "The Greatness of *Measure for Measure*." *Scrutiny* 10: 234–47.

Lever, J. W., ed. *Measure for Measure*. William Shakespeare. Arden ed. London: Methuen, 1967.

Lévinas, Emmanuel. *The Lévinas Reader*. Ed. Seán Hand. Oxford: Basil Blackwell, 1989.

——. "The Pact." In *The Lévinas Reader*. 211–26.

——. "Une religion d'adultes." In *Difficile liberté: Essais sur le judaïsme*. 3rd ed. Éditions Albin Michel, 1976. 24–22.

"Substitution." In *The Lévinas Reader*. 88–125.

Lipking, Lawrence. *The Ordering of the Arts in Eighteenth-Century England*. Princeton: Princeton University Press, 1970.

Lloyd-Jones, Hugh. "Biographical Memoir." In Edgar Wind, *The Eloquence of Symbols: Studies in Humanist Art*. Ed. Jaynie Anderson. Oxford: Clarendon Press, 1983. xiii–xxxvi.

Löwith, Karl. *Meaning in History*. Chicago: University of Chicago Press, 1949.

——. *Mein Leben in Deutschland vor und nach 1933*. Stuttgart: J. B. Metzlersche Verlagsbuchhandlung, 1986.

Lugli, Adalgisa. "Inquiry as Collection: The Athanasius Kircher Museum in Rome." *Res* 12 (Autumn 1986): 109–24.

Lupton, Julia Reinhard. "Home-Making in Ireland: Virgil's Eclogue I and Book VI of *The Faerie Queene*." *Spenser Studies* 8. New York: AMS Press, 1990. 119–45.

——, and Kenneth Reinhard. *After Oedipus: Shakespeare in Psychoanalysis*. Ithaca: Cornell University Press, 1993.

Luther, Martin. *Biblia, das ist die gantze Heilige Schrifft, deudsch auff new zugericht.* Wittenberg, 1545. 3 vols. Ed. Hans Volz. Munich: Deutscher Taschenbuch Verlag, 1974.

Lyotard, Jean-François. *The Post-Modern Condition: A Report on Knowledge.* Trans. Geoff Bennington and Brian Massumi. Minneapolis: University of Minnesota Press, 1984.

MacCannell, Juliet Flower. *The Regime of the Brother: After the Patriarchy.* London: Routledge, 1991.

Marcus, Millicent Joy. *An Allegory of Form: Literary Self-Consciousness in the Decameron.* Saratoga, Calif.: Anma Libri, 1979.

Marguerite de Navarre. *The Heptameron.* Trans. P. A. Chilton. Harmondsworth, Middlesex: Penguin, 1984.

Marin, Louis. *Food for Thought.* Trans. Mette Hjort. Baltimore: Johns Hopkins University Press, 1989.

Marlowe, Christopher. *The Jew of Malta.* In Russell A. Fraser and Norman Rabkin, eds., *Drama of the English Renaissance, Volume 1: The Tudor Period.* New York: Macmillan, 1976. 263–94.

Mazzotta, Giuseppe. *Dante, Poet of the Desert: History and Allegory in the Divine Comedy.* Princeton: Princeton University Press, 1979.

———. "The Marginality of Literature." In Dombrowski, ed., *Critical Perspectives.* 129–43.

———. *The World at Play in Boccaccio's Decameron.* Princeton: Princeton University Press, 1986.

McLuskie, Kathleen. "The Patriarchal Bard: Feminist Criticism and Shakespeare: *King Lear* and *Measure for Measure.*" In Dollimore and Sinfield, eds., *Political Shakespeare.* 88–108.

McNamara, Jo Ann, and John E. Halborg, ed. and trans., with E. Gordon Whatley. *Sainted Women of the Dark Ages.* Durham, N.C.: Duke University Press, 1992.

Miller, J. Abbott, ed. *Printed Letters: The Natural History of Typography.* Jersey City, N.J.: Jersey City Museum, 1992.

Miller, J. Hillis. *Versions of Pygmalion.* Cambridge, Mass.: Harvard University Press, 1990.

Miller, Jacques-Alain. "Extimité." *Prose Studies* 11 (1988): 121–30.

———. "Reflections on the Formal Envelope of the Symptom." *lacanian ink* 4 (Fall 1991): 13–21.

———. "Du symptôme au fantasme et retour." 2 vols. Seminar given 1982–83. Unpublished.

Milton, John. *Paradise Lost.* Ed. Scott Elledge. New York: Norton, 1975.

Morse, William R. "Metacriticism and Materiality: The Case of Shakespeare's *The Winter's Tale.*" *ELH* 58.2 (1991): 283–304.

Mouffe, Chantal. *The Return of the Political.* London: Verso, 1993.

Musa, Mark, and Peter E. Bondanella, ed. and trans. *The Decameron.* New York: Norton Critical Editions, 1977.

Musurillo, Herbert, ed. and trans. *The Acts of the Christian Martyrs.* London: Clarendon Press, 1972.

Nägele, Rainer. "Reading Benjamin." In Nägele, ed., *Benjamin's Ground: New Readings of Walter Benjamin.* Detroit: Wayne State University Press, 1988. 7–37.

————. *Theater, Theory, Speculation: Walter Benjamin and the Scenes of Modernity.* Baltimore: The Johns Hopkins University Press, 1991.

Neely, Carol Thomas. "Women and Issue in *The Winter's Tale.*" In Bloom, ed., *Shakespeare's "The Winter's Tale."* 75–88.

Neusner, Jacob. *Introduction to Rabbinic Literature.* New York: Doubleday, 1994.

Nicholson, Eric. "The *Decameron's* Magic Theatre." Paper delivered at Kalamazoo Medieval Conference, 1986.

Nietzsche, Friedrich. *The Birth of Tragedy.* Trans. Walter Kaufman. New York: Random House, 1967.

O'Connell, Canon J. B., ed. *The Roman Martyrology, in Which Are To Be Found the Eulogies of the Saints and Blessed Approved by the Sacred Congregation of Rites Up to 1961.* Westminster, Md.: Newman Press, 1962.

O'Connell, Michael. "The Idolatrous Eye: Iconoclasm, Anti-Theatricalism, and the Image of the Elizabethan Theatre." *ELH* 52.2 (1985): 279–310.

Orgel, Stephen. "The Poetics of Incomprehensibility." *Shakespeare Quarterly* 42.4 (Winter 1991): 431–37.

Ovid. *Fasti.* Trans. Sir James Frazer. 1931. Second ed., 1989. Cambridge, Mass.: Harvard / Loeb Classics, 1989.

————. *Metamorphoses.* 2 vols. 1916. Trans. Frank Justus Miller. Cambridge, Mass.: Harvard / Loeb Classics, 1976.

Pafford, J. H., ed. *The Winter's Tale.* William Shakespeare. Arden ed. London: Methuen, 1963.

Pagels, Elaine. *Adam, Eve, and the Serpent.* New York: Random House, 1988.

Panofsky, Erwin. *Early Netherlandish Painting.* 2 vols. 1953. New York: Harper and Row, 1971.

————. "Iconography and Iconology: An Introduction to the Study of Renaissance Art." In Panofsky, *Meaning and the Visual Arts.* Chicago: University of Chicago Press, 1955. 26–54.

————. *Renaissance and Renascences in Western Art.* Stockholm: Almquist and Wiksell, 1960.

Patterson, Annabel. "Vergil's *Eclogues*: Images of Change." In Patterson, ed., *Roman Images*. Baltimore: Johns Hopkins University Press, 1982. 165–86.

Paulinus. "Life of St. Ambrose." Trans. John A. Lacy. In Roy J. Deferrari, ed., *Early Christian Biographies*. The Fathers of the Church, vol. 15. Washington, D.C.: Catholic University Press, 27–66.

Phillippy, Patricia. "Love's Remedies: Palinodic Discourse in Renaissance Literature." Dissertation. Yale University, 1988.

Pliny the Elder. *Natural History*. 9 vols. Trans. H. Rackham. Cambridge, Mass.: Harvard / Loeb Classics, 1952.

Porter, J. R. *Leviticus*. (Commentary.) Cambridge, Eng.: Cambridge University Press, 1976.

Potter, Joy Hambuechen. *Five Frames for the Decameron: Communication and Social Systems in the Cornice*. Princeton: Princeton University Press, 1982.

Preziosi, Donald. *Rethinking Art History: Meditations on a Coy Science*. New Haven: Yale University Press, 1989.

Quilligan, Maureen. *The Allegory of Female Authority: Christine de Pizan's "Cité des Dames."* Ithaca: Cornell University Press, 1991.

Rajna, Pio. *Le fonte dell' Orlando Furioso*. Ed. Francesco Mazzoni. Florence: Sansoni, 1975.

Raymond of Capua. *The Life of St. Catherine of Siena*. Trans., ed., and introduced by Conleth Kearns, O. P. Wilmington, Del.: Michael Glazier, 1980.

Reames, Sherry L. *The Legenda Aurea: A Reexamination of Its Paradoxical History*. Madison: University of Wisconsin Press, 1985.

Regosin, Richard L. "Critical Discussions." *Philosophy and Literature* 16 (1992): 134–49.

Rose, Gillian. *Judaism and Modernity: Philosophical Essays*. Oxford: Blackwell, 1993.

Rose, Jacqueline. "Sexuality in the Reading of Shakespeare: *Hamlet* and *Measure for Measure*." In Drakakis, ed., *Alternative Shakespeares*. 95–118.

———. "Shakespeare and the Death Drive." Unpublished paper.

Rosenzweig, Franz. *The Star of Redemption*. Trans. William W. Hallo. Notre Dame: University of Notre Dame Press, 1985.

Saxl, Fritz. "The History of Warburg's Library." In Gombrich, *Aby Warburg*. 325–38.

Schama, Simon. *The Embarrassment of Riches: An Interpretation of Dutch Culture in the Golden Age*. Berkeley: University of California Press, 1988.

Schell, Edgar. "Fulfilling the Law in the Brome *Abraham and Isaac*." *Leeds Studies in English*. New Series 25 (1994): 149–58.

Schlaffer, Hannelore, and Heinz Schlaffer. *Studium zum ästhetischen Historismus*. Frankfurt: Suhrkamp, 1975.

Schleifer, Ronald. *A. J. Greimas and the Nature of Meaning: Linguistics, Semiotics and Discourse Theory*. Lincoln: University of Nebraska Press, 1987.

Schmitt, Carl. *Political Theology: Four Chapters in the Concept of Sovereignty*. Trans. George Schwab. Cambridge, Mass.: MIT Press, 1988.

Schwartz, Murray, and Copelia Kahn, eds. *Representing Shakespeare: New Psychoanalytic Essays*. Baltimore: Johns Hopkins University Press, 1980.

Severs, J. Burke. *The Literary Relationships of Chaucer's "Clerkes Tale."* New Haven: Yale University Press, 1942. Reprinted Hamden, Conn.: Archon Books, 1972.

Shakespeare, William. *Measure for Measure*. Ed. J. W. Lever. Arden ed. London: Methuen, 1967.

———. *The Riverside Shakespeare*. Ed. G. Blakemore Evans. Boston: Houghton Mifflin, 1974.

———. *The Winter's Tale*. Ed. J. H. Pafford. Arden ed. London: Methuen, 1963.

Shaner, M. C. E., ed. "The Legend of Good Women." In *The Riverside Chaucer*. General ed. Larry D. Benson. Boston: Houghton Mifflin, 1987. Text, 587–630. Notes, 1059–75, 1178–84.

Shell, Marc. *The End of Kinship: Measure for Measure, Incest, and the Ideal of Universal Siblinghood*. Stanford, Calif.: Stanford University Press, 1988.

Shuger, Debora. *Habits of Thought in the English Renaissance: Religion, Politics, and the Dominant Culture*. Berkeley: University of California Press, 1990.

Siemon, James R. *Shakespearean Iconoclasm*. Berkeley: University of California Press, 1985.

———. "'But It Appears She Lives': Iteration in *The Winter's Tale*." In Bloom, ed., *Shakespeare's "The Winter's Tale."* 47–58.

Smith, John. *The Spirit and Its Letter: Traces of Rhetoric in Hegel's Philosophy of Bildung*. Ithaca: Cornell University Press, 1988.

Speiser, E. A. *The Anchor Bible: Genesis*. Vol. 1. New York: Doubleday, 1964.

Spenser, Edmund. *The Faerie Queene*. Ed. A. C. Hamilton. London: Longman, 1977.

———. *Poetical Works*. Ed. J. C. Smith and E. de Selincourt. Oxford: Oxford University Press, 1912.

Steiner, George. *Antigones*. Oxford: Clarendon Press, 1986.

Tertullian. "On Idolatry." In S. L. Greenslade, ed. and trans., *Early Latin Theology*. Philadelphia: Westminster Press, 1956.

Vasari, Giorgio. *Le Vite de' più eccelenti architetti, pittori, et scultori italiani, da Cimabue insino a' tempi nostri*. First ed., 1550. Ed. Licia and Carlo L. Ragghianti, 4 vols. Milan: Rizzoli, 1971 (rpt.). Second ed., 1568. Ed. Luciano Bellosi and Aldo Rossi. Turin: Giulio Einaudi, 1986 (rpt.).

————. *Lives of the Artists.* Selected and trans. George Bull, 2 vols. Harmondsworth: Penguin, 1987.

————. *Vasari on Technique.* Orig. "Introduzione . . . alle tre arti del disegno," from *Le Vite.* Trans. Louisa S. Maclehose, ed. G. Baldwin Brown. New York: Dover, 1960.

Voragine, Jacobus de. *Legenda Aurea.* Ed. Thomas Graesse. 1890. Rpt. Osnabrück: Otto Zeller Verlag, 1969.

————. *The Golden Legend.* Trans. and adapted by Branger Ryan and Helmut Ripperger. Salem, N.H.: Ayer, 1969.

Walton, John H. *Ancient Israelite Literature in Its Cultural Context: A Survey of Parallels Between Biblical and Ancient Near Eastern Texts.* Grand Rapids, Mich.: Regency Reference Library, 1989.

Ward, Benedicta, S.L.G. *Harlots of the Desert: A Study of Repentance in Early Monastic Sources.* Kalamazoo, Mich.: Cisterian Publications, 1987.

————. Introduction. *Lives of the Desert Fathers: The Historia Monachorum in Aegypto.* Trans. Norman Russell. London: Mowbray, 1981. 1–46.

Warburg, Aby. *Gesammelte Schriften.* 2 vols. Ed. Gertrud Bing. Berlin: B. G. Teubner, 1932.

Watson, Francis. *Paul, Judaism, and the Gentiles: A Sociological Approach.* Cambridge, Eng.: Cambridge University Press, 1986.

Watson, Robert N. "False Immortality in *Measure for Measure*: Comic Means, Tragic Ends." *Shakespeare Quarterly* 41.4 (Winter 1990): 411–32.

Weber, Samuel. "Taking Exception to the Decision: Walter Benjamin and Carl Schmitt." *Diacritics* 22.3–4 (Fall and Winter 1992): 5–18.

Wenham, Gordon J. *The Book of Leviticus.* (Commentary.) Grand Rapids, Mich.: William B. Eerdmans, 1979.

White, Hayden. *Metahistory: The Historical Imagination in Nineteenth-Century Europe.* Baltimore: The Johns Hopkins University Press, 1973.

White, Helen. *Tudor Books of Saints and Martyrs.* Madison: University of Wisconsin Press, 1963.

Wickler, Wolfgang. *The Biology of the Ten Commandments.* New York: McGraw-Hill, 1972.

Wilde, Oscar. "The Decay of Lying." In Hazard Adams, ed., *Critical Theory Since Plato.* Rev. ed. Fort Worth, Tex.: Harcourt Brace Jovanovich, 1992. 658–70.

Winckelmann, Johann Joachim. *Ausgewählte Schriften und Briefe.* Ed. Walther Rehm. Wiesbaden: Dieterich, 1948.

Wind, Edgar. "Michelangelo's Prophets and Sibyls." *Proceedings of the British Academy* 44, 1958.

————. *Pagan Mysteries in the Renaissance.* New York: Norton, 1958.

Wittkower, Rudolph. *Allegory and the Migration of Symbols.* London: Thames and Hudson, 1977.

————, and Margot Wittkower. *Born Under Saturn: The Character and Conduct of Artists: A Documented History from Antiquity to the French Revolution.* New York: Random House, 1963.

Wyschogrod, Edith. *Saints and Postmodernism: Revisioning Moral Philosophy.* Chicago: University of Chicago Press, 1990.

Zizek, Slavoj. *Enjoy Your Symptom!: Jacques Lacan in Hollywood and Out.* New York: Routledge, 1992.

————. *The Sublime Object of Ideology.* London: Verso, 1989.

Index

In this index, an "f" after a number indicates a separate reference on the next page, and an "ff" indicates separate references on the next two pages. A continuous discussion over two or more pages is indicated by a span of page numbers, e.g., "52–55." *Passim* is used for a cluster of references in close but not consecutive sequence.

Aaron, 195
Abraham, 152f
Adonis, 99
Agatha, St., 62–63
Alberti, Leon Baptista, 158, 238n, 239n
alienation and separation, 56–59, 101, 139
All Saints' Day, 64, 204–5
allegory, xix–xx, 9–10, 24–36, 42, 135–37, 176, 207
Anastasia, St., 117
Andrew, St., 64
Anectus, St., 55
annunciations, xxi, 112–16, 155–56, 225n, 233n, 238n
Anthony, St., xxiii, 121–26 *passim*, 235n
Antigone, 60–61, 205

Apsu, 146, 237n
Ariosto, 125–26
Aristotle, 151, 198
Aston, Margaret, 180
Auerbach, Eric, xviii, xix, xxix, 20–21, 23, 221n, 225n, 240n
Augustine, St., xv, 3f, 12, 30, 86, 157, 159, 182, 226n, 235n

Bann, Stephen, 213
baptism, 58
Barabbas, 138–40
Barbara, St., 48, 95, 114, 125
Barkan, Leonard, 207–8, 212
Barnardine, xxxi, 138–40, 157
Barolsky, Paul, 156
Baroque, xix–xx, 34–36, 42, 209
Bartholomew, St., xv–xx, 44ff, 48, 52–53, 211, 232n

Library of Congress Cataloging-in-Publication Data

Lupton, Julia Reinhard
Afterlives of the saints : hagiography, typology, and
Renaissance literature / Julia Reinhard Lupton.
p.   cm.
Includes bibliographical references and index.
ISBN 0-8047-2643-4 (cloth)
1. European literature—Renaissance, 1450–1600—History and
criticism. 2. Religious literature—History and criticism.
3. Saints in literature. 4. Hagiography. 5. Typology (Theology)
I. Title.
PN721.L87   1996
809'.93382'09031—dc20
95-50474   CIP

∞ This book has been printed on acid-free paper

Original printing 1996
Last figure below indicates year of this printing
05   04   03   02   01   00   99   98   97   96